# THE
# COVENANTERS
# OF
# SCOTLAND

## 1638 - 1690

By
David Dobson

CLEARFIELD

Copyright © 2023
by David Dobson
All Rights Reserved


Published for Clearfield Company by
Genealogical Publishing Company
Baltimore, Maryland
2023


ISBN: 9780806359564

# INTRODUCTION

The Wars of the Covenant covered the years between 1639 and 1651, when Scotland and England were two independent countries, though both were subject to King Charles 1. The cause of the Covenanter movement lay in the attempts of the Stuart kings to impose Anglicanism on a basically Presbyterian Church of Scotland and to make the Stuart kings head of the Church of Scotland in line with their position in the Church of England. This would give King Charles I greater power over his Scottish subjects.

In 1638 a National Covenant was subscribed, initially in Greyfriars kirkyard in Edinburgh and thereafter throughout Scotland, which demanded general assemblies and parliaments free of royal control. Charles, realising this threat to his objectives, set about raising an army in England to subdue the Scots. As there was no standing army in Scotland the Covenanters were faced with raising one from scratch. However, there were thousands of Scottish soldiers of fortune in the service of the Netherlands, Sweden and Denmark, who were persuaded to return to form the basis of a Scottish army to face the army of King Charles. Besides the former mercenaries, this Scottish army was composed of Lowlanders and Highlanders from Argyll

The First Bishop's War of 1639 ended with the two armies facing each other at Kelso, and the Pacification of Berwick whereby the Scots were permitted to hold a parliament and a general assembly of the church. The Second Bishop's War from 1640 to 1641 was a further attempt by King Charles to impose his will on the Scots. On 28 August 1640, the Royalist army was defeated by the Scots at Newburn and thereafter the Covenanters overran much of northern England, including Newcastle. Again, the king had to agree to the Scots demands, such as regular parliaments, the removal of bishops, and other reductions of the royal authority.

The outbreak of the Irish Rebellion in 1641 led to Scottish soldiers being stationed in Ulster to defend the settlers there. Under the Solemn League and Covenant of 1643-1644, the Scots agreed to support the English Parliament in its struggle with the King known as the English Civil War. In January 1644 the Army of the

Covenant, with over 20,000 men, marched into England to aid the English Parliamentary forces. On 2 July 1644 it made a major contribution to the defeat of a Royalist army at Marston Moor. James Graham, Marquis of Montrose, who formerly fought for the Covenanters, became a Royalist leader in Scotland; he led a mainly Irish Catholic army to several victories over the Covenanters in Scotland between 1644 and 1645, until his defeat at Philiphaugh on 13 September 1645.

In 1647 King Charles admitted defeat and surrendered to the Scottish Army in England; however, it returned home and handed the King over to Oliver Cromwell. King Charles I was duly executed in London, an event which was considered excessive by most Scots. England became a republic while Scotland chose to remain a kingdom. Charles's son, then in exile in the Netherlands, was brought to Scotland and crowned at Scone as King Charles II of Scotland.

Cromwell could not accept this and brought an army north to face the Scots. He laid siege to Edinburgh but could not break through the defences and retreated to the port of Dunbar where his ships lay. The Scottish Army of the Covenant followed the Parliamentary forces but made a major tactical error whereby the Scots suffered a major defeat on 3 September 1650. Thousands of Scots were taken prisoner, and many were transported for sale to the colonies or plantations, and elsewhere.

In 1651 the Covenanters agreed to support King Charles II, and his Royalist supporters, on his invasion of England, on the condition that Presbyterianism would be the Established Church in Scotland and the Church of England would become Presbyterian. The army then marched south to Worcester, where it was besieged by Cromwell's Army, and forced to surrender in September 1651. King Charles II escaped to exile in Holland where he remained until the Restoration in 1662. Again, many prisoners were captured and sent as indentured servants to the colonies or Plantations, especially to New England.

During the Stuart Inter Regnum (Oliver Cromwell and his son Richard were Lord Protectors of the British Isles), the Church of Scotland was allowed to retain its Presbyterian structure. Cromwell died in 1658 to be briefly succeeded by Richard. But when the monarchy was restored in 1660 the Covenanters, who were militant Presbyterians, were subject to policies which conflicted with them. This led to armed Covenanter risings in Scotland. Episcopacy was imposed on the Kirk, which led to hundreds of Scottish ministers being deprived of their parishes. Many of them moved to Holland or to Ulster.

King Charles II took vengeance on leading Covenanters, such as Archibald Johnston of Warriston, who had contributed to his father's execution; Johnston was kidnapped in Holland and executed in Scotland. All legislation passed by the Covenanting parliaments between 1639 and 1651 were annulled, and in 1662 bishops were restored to the Kirk, putting the church under the authority of the king. In the heartlands of the Covenanters (i.e., south west Scotland) around 275 ministers left their charges and operated through conventicles, or open-air services. The army was used to enforce the new ecclesiastical regime, with dragoons hunting fugitives.

In the aftermath of the early Covenanter risings, executions, deportations and fines were used to impose the policy of King Charles II. One of the chief persecutors was Archbishop James Sharp, who was assassinated 3 May 1679. This was followed by an armed rising of the Covenanters which was defeated at Bothwell Bridge on 22 June 1679. The Sanquhar Declaration on 22 June 1680, in which various Presbyterians renounced their allegiance to Charles II, resulted in a guerrilla war. Many Covenanters opted to go abroad, mainly to the Netherlands and Ireland. The government also banished significant numbers of Covenanters to the Plantations or colonies in America and the West Indies. Some prisoners were released provided they subscribed to a specific oath and undertook to live within the law, subject to a financial penalty. For example, John Heislop and Robert Eliott, from Cavers, Roxburghshire, prisoners in Edinburgh Tolbooth, having taken the Test Act and subscribed to bonds committing them to live regularly and attend the parish church, subject to a penalty of 500 Scots merks if they failed to do so, were released on 21 July 1685. Greyfriars churchyard, Edinburgh, was used as a prison for four months in 1679, for 1,000 Covenanters captured after the Battle of Bothwell Bridge. 258 of them were put aboard ship bound for America. On 24 October

1679, the <u>Crown of London</u> set sail from Leith with 258 Covenanter prisoners aboard bound for sale in the West Indies; however, the ship struck a rock off Deerness in the Orkney Islands and most of the prisoners drowned. Many of these men had fought at the Battle of Bothwell Bridge on 12 June 1676.

King Charles II died on 6 February 1685 and was succeeded by his brother as King James VII of Scotland and King James II of England and Ireland. King James, however, was a Catholic--something unacceptable to the Protestants of England and of Scotland. In Scotland the Covenanter Earl of Argyll returned from exile to lead a rebellion from Argyll in 1685. When the rebellion failed, he and other leaders were executed and 150 of his men were transported to Jamaica. In England, a similar rebellion led by the Duke of Monmouth was defeated at Sedgemoor on 6 July 1685.

In 1689 the Scots Parliament offered the crown to William of Orange and his wife Mary Stuart. This was opposed by followers of King James, especially among Catholic and Episcopalian clans led by John Graham of Claverhouse, [Viscount Dundee]. This Jacobite Army clashed with a government army [that included the Cameronians, who had been raised among former Covenanters], in 1689 at Killiecrankie in Perthshire, which was followed by the Siege of Dunkeld. This, and the Battle of the Boyne in Ireland in 1690 effectively ended the rule of the Stuart kings. In addition, by 1689 the Scottish Parliament had stripped the crown of some prerogative powers and had given greater protection for the rights and liberties of its subjects.

David Dobson, Dundee, 2023

REFERENCES

AGA  Acts of the General Assembly of the Church of Scotland

APS  Acts of the Parliament of Scotland

BK  Battle of Killiecrankie, [Warwick, 2018]

BMF  Belfast Merchant Families in the 17$^{th}$ Century, [Dublin, 1996]

CEC  Exiles of the Covenant, [Helensburgh, 1908]

CKC  Clan, King and Covenant, [Edinburgh, 2000]

CS  Civil Survey of Donegal, Londonderry, and Tyrone, [Dublin, 1937]

EJD  East Jersey Deeds, Trenton, New Jersey

ETR  Edinburgh Tolbooth Records

F  Fasti Ecclesiae Scoticanae, H. Scott, [Edinburgh]

FI  Fasti of the Irish Presbyterian Church

GC  Galloway and the Covenanters, [Paisley, 1914]

HD  History of Dumfries

LC  Lamont Clan, [Edinburgh, 1938]

LJ  Letters and Journals 1663-1887, [London, 1953]

NRS  National Records of Scotland, Edinburgh

NWI  New World Immigrants, [Baltimore, 1980]

NYD  New York Documents

PCC  Prerogative Court of Canterbury

RGS  Register of the Great Seal of Scotland, [Edinburgh]

RHCA Regimental History of the Covenanting Armies 1639-1651. [Edinburgh, 1990]

RSA  Records of the Synod of Argyll, 1639-1662

RPCS Register of the Privy Council of Scotland, [Edinburgh]

SCF  Suffolk Court Files, Massachusetts

SCIC Scottish Covenanters and Irish Confederates

SD Suffolk Deeds, Massachusetts

SD  Scots on the Dyke

SEC  Scottish Exile Community in the Netherlands, 1660-1690

SHR  Scottish Historical Review, vol.99

SPC  Calendar of State Papers, Colonial, [London]

SPDom  Calendar of State Papers, Domestic, [London]

SP.Ire  Calendar of State Papers, Ireland

SW  Standing Witnesses, [Edinburgh, 1996]

UJA  Ulster Journal of Archaeology, [Belfast]

Z  Zealots, [Amberley, 2018]

GLOSSARY

Conventicle  a clandestine, generally oudoor, religious meeting

Tolbooth  a burgh jail

Warded  to put in custody

Covenanter Flag

The National Covenant of 1638

Covenanter Memorial, Greyfriars Kirkyard, Edinburgh

Signing the Covenant, Greyfriars Kirkyard, Edinburgh

A field communion

Gordon of Rothiemay's map of Edinburgh, 1647, as re-engraved after de Wit, 1710

Edinburgh Tolbooth

Glasgow Tolbooth

Execution of the Earl of Argyle

Blackadder's gravestone, North Berwick (East Lothian)

Murder of James Sharp, Lord Arch-Bishop of St. Andrews

Greyfriars Church, 1640

# THE COVENANTERS OF SCOTLAND, 1638-1690

ABERCROMBIE, THOMAS, was warded in Edinburgh Tolbooth on 22 July 1685. [RPCS.IX.163]

ADAIR, PATRICK, son of William Adair in Ayr, was educated t Glasgow University, minister at Cairncastle from 146 until 1674 when he moved to Belfast, he died in 1694. [F.7.527]

ADAIR, ROBERT, settled in Ulster, returned to Scotland in 1639, was accused of signing the National Covenant in June 1639 and of planning a Scottish invasion of Ireland together with a rising at Ballymena, County Antrim, but was found not guilty and pardoned.

ADAIR, WILLIAM, born 1615, son of William Adair of Kinhilt, and brother of Sir Robert Adair of Kinhilt and Ballymena, minister at Ayr from 1648 until 1682, was deposed in 1648 for non-conformity, he fought at the Battle of Mauchline Moor, and died on 12 February 1684. [F.III.9][RPCS.VI.406]

ADAM, COLIN, born 1603, was educated at the University of St Andrews, minister at Kilrenny, Fife, from 1634 until his death in March 1677, he declined to convert to Episcopacy and was confined to his parish. [F.V.180]

ADAM, JAMES, was captured at the Battle of Dunbar in 1650, and was transported via London aboard the Unity of Boston bound for New England in November 1650. [SCF.1226]

ADAM, JOHN, and his brother FRANCIS ADAM, in Ballie, for attending conventicles, were outlawed on 29 August 1672. [RPCS.III.583]

ADAM, JOHN, from Ormadale, guilty of participation in Argyll's Rebellion, was banished to the American Plantations and transported via Leith to Jamaica on 7 August 1685. [RPCS.II.329]

ADAM, ROBERT, a Covenanter who was banished to the American Plantations on 25 August 1685, who was transported via Leith aboard the Henry and Francis to East New Jersey on 5 September 1685. [RPCS.XI.162/336]

ADAM, WILLIAM, a merchant from Culross, Fife, who was banished to America in 1670. [RPCS.III.204]

ADAMSON, WILLIAM, a smith from Williamston, was in the rebellion of 1666, was transported aboard the Convertin to Virginia in September 1668. [RPCS.II.470/507/534]

ADDIE, JOHN, from Torpichen, West Lothian, was transported via Leith aboard the Crown of London bound for Barbados on 27 November 1679, was shipwrecked and drowned off Orkney on 10 December 1679. [RBM]

AFFLECK, WILLIAM, and Isobel Affleck, children of John Affleck in Buittle, Kirkcudbrightshire, fanatics and fugitives in 1684. [RPCS.IX.571]

AGNEW, NIVEN, captured at the Battle of Dunbar in 1650, was transported via London aboard the Unity of Boston bound for Boston, New England, in November 1650. [Probate, 1687, Maine]

AIR, PATRICK, Quartermaster of the Angus Regiment, of the Army of the Solemn League and Covenant, fought at the Siege of York, the Siege of Newcastle and at the Battle of Marston Moor in 1646, testament, 1675, Comm. Brechin. [NRS]

AITCHISON, JAMES, from Nethen, Berwickshire, was captured after the Battle of Bothwell Bridge, was transported via Leith aboard the Crown of London bound for Barbados on 27 November 1679, was shipwrecked and drowned off Orkney on 10 December 1679. [RBM][CEC.212/5][SW.203]

AITKEN, ALLEN, was warded in Edinburgh Tolbooth on 28 May 1685. [ETR]

AITKEN, JAMES, born in Bughtrig, a prisoner in Canongait Tolbooth, having signed a bond was released on 23 August 1684. [RPCS.IX.315]

AITKEN, JANET, a widow, was accused of rioting in Kirkcudbright in the parish of Irongray, in 1663. [RPCS.I.373]

AITKEN, JOHN, from Shotts, Lanarkshire, was transported via Leith aboard the <u>Crown of London</u> bound for Barbados on 27 November 1679, was shipwrecked and drowned off Orkney on 10 December 1679. [RBM]

AITON, ANDREW, from Avondale, Lanarkshire, was transported via Leith aboard the <u>Crown of London</u> bound for Barbados on 27 November 1679, was shipwrecked and drowned off Orkney on 10 December 1679. [RBM]

AITON, JOHN, from Heuchheid, Avondale, Lanarkshire, was banished to the American Plantations in October 1684. [RPCS.X.258]

ALBERTUS, DERICK, a Dutchman, was warded in Edinburgh Tolbooth on 11 August 1685 for his part in Argyll's Rebellion, was liberated on 30 March 1686. [ETR]

ALDCORN, ADAM, chaplain to Lady Cavers, a Covenanter, was transported via Leith to the West Indies on 12 December 1678. [RPCS.VI.76]

ALEXANDER, DUNCAN, having taken part in Argyll's Rebellion in 1685, was banished to the American Plantations on 24 July 1685, and was transported via Leith bound for Jamaica on 7 August 1685. [RPCS.XI.329]

ALEXANDER, GEORGE, from Newburgh, Fife, was banished to the American Plantations on 1 August 1678, and transported via Leith aboard the <u>St Michael of Scarborough</u> to Jamaica on 12 December 1678. [RPCS.VI.76]

ALEXANDER, JOHN, from Mauchline, Ayrshire, a rebel in Glasgow Tolbooth, was transported via Port Glasgow aboard the <u>Pelican of Glasgow</u> bound for Carolina in June 1684. [RPCS.IX.208] [Woodrow.iv.10]

ALGEO, JAMES, a writer in Minnigaff, was accused, in Kirkcudbright on 4 October 1684, of conversing with rebels,

James Gordon the younger of Craiglaw and James Mertison in Glencapel in 1682. [RPCS.IX.375]

ALGIE, JAMES, tenant of Kennishead farm, Eastwood, Renfrewshire, refused to take the Test Act Oath, consequently he was hanged on Paisley Green on 3 July 1685. [Woodside gravestone, Paisley, Renfrewshire]

ALLISON, ADAM, a minister in Galloway, was accused of holding conventicles within the Presbytery in 1666. [GC.107]

ALISON, COLIN, was banished to the American Plantations on 11 October 1684, was taken from Leith Tolbooth, put in irons and imprisoned in Edinburgh Tolbooth on 31 October 1685, [ETR], and was transported via Leith to East New Jersey. [RPCS.XI.155]

ALISON, PATRICK, in Carnwath, Lanarkshire, a rebel, was warded in Edinburgh Tolbooth, was banished to the Plantations on 2 July 1684. [RPCS.IX.28][ETR]

ALISON, ROBERT, from Avondale, Lanarkshire, was transported via Leith aboard the Crown of London bound for Barbados on 27 November 1679, was shipwrecked and drowned off Orkney on 10 December 1679. [RBM]

ALISON, WILLIAM, from Avondale, Lanarkshire, was transported via Leith aboard the Crown of London bound for Barbados on 27 November 1679, was shipwrecked and drowned off Orkney on 10 December 1679. [RBM]

ALLAN, ADAM, in Dalmellington, Ayrshire, a rebel in Glasgow Tolbooth, was banished to the Plantations in June 1684, and transported via Glasgow aboard the Pelican bound for Carolina, bond by Walter Gibson, a merchant in Glasgow, dated 20 June 1684. [RPCS.IX.208]

ALLAN, GEORGE, from Penpont, Dumfries-shire, was captured at the Fans of Altry and shot, in 168-. [Allan's Cairn, Polskeoch, Penpont, Dumfries-shire] [Nithsdale Martyrs Cross, Dumfries]

ALLAN, JOHN, from Torpichen, West Lothian, was transported via Leith aboard the Crown of London bound for Barbados on 27

November 1679, was shipwrecked and drowned off Orkney on 10 December 1679. [RBM]

ALLAN, JOHN, from Cumnock, Ayrshire, then in Edinburgh Tolbooth, was put in irons and imprisoned in Canongait Tolbooth on 29 July 1685, then transported via Leith bound for Jamaica on 7 August 1685. [ETR][RPCS.II.330]

ANDERSON, ALASTAIR, captured at the Siege of Worcester and transported via Gravesend, London, aboard the John and Sarah bound for Boston, New England, in November 1651. [SD.1/6-6]

ANDERSON, ALEXANDER, servant of George Anderson in Kirkliston, Mid Lothian, was banished to the Plantations on 13 June 1678, transported via Leith aboard the St Michael of Scarborough on 12 December 1678. [RPCS.VI.76]

ANDERSON, ARCHIBALD, a prisoner of war employed at the Lyn Ironworks in Massachusetts, died in 1662, probate, Essex County, on 27 September 1662.

ANDERSON, DAVID, was captured at the Siege of Worcester and transported via Gravesend, London, aboard the John and Sarah bound for Boston, New England, in November 1651. [SD1/5-6]

ANDERSON, HARRY, a rebel imprisoned in Edinburgh Tolbooth, was released on 25 September 1684. [RPCS.IX.180]

ANDERSON, ISOBEL, spouse of James Hunter, was accused of rioting in Kirkcudbright in the parish of Irongray, in 1663. [RPCS.I.373]

ANDERSON, JAMES, a rebel in 1666, imprisoned in Edinburgh Tolbooth, was banished to Virginia on 4 August 1668 and transported via Leith aboard the Convertin, Captain Lightfoot, bound for Virginia in September 1668. [RPCS.II.507/534]

ANDERSON, JAMES, from Kilmarnock, Ayrshire, captured after the Battle of Bothwell Bridge on 22 June 1679, was transported via Leith aboard the Crown of London bound for Barbados on 27

November 1679 was shipwrecked and drowned off Orkney on 10 December 1679. [RBM][Kilmarnock gravestone]

ANDERSON, JOHN, was captured at the Siege of Worcester and transported via Gravesend, London, aboard the John and Sarah bound for Boston, New England, in November 1651. [SD1/5-6]

ANDERSON, JOHN, a servant of George Winget a maltman in Glasgow, was banished to the American Plantations on 13 June 1678, and was transported via Leith aboard the St Michael of Scarborough on 12 December 178. [RPCS.VI.76]

ANDERSON, JOHN, was banished to the Plantations in the West Indies or elsewhere and was transported there by a Leith shipmaster on 11 October 1681. [RPCS.VII.219]

ANDERSON, JOHN, in Ironspie, was accused in Kirkcudbright of conversing with a rebel and fugitive, William Russell, in 1684. [RPCS.IX.374]

ANDERSON, JOHN, from Lanark, a prisoner in Edinburgh Tolbooth, was banished to the Plantations on 12 December 1685, and was transported via Leith aboard the John and Nicolas bound for Barbados on 17 December 1685. [RPCS.XI.384] [NRS.HH.11] [ETR]

ANDERSON, JOHN, of Westerton the younger, was accused of treason in 1687 having stated that it was lawful for subjects to rise in arms against the king. [NRS.JC39.98]

ANDERSON, MARGARET, late servant to James Oswell in Edinburgh, imprisoned in Edinburgh Tolbooth for the part in the attempted escape of Alexander Gordon of Earlston, was freed on 31 January 1684. [ETR]

ANDERSON, ROBERT, from Kilmarnock, Ayrshire, was transported via Leith aboard the Crown of London bound for Barbados on 27 November 1679, was shipwrecked and drowned off Orkney on 10 December 1679. [RBM]

ANDERSON, WILLIAM, was captured at the Siege of Worcester in 1651 and transported via Gravesend, London, aboard the John and Sarah bound for Boston, New England, in December 1651. [SD.1/5-6]

ANDERSON, WILLIAM, from Shalloch, a rebel, having taken the Bond for Peace, was pardoned in February 1669. [RPCS.II.612]

ANDREW, JOHN, servant to Sir John Cochrane of Ochiltree, Ayrshire, a prisoner in Canongait Tolbooth, having signed a bond was released on 23 August 1684. [RPCS.IX.315]

ANDREW, WILLIAM, a shoemaker in Greenock, who attended a conventicle near Greenock, was to be captured and imprisoned in Edinburgh Tolbooth in August 1684. [RPCS.IX.131]

ANDREW, WILLIAM, from Linlithgow, West Lothian, was banished to the American Plantations on 27 May 1684, was transported via Leith to Carolina in 1684. [RPCS.VIII.526]

ANGUS, HENRY, in Kinross, for attending conventicles, was outlawed on 29 August 1672. [RPCS.III.583]

ANGUS, WILLIAM, from Abercorn, West Lothian, was banished to the American Plantations on 1 August 1678, and was transported via Leith aboard the St Michael of Scarborough on 12 December 1678. [RPCS.VI.76]

ANNAND, WALTER, was transported via Leith to East New Jersey on 7 August 1685. [RPCS.XI.137]

ANNAND, WILLIAM, in Fordell, Fife, for attending conventicles, was outlawed on 29 August 1672. [RPCS.III.583]

ARBUCKLE, JOHN, a prisoner in Canongait Tolbooth, who refused to take an Oath of Allegiance, was banished to the American Plantations on 17 December 1685. [ETR]; and was transported via Leith aboard the John and Nicolas bound for Barbados on 17 December 1685. [RPCS.XI.386]

ARBUTHNOTT, JOHN, of Cairngall, and his deceased wife Anna Farquharson, had attended conventicles in 1683, for which he was he was fined on 7 October 1684. [RPCS.IX.713]

ARCHER, THOMAS, a minister in exile in Rotterdam, Holland, from 1676 until 1685. [SEC]; was accused of participating in the Earl of

Argyll's Rebellion, in 1685. [NRS.JC39.72], and was warded in Edinburgh Tolbooth on 11 August 1685, found guilty of treason and rebellion, was sentenced to be hung in the Grassmarket of Edinburgh on 14 August 1685. [ETR]

ARCHIBALD, ANDREW, in Orphat, for attending conventicles, was outlawed on 29 August 1672. [RPCS.III.583]

ARCHIBALD, HUGH, was educated at Glasgow University, minister at Strathaven from 1648 until 1658, he refused to conform to Episcopacy, he died in 1679. [F.III.222]

ARCHIBALD, JOHN, born 1627, was captured at the Battle of Dunbar in August 1650, and transported via London aboard the Unity of Boston bound for Boston, New England, in November 1650. [SCF.1226]

ARCHIBALD, ROBERT, late minister at Dunscore, was accused of holding conventicles, in 1666. [GC.114]; a minister in exile in Rotterdam, Holland, from 1685 until 1686. [SEC]

ARMOR, JAMES, a merchant imprisoned in Hutcheson's Hospital and Glasgow Tolbooth, was released on 27 March 1685 to go to America from Leith aboard the Henry and Francis bound for East New Jersey in September 1685. [NRS.E72.15.32]

ARMSTRONG, GEORGE, of Kinmont, a refugee in Ireland in 1679. [RPCS.VI.159]

ARMSTRONG, ROBERT, a prisoner from Jedburgh Tolbooth, Roxburghshire, later in Edinburgh Tolbooth, was transported via Leith aboard the Phoenix of Leith bound for Virginia on 24 April 1666. [ETR.106]

ARNOT, Captain ALEXANDER, of Lochridge, fought at Rullion Green in 1666, a prisoner in Edinburgh Tolbooth, having taken the Test Oath was released on 16 December 1684. [ETR]

ARNOT, JOHN, a tenant farmer of Balgedy, Milnathort, Kinross, was banished to the American Plantations on 13 June 1678, and was transported via Leith aboard the St Michael of Scarborough on 12 December 1678. [RPCS.VI.76]

ARNOT, ROBERT, and WILLIAM ARNOT, in Kinswaid, for attending conventicles, was outlawed on 29 August 1672. [RPCS.III.583]

ARNOT, SAMUEL, a minister in Kirkpatrick-Durham, Galloway, was accused of holding conventicles within the Presbytery in 1666. [GC.107/114]; was sought by the Justice Court in August 1667 for his part in the late rebellion. [GC.123] [RPCS.II.345]

AUCHINCLOSE, WILLIAM, from Paisley, Renfrewshire, was transported via Leith aboard the Crown of London bound for Barbados on 27 November 1679, was shipwrecked and drowned off Orkney on 10 December 1679. [RBM]

AULD, ROBERT, from Kilbride, Lanarkshire, was transported via Leith aboard the Crown of London bound for Barbados on 27 November 1679, was shipwrecked and drowned off Orkney on 10 December 1679. [RBM]

BAIKER, JACOB, a Dutchman, was warded in Edinburgh Tolbooth on 11 August 1685 for his part in Argyll's Rebellion, was liberated on 30 March 1686. [ETR]

BAIRD, GEORGE, a prisoner in Edinburgh Tolbooth in May 1685. [ETR]

BAIRD, JAMES, from Calderwater, Lanarkshire, was banished to the American Plantations on 2 July 1684, and was transported via Leith to Carolina in August 1684. [RPCS.XI.330]

BAIRD, JAMES, in Calder Water, a rebel, a prisoner in Edinburgh or Canongait Tolbooth, was banished to the Plantations on 2 July 1684. [RPCS.IX.28]

BAIRD, JAMES, from Kirkhousell, Kintyre, Argyll, in Argyll's Rebellion in 1685, was banished to the Plantations on 31 July 1685, and transported via Leith to Jamaica in August 1685. [RPCS.II.330]

BAIRD, WILLIAM, a journeyman shoemaker in the service of William Andrew in Greenock, who attended a conventicle near Greenock, was to be captured and imprisoned in Edinburgh Tolbooth in August 1684. [RPCS.IX.131]

BAITTIE, JOHN, a prisoner in Edinburgh Tolbooth was released on 30 July 1685 having taken an Oath of Allegiance. [ETR]

BALFOUR, ALEXANDER, from Fife, was banished to the American Plantations in June 1684, and was transported to New York in June 1684. [RPCS.VIII.516]

BALFOUR, GEORGE, an alleged assassin of Archbishop Sharp, fled to Ireland on 7 October 1680. [RPCS.VI.560]

BALFOUR, JAMES, from Fife, was banished to the American Plantations in June 1684, and was transported to New York in June 1684. [RPCS.VIII.516]

BALFOUR, JOHN, of Kinloch, Fife, an alleged assassin of Archbishop Sharp, fled to Ireland on 7 October 1680. [RPCS.VI.560][Z.201]

BALMANNO, WILLIAM, was transported via Leith aboard the Phoenix of Leith bound for Virginia in April 1666. [ETR]

BALMENIE, JAMES, in Blairhead, for attending conventicles, was outlawed on 29 August 1672. [RPCS.III.583]

BANKE, JOHN, was captured after the Battle of Dunbar in 1650, and transported via London to Boston, New England, in November 1650. [SCF.1226]

BANKIER, JAMES, in Calder, Mid Lothian, a prisoner in 1683. [RPCS.VIII.643]

BANNATYNE, GEORGE, from Craigmuir, was transported to the American Plantations in December 1684. [RPCS.X.77]

BANNATYNE, JOHN, of Corhouse, was warded in Edinburgh Tolbooth on 13 November 1684. [ETR]

BANNATYNE, JOHN, of Craigmuir, was transported to the Plantations in December 1684. [RPCS.X.77]

BARBER, JAMES, in Arderroch, was accused, in Kirkcudbright in 1684, of aiding rebel James McMichael. [RPCS.IX.376]

BARR, JAMES, in Fenwick, a rebel in 1666, imprisoned in Edinburgh Tolbooth or Canongait Tolbooth, having taken the Oath of Allegiance, was released on 11 July 1667. [RPCS.II.308]

BARR, ....., a rebel who fled to Ireland on 7 October 1680. [RPCS.V.560]

BARRIE, THOMAS, a weaver in Stonehouse, Lanarkshire, imprisoned in Canongait Tolbooth, subscribed to a bond on 8 July 1684. [RPCS.IX.211]

BARTON, THOMAS, from Monklands, Lanarkshire, was transported via Leith aboard the Crown of London bound for Barbados on 27 November 1679, was shipwrecked and drowned off Orkney on 10 December 1679. [RBM]

BAYNE, WALTER, a pedlar in Kinswaid, for attending conventicles, was outlawed on 29 August 1672. [RPCS.III.583]

BEAL, JOHN, from Newburn, Fife, was transported via Leith aboard the Crown of London bound for Barbados on 27 November 1679, was shipwrecked and drowned off Orkney on 10 December 1679. [RBM]

BECK, SAMUEL, from Kirkmabreck, Galloway, was transported via Leith aboard the Crown of London bound for Barbados on 27 November 1679, was shipwrecked and drowned off Orkney on 10 December 1679. [RBM]

BELL, JAMES, was educated at Glasgow University, chaplain to Colonel Campbell's Regiment, minister at Kirkcolm, Wigtownshire, from 1644 until 1663 when deprived for not conforming to Episcopacy, in 1689 he returned to the parish and died on 30 July 1698. [F.II.339]

BELL, JOHN, of Whiteside, Anwoth, who fought at the Battle of Bothwell Bridge on 22 June 1679. was killed on Kirkconnell Moor, Kirkcudbrightshire, in 1685. [Kirkconnell Moor Monument] [Anwoth gravestone, Gatehouse of Fleet, Kirkcudbrightshire] [GC.301]

BELL, JOHN, from Livingstone, West Lothian, was transported via Leith aboard the Crown of London bound for Barbados on 27 November 1679, was shipwrecked and drowned off Orkney on 10 December 1679. [RBM]

BENNET, WILLIAM, in Lyne parish in 1684, fought at the Battle of Bothwell Bridge in 1678. [RPCS.IX.501]

BENNETTIE, JAMES, in Belladoes, for attending conventicles, was outlawed on 29 August 1672. [RPCS.III.583]

BENNIE, JAMES, was captured at the Siege of Worcester and transported via Gravesend, London, aboard the John and Sarah bound for Boston, New England, in December 1651, landed there in February 1652. [SD.1.58]

BENNIE, JOHN was captured at the Siege of Worcester and transported via Gravesend, London, aboard the John and Sarah bound for Boston, New England, in December 1651, landed there in February 1652. [SD.1.58]

BENNOCH, CUTHBERT, and his spouse Marion Wilson, for aiding rebel James Douglas, and failing to report it was declared to be a rebel and fugitive in October 1684. [RPCS.IX.365]

BENNOCH, JAMES, was killed at Ingliston, Dumfries-shire, in 1685. [Nithsdale Martyrs Cross, Dumfries]

BENNOCH, MALCOLM, servant of the laird of Barjarg, was imprisoned in the castle in October 1684. [RPCS.IX.696]

BEREERE THOMAS, was captured at the Siege of Worcester and transported via Gravesend, London, aboard the John and Sarah bound for Boston, New England, in December 1651, landed there in February 1652. [SD.1.58]

BERTRAM, ALEXANDER, of Dambrae, Coulter, Lanarkshire, was born in the 1620s, a minister in exile in the Netherlands around 1676. [SEC]

BEVERIDGE, JOHN, from Islay, Argyll, for participation in Argyll's Rebellion in 1685, he was banished to the American Plantations on 30 July 1685, and transported via Leith aboard the Henry and

Francis bound for East New Jersey in August 1685. [RPCS.XI.126/137/320/330]

BIGGAR, JAMES, from Marglolly, a rebel, having subscribed to a bond of peace, was pardoned in March 1669. [RPCS.II.622]

BIGGAR, JAMES, from Ettrick Forest, was warded in Edinburgh Tolbooth on 20 May 1685, but, having subscribed to the Test Act was released on 28 May 1685. [ETR]

BIGLAW, JANET, daughter of James Biglaw in Kirkcudbright, was accused of rioting in Kirkcudbright in the parish of Irongray, in 1663. [RPCS.I.373/408]; a rioter, was imprisoned in Kirkcudbright Tolbooth, then to stand at the market cross there on two days in September 1683. [GC.105]

BINSTON, JOHN, was warded in Edinburgh Tolbooth on 11 August 1685. [ETR]

BISHOP, ALEXANDER, from Torpichan, West Lothian, was transported via Leith aboard the Crown of London bound for Barbados on 27 November 1679, was shipwrecked and drowned off Orkney on 10 December 1679. [RBM]

BISSETT, ALEXANDER, from West Calder, Midlothian, was transported via Leith aboard the Crown of London bound for Barbados on 27 November 1679, was shipwrecked and drowned off Orkney on 10 December 1679. [RBM]

BISSETT, JOHN, in Laicht, to be tried accused of rebellion, 3 June 1684. [RPCS.IX.205]

BITCHET, DAVID, from Fenwick, Ayrshire, was transported via Leith aboard the Crown of London bound for Barbados on 27 November 1679, was shipwrecked and drowned off Orkney on 10 December 1679. [RBM]

BITCHET, WILLIAM, from Fenwick, Ayrshire, was transported via Leith aboard the Crown of London bound for Barbados on 27 November 1679, was shipwrecked and drowned off Orkney on 10 December 1679. [RBM]

BLACK, DANIEL, was captured at the Siege of Worcester in 1651 and transported via Gravesend, London, aboard the John and Sarah bound for Boston, New England, in December 1651, landed there in February 1652. [SD.1.58]

BLACK, GAVIN, from Monklands, Lanarkshire, a rebel imprisoned in Glasgow Tolbooth, was banished to the American Plantations in June 1684, and transported via Leith aboard the Pelican bound for Carolina in June 1684. [RPCS.IX.208]

BLACK, JOHN, in Glen Gour, for aiding rebel James Douglas, was declared a rebel and fugitive in October 1684. [RPCS.IX.365]

BLACK, JOHN, from the Water of Orr in Dumfriesshire, was transported via Leith aboard the Henry and Francis bound for East New Jersey in August 1685. [RPCS.XI.154/291] [NWI.I.422]

BLACK, MALCOLM, from Auchahoish, Argyll, a tenant of the laird of Craigintyrey, for participating in Argyll's Rebellion in 1685, he was imprisoned in Canongate Tolbooth, and in Paul's Hospital in Edinburgh, then banished to the Plantations on 30 July 1685 and transported via Leith to Jamaica in 1685. [RPCS.XI.136]

BLACK, NEIL, from Melford, Glenbeg, Argyll, was transported via Leith to Jamaica in August 1685. [RPCS.II.329]

BLACKADDER, Reverend JOHN, born 1615 in Blairhall, Dunfermline, Fife, from Troqueer, Kirkcudbrightshire, minister at Dumfries from 1652 until 1662, when he was ousted, was accused of holding conventicles within the Presbytery in 1666. [GC.107/111]; a field preacher, at a conventicle on Beak Hill, Dunfermline, in 1670, who fled to Holland, a minister in Leiden and in Rotterdam from 1678 to 1680, returned by 1681, was warded in Edinburgh Tolbooth on 11 August 1685, [ETR]; then imprisoned on the Bass Rock in the Firth of Forth, died there in 1685. [NRS.E100.39.1] [North Berwick gravestone, East Lothian] [SEC] [Z.199][GC.397/398][Z.199/201]

BLACKADDER, JOHN, imprisoned in Edinburgh Tolbooth for being in Argyll's Rebellion, was released on 25 March 1686. [ETR]

BLACKADDER, ROBERT, from Troqueer, Kirkcudbrightshire, a minister in exile in the Netherlands from 1681 to 1689. [SEC]

BLACKATTER, Dr WILLIAM, was warded in Edinburgh Tolbooth on 6 June 1685, was taken to Edinburgh Castle on 17 June 1685 and returned on 20 June 1685. [ETR]

BLACKWOOD, JAMES, from Carmannock in Lanarkshire, was transported via Leith aboard the St Michael of Scarborough bound for the Plantations on 12 December 1678. [RPCS.VI.76]

BLACKWOOD, THOMAS, a tenant in Muirkirk, imprisoned in Canongait Tolbooth, having signed a bond was released on23 August 1684. [RPCS.IX.314]

BLAIKIE, JOHN, was warded in Edinburgh Tolbooth on 3 February 1686. [ETR]

BLAIR, ALEXANDER, born 1618, was educated at St Andrews University, minister at Galston, Ayrshire, from 1643, until 1662, for refusing to take the Oath of Allegiance, was deposed and order to move out of the parish, on 16 September 1662. [RPCS.I263]; he fought at Mauchline Moor, was imprisoned in 1673, died in January 1674. [F.3.39]

BLAIR, DAVID, born 1637, from St Andrews, Fife, a minister in exile in Den Haag and Leiden, in the Netherlands, before 1688, returned with William of Orange in 1688. [SEC]

BLAIR, JOHN, a minister in Mauchline, Ayrshire, was deposed and ordered to move beyond the River Ness in August 1663. [RPCS.I.408]

BLAIR, Reverend ROBERT, born in Irvine, Ayrshire, was educated at Glasgow University, minister at Bangor, Ireland, from 1623 until 1638, returned to Scotland, a minister in Ayr in 1638, and in St Andrews, Fife, in 1639, died 27 August 1666 at Coustoun Castle, Fife. [Aberdour gravestone, Fife][F.7.527]

BOGIE, ROBERT, a prisoner in Edinburgh Tolbooth, was transported via Leith to the colonies on 15 November 1679. [ETR]

BOGIE, ROBERT, in Armicanie, was accused, in Kirkcudbright on 4 October 1684 of aiding Mr Renwick and other rebels in 1684. [RPCS.IX.377]

BOICK, WILLIAM, was executed in Glasgow on 14 June 1673. [Clachan of Campsie gravestone, Stirlingshire]

BOIG, Mrs, servant to Mrs Duncan, a rebel, was banished and transported to Virginia, on 30 July 1668. [RPCS.II.503]

BOOGE, PATRICK, imprisoned in Edinburgh Tolbooth, was transported via Leith aboard the Phoenix of Leith bound for Virginia in April 1666. [ETR]

BOOG, ROBERT, from Strathmiglo, Fife, was transported via Leith aboard the Crown of London bound for Barbados on 27 November 1679, was shipwrecked and drowned off Orkney on 10 December 1679. [RBM]

BORTHWICK, THOMAS, from Linlithgow, West Lothian, was transported via Leith aboard the Crown of London bound for Barbados on 27 November 1679, was shipwrecked and drowned off Orkney on 10 December 1679. [RBM]

BORTHWICK, WILLIAM, of Johnstonburg, a Captain a Grenadier company of Lord Angus's Regiment, [the Cameronians], who fought at the Battle of Killiecrankie in 1689. [BK]

BORTHWICK, Major, of the Earl of Lindsay's Regiment, bound from Aberdeen for Ulster in 1641.

BOSTOUN, JAMES, from Dreghorn, Ayrshire, was transported via Leith aboard the Crown of London bound for Barbados on 27 November 1679, was shipwrecked and drowned off Orkney on 10 December 1679. [RBM]

BOUNTY, JAMES, in Kinswaid, for attending conventicles, was outlawed on 29 August 1672. [RPCS.III.583]

BOWIE, JOHN, from Glasgow, was banished to the Plantations in the [West] Indies, then transported via Leith aboard the St Michael of Scarborough on 12 December 1678. [RPCS.VI.76]

BOY, JOHN, was captured at the Siege of Worcester and transported via London aboard the John and Sarah bound for New England in December 1651, landed in Boston in February 1652. [SD.1.5-6]

BOYD, JOHN, was warded in Edinburgh Tolbooth, on 11 December 1684. [ETR]

BOYD, JOHN, an Ensign of Lord Angus's Regiment, [The Cameronians], fought at the Battle of Dunkeld in August 1679. [BK]

BOYD, ROBERT, of Portincrosss, was accused of participating in the Rebellion of 1679, was tried in 1680. [NRS.JC39.92]; was warded in Edinburgh Tolbooth on 2 December 1685, liberated on 8 February 1686. [ETR]

BOYD, ROBERT, former minister at Kilbride, imprisoned in Edinburgh Tolbooth was released on parole, to be resident with Hugh Blackie a merchant in Edinburgh, on 8 January 1685. [ETR]

BOYD, ROBERT, son of Robert Boyd of Portincrose, having subscribed to the Test Act, was released on 20 March 1685. [ETR]

BOYLE, JAMES, was tried for attending conventicles in 1687. [NRS.JC39.97]

BRABAND, ALEXANDER, was captured at the Battle of Dunbar in 1650, the transported via London aboard the Unity of Boston bound for New England in November 1650. [SCF.1226]

BRAID, JOHN, in Handistoun, for attending conventicles, was outlawed on 29 August 1672. [RPCS.III.583]

BRAIDWOOD, JAMES, from Carmannock, Lanarkshire, was banished to the Plantations in the [West] Indies on 1 August 1678 and transported via Leith aboard the St Michael of Scarborough on 12 December 1678. [RPCS.VI.76]

BRECKENRIDGE, WILLIAM, from Bothwell, Lanarkshire, was transported via Leith aboard the Crown of London bound for

Barbados on 27 November 1679, was shipwrecked and drowned off Orkney on 10 December 1679. [RBM]

BRIG, JOHN, in Bahassie, was accused, in Kirkcudbright in October 1684, of conversing with rebel Archibald McChesnuy in October 1683. [RPCS.IX.376]

BRISBANE, JOHN, of Freeland, was accused of frequenting conventicles, withdrawing from public ordinances and disorderly baptisms, on 22 July 1684. [RPCS.IX.52]; was fined £500 for attending conventicles between 1679 and 1682, and having his children irregularly baptised, as well as withdrawing from church, and imprisoned in Edinburgh Tolbooth until the fine was paid, July 1684, was liberated on 15 August 1684. [RPCS.IX.68] [ETR]

BROADFOOT, JAMES, in Glen Whargan, having aided Gilbert Gilchrist and three other rebels in April 1684, was declared a rebel and a fugitive in October 1684. [RPCS.IX.363]

BRODIE, ANDREW, was killed near Culteuchar Hill in 1678. [Forgandenny gravestone, Perthshire]

BROTHERSTAINES, JAMES, chaplain of Darroch's Regiment of Foot soldiers in 1659. [RHCA]

BROUNELL, HENRY, was captured at the Siege of Worcester in 1651 and transported via London aboard the _John and Sarah of London_ bound for New England, landed in Boston in February 1652. [SD.1.5-6]

BROWN, ARCHIBALD, fought in Argyll's Rebellion in 1685, was captured and banished to the Plantations on 30 July 1685, then transported via Leith bound for Jamaica in August 1685. [RPCS.XI.330]

BROWN, GEORGE, a journeyman tailor in Edinburgh, a rebel who refused to retract his Covenanting principles, was imprisoned in Edinburgh Tolbooth on 25 September 1684, [RPCS.IX.181]; then in Edinburgh Tolbooth, was transferred to Dunnottar Castle, Kincardineshire, on 29 July 1685. [ETR]; was banished to the American Plantations on 13 August 1685, and was transported via

Leith to East New Jersey in August 1685, landed there on 7 December 1685. [RPCS.XI.154] [NWI.I.422]

BROWN, JAMES, from Frosk, was banished to the Plantations in the [West] Indies on 1 August 1678 and transported via Leith aboard the St Michael of Scarborough on 12 December 1678. [RPCS.VI.76]

BROWN, JAMES, born 1634, a minister in exile in Rotterdam, Holland, from 1687 to 1690. [SEC]

BROWN, JOHN, was captured at the Siege of Worcester in 1651, and was transported via Gravesend, London, on board the John and Sarah of London bound for Boston, New England, in November 1651. [SD.1.5-6]

BROWN, JOHN, from Buchlyvie, Stirlingshire, was transported via Leith aboard the St Michael of Scarborough bound for the Plantations in the [West Indies] on 12 December 1678. [RPCS.VI.76]

BROWN, JOHN, from Midcalder, Midlothian, was transported via Leith aboard the Crown of London bound for Barbados on 27 November 1679, was shipwrecked and drowned off Orkney on 10 December 1679. [RBM]

BROWN, JOHN, of Priesthill, Muirkirk, Ayrshire, was killed at the Battle of Aird's Moss in July 1680.

BROWN, JOHN, a tailor in Kirkcudbright, was imprisoned in the Tolbooth there, then banished to the Plantations on 13 October 1684. [RPCS.X.258]

BROWN, JOHN, was warded in Edinburgh Tolbooth on 28 November 1684. [ETR]

BROWN, JOHN, was killed in March or April 1685. [Blackwood Estate gravestone, Kirkmuirhill, Lanarkshire]

BROWN, JOHN, was educated at Edinburgh University, minister at Wamphrey, Dumfries-shire, from 1655 until he was deprived in 1662, was imprisoned in Edinburgh Tolbooth, fled to Holland where he became minister of the Scots Kirk in Rotterdam in the Netherlands from 1663 until 1677, died there in September 1679. [F.II.224][SD.12] [SEC]

BROWN, JOHN, was warded in Edinburgh Tolbooth on 28 May 1685. [ETR] then in Edinburgh Tolbooth, was transferred to Dunnottar Castle, Kincardineshire, on 29 July 1685. [ETR]

BROWN, MARION, a widow, was accused of rioting in Kirkcudbright in the parish of Irongray, in 1663. [RPCS.I.373/408]; a rioter, was imprisoned in Kirkcudbright Tolbooth, then to stand at the market cross there on two days in September 1683. [GC.105]

BROWN, ROBERT, chaplain of Caithness's Regiment of Foot, a prisoner after the Siege of Worcester in 1651. [RHCA.365]

BROWN, ROBERT, from Kirkmabreck, Galloway, was transported via Leith aboard the Crown of London bound for Barbados on 27 November 1679, was shipwrecked and drowned off Orkney on 10 December 1679. [RBM]

BROWN, THOMAS, from Edinburgh, one of the assassins of Archbishop Sharp on Magus Moor, Fife, on 3 May 1679, was executed on 25 November 1679. [Magus Moor memorial][Z.203]

BROWN, THOMAS, from Gargunnock, Stirlingshire, was transported via Leith aboard the Crown of London bound for Barbados on 27 November 1679, was shipwrecked and drowned off Orkney on 10 December 1679. [RBM]

BROWN, THOMAS, in Branrig, for communing with William Harkness a rebel, was declared a rebel and fugitive in 1684, [RPCS.IX.359]; was transported to the colonies in July 1685. [RPCS.XI.114]

BROWN, WILLIAM, for his part in the recent rebellion was imprisoned in Edinburgh Tolbooth, having subscribed to a bond was released on 18 February 1669. [RPCS.II.602]

BROWN, WILLIAM, from Kilmarnock, Ayrshire, fought at the Battle of Bothwell Bridge, imprisoned in Edinburgh Tolbooth, was transported via Leith aboard the Crown of London bound for Barbados on 27 November 1679, was shipwrecked and drowned off Orkney on 10 December 1679. [RBM] [ETR]

BROWN, WILLIAM, servant of John Howatson, for aiding rebels and fugitives, was declared a rebel and fugitive in October 1684. [RPCS.IX.372]

BROWN, WILLIAM, was killed at Sanquhar, Dumfries-shire, in 1685. [Nithsdale Martyrs Cross, Dumfries]

BROWNING, WILLIAM, in Caldcoats, a rebel, subscribed to a bond of the peace in October 1668. [RPCS.II.548]

BROWNLIE, ROBERT, born 1589, was educated at the University of St Andrews, minister at Kirkton, Roxburghshire, from 1620 until September 1645 when he was murdered in his manse, after the Battle of Philiphaugh, by followers of the Marquis of Montrose. [F.II.129]

BROWNLEE, THOMAS, from Avondale, Lanarkshire, was transported via Leith aboard the Crown of London bound for Barbados on 27 November 1679, was shipwrecked and drowned off Orkney on 10 December 1679. [RBM][ETR]

BRUCE, ALEXANDER, a servant of mason John Hamilton, a rioter in Edinburgh, imprisoned in Edinburgh Tolbooth, was transported via Leith aboard the Phoenix of Leith bound for Virginia in April 1666. [ETR] [RPCS.II.195]

BRUCE, ARTHUR, fought at the Battle of Bothwell Bridge, Lanarkshire, on 22 June 1679, was executed at the Cross of Edinburgh on 30 November 1683, a confession and testimony. [RPCS.VIII.636]

BRUCE, MICHAEL, was educated at Edinburgh University in 1650s, minister at Killinchy, County Down, from 1657 until 1661, held conventicles, was sought in Scotland in 1664. [RPCS.I.551], was transferred from prison in Stirling Castle to Edinburgh Tolbooth in August 1668, [RPCS.II.459/s471]; to be transported to Barbados or Virginia in 1668. [RPCS.II.478]; to be transported via

Prestonpans aboard the John of Prestonpans, master John Jollie, bound for London in September 1668, [RPCS.II.535]; minister in Killinchy, County Down, from 1670 until 1689, died and buried in Scotland. [NRS.RD3.76.26; RD4.77.406][Killinchy gravestone]

BRUCE, ....., a servant in Edinburgh and a rioter there, was transported via Leith bound for Barbados in September 1666. [

BRUNTLEY, JAMES and JOHN, in Cothill, for attending conventicles, was outlawed on 29 August 1672. [RPCS.III.583]

BRUNTON, JANET, a prisoner in Edinburgh Tolbooth, was transported via Greenock to New York on 21 October 1682. [NRS.HH.11] [ETR.221]

BRUNTON, ROBERT, for his part in the Pentland Rising of 1666, was hanged in Glasgow on 19 December 1666. [Glasgow Cathedral]

BRYCE, JANET, a widow in Rotraw, was accused, in Kirkcudbright in October 1684, of conversing with rebel Gilbert McGie. [RPCS.IX.374]

BRYCE, JOHN, a mealmaker from Cambusnethan, Lanarkshire, a rebel in 1666, was banished to the Plantations in Virginia, was transported via Leith aboard the Convertin bound for Virginia on 18 June 1668. [RPCS.II.470/534]

BRYCE, JOHN, from Borgue, Kirkcudbrightshire, was transported via Leith aboard the Crown of London bound for Barbados on 27 November 1679, was shipwrecked and drowned off Orkney on 10 December 1679. [RBM]

BRYCE, JOHN, from Kirkmichael, Ayrshire, was transported via Leith aboard the Crown of London bound for Barbados on 27 November 1679, was shipwrecked and drowned off Orkney on 10 December 1679. [RBM]

BRYCE, MALCOLM, was banished to the Plantations on 30 July 1685, and stigmatised on 4 August 1685. [RPCS.XI.330]

BRYCE, MATTHEW, was accused of participating in the Earl of Argyll's Rebellion, in 1685. [NRS.JC39.72]

BRYCE, ROBERT, from Borgue, Galloway, was transported via Leith aboard the Crown of London bound for Barbados on 27 November 1679, was shipwrecked and drowned off Orkney on 10 December 1679. [RBM]

BRYCE, THOMAS, in Rotraw, was accused, in Kirkcudbright in October 1684, of conversing with rebel Gilbert McGie. [RPCS.IX.374]

BRYCE, THOMAS, a maltman from Irvine, Ayrshire, later in Glasgow, a rebel imprisoned in Glasgow Tolbooth, was banished to the Plantations in June 1684, and transported via Port Glasgow aboard the Pelican bound for Carolina in June 1684. [RPCS.IX.208]

BRYDEN, JAMES, was warded in Edinburgh Tolbooth on 20 May 1685, but having subscribed to the Test Act was released on 28 May 1685. [ETR]

BRYDEN, ROBERT, was warded in Edinburgh Tolbooth on 20 May 1685, but having subscribed to the Test Act was released on 28 May 1685. [ETR]

BUCHAN, WILLIAM, from Paisley, Renfrewshire, was transported via Leith aboard the Crown of London bound for Barbados on 27 November 1679, was shipwrecked and drowned off Orkney on 10 December 1679. [RBM]

BUCHANAN, ALEXANDER, from Buchlyvie, Stirlingshire, was transported via Leith aboard the St Michael of Scarborough bound for the Plantations in the West Indies on 12 December 1678. [RPCS.VI.76]

BUCHANAN, ANDREW, from Shirgarton, was transported via Leith aboard the St Michael of Scarborough bound for the Plantations in the West Indies on 12 December 1678. [RPCS.VI.76]

BUCHANAN, ANDREW, from Kippen, Stirlingshire, was transported via Glasgow aboard the Carolina Merchant bound for Carolina in June 1684. [RPCS.VIII.710]

BUCHANAN, DAVID, was captured at the Siege of Worcester in 1651 and transported via Gravesend, London, aboard the John and Sarah bound for Boston, New England, in December 1651. [SD.1.5-6]

BUCHANAN, GEORGE, of Buchanan, Colonel of a Regiment of Foot in the Army of the Covenant from 1648 until 1650, fought at the Battle of Dunbar in 1650 and at Inverkeithing on 20 July 1651 where he was captured and died later that year. [RHCA]

BUCHANAN, GEORGE, from Kippen, Stirlingshire, was transported via Glasgow aboard the Carolina Merchant bound for Carolina in June 1684. [RPCS.VIII.710] [ECJ.72]

BUCHANAN, GILBERT, a baker, son of Walter Buchanan in Glasgow, was banished to the [West] Indies on 13 June 1670. [RPCS.V.474]

BUCHANAN, JAMES, from Gargunnock, Stirlingshire, was transported via Leith aboard the Crown of London bound for Barbados on 27 November 1679, was shipwrecked and drowned off Orkney on 10 December 1679. [RBM]

BUCHANAN, JOHN, was captured at the Siege of Worcester in 1651 and transported via Gravesend, London, aboard the John and Sarah bound for Boston, New England, in December 1651, landed there in February 1652. [SD.1.5-6]

BUCHANAN, JOHN, son of John Buchanan, a cooper in Glasgow, a rebel imprisoned in Glasgow Tolbooth, was banished in June 1684 and transported via Glasgow aboard the Pelican bound for Carolina in June 1684. [RPCS.IX.208]

BUCHANAN, MARION, a prisoner in Edinburgh Tolbooth was transported via Greenock bound for New York on 21 October 1682. [ETR.221] [NRS.HH11]

BUCKLE, ANDREW, from Fenwick, Ayrshire, was transported via Leith aboard the Crown of London bound for Barbados on 27 November 1679, was shipwrecked and drowned off Orkney on 10 December 1679. [RBM]

BUGLASS, JAMES, a minister in Galloway, was accused of holding conventicles within the Presbytery in 1666. [GC.107]

BUNTON, ROBERT, fought at Bothwell Bridge, Lanarkshire, on 22 June 1679, was tried in Glasgow on 1 March 1684, and executed on 19 March 1684. [Glasgow Cathedral plaque]

BUNTRUM, JOHN, a baker in Strathmiglo, Fife, for attending conventicles, was outlawed on 29 August 1672. [RPCS.III.583]

BURDEN, ALEXANDER, from Barr, Ayrshire, was transported via Leith aboard the Crown of London bound for Barbados on 27 November 1679, was shipwrecked and drowned off Orkney on 10 December 1679. [RBM]

BURGESS, ALEXANDER, was captured at the Battle of Dunbar in September 1650 and transported via London aboard the Unity of Boston bound for New England in November 1650. [SCF.1226]

CAIRNCROSS, ...., a Lieutenant of the Covenanter Garrison at Spynie Castle in 1640. [NRS.GD188.19.1.8]

CAIRNDUFF, JOHN, from Avondale, Lanarkshire, was transported via Leith aboard the Crown of London bound for Barbados on 27 November 1679, was shipwrecked and drowned off Orkney on 10 December 1679. [RBM]

CAIRNS, ALEXANDER, factor to Kenmure, was accused, in Kirkcudbright in October 1684, of aiding rebels .... Gordon of Craig, MacCormack of Barley, and Mr Thomas Vernor. [RPCS.IX.377]

CAIRNS, JAMES, in Ironspie, was accused in Kirkcudbright of conversing with a rebel and fugitive, William Russell, in 1684. [RPCS.IX.374]

CAIRNS, MARGARET, spouse of Andrew Carsane in Meikle Careltoune, was accused, in Wigtown in October 1684, of aiding rebel Gilbert McGie, and supplying money for the prisoners on the Bass Rock in the Firth of Forth, [RPCS.IX.374] transported via Leith aboard the Crown of London bound for Barbados on 27 November 1679, was shipwrecked and drowned off Orkney on 10 December 1679. [RBM]

CALDERWOOD, Reverend WILLIAM, minister of Legerwood, Berwickshire, from 1655 until 1662 when he was ejected, died in 1709. [F.XI.]

CALDOW, ROBERT, from Balmaghie, Galloway, fought at the Battle of Bothwell Bridge on 22 June 1679, was transported via Leith aboard the Crown of London bound for Barbados on 27 November 1679, was shipwrecked and drowned off Orkney on 10 December 1679. [RBM]

CALDWELL, JOHN, of Caldwell, was warded in Edinburgh Tolbooth on 13 November 1684. [ETR]

CALDWELL, JOHN, a Captain of Lord Angus's Regiment, [the Cameronians], who fought at the Battle of Killiecrankie in 1689, died of wounds in Dunkeld. [BK]

CALDWELL, WILLIAM, from Girvan, Ayrshire, was transported via Leith aboard the Crown of London bound for Barbados on 27 November 1679, was shipwrecked and drowned off Orkney on 10 December 1679. [RBM]

CALLEND, JAMES, a glover, was transported via Glasgow bound for the American Plantations in May 1685. [RPCS.VIII.516]

CALLENDAR, ALESTAR, was captured at the Siege of Worcester in September 1651 and transported via London aboard the John and Sarah bound for New England in December 1651, landed in Boston in February 1652. [SD.1.5-6]

CALLENDAR, DAVID, was captured at the Siege of Worcester in September 1651 and transported via London aboard the John and Sarah bound for New England in December 1651, landed in Boston in February 1652. [SD.1.5-6]

CALLENDAR, JAMES, was captured at the Siege of Worcester in September 1651 and transported via London aboard the John and Sarah bound for New England in December 1651, landed in Boston in February 1652. [SD.1.5-6]

CALLUM, JAMES, a glover from Dumfries, was transported in 1666, and died in Carolina. [HD.443]

CAMERON, Reverend ALEXANDER, a minister in Kilbride, Argyll, later in Rasharkan, Ireland, a sasine, 1683. [NRS.RS59.2.76]

CAMERON, HUGH, from Dalmellington, Ayrshire, fought at the Battle of Bothwell Bridge in 1679. was transported via Leith aboard the Crown of London bound for Barbados on 27 November 1679, was shipwrecked and drowned off Orkney on 10 December 1679. [RBM]

CAMERON, MICHAEL, was killed at the Battle of Aird's Moss on 22 July 1680. [Muirkirk Monument, Ayrshire]

CAMERON, RICHARD, born 1640s, from Falkland, Fife, a minister in exile in Rotterdam, Holland, in 1679. [SEC]

CAMERON, Reverend RICHARD, born in Falkland, Fife, author of the Sanquhar Declaration, renounced all allegiance to King Charles II, was killed at the Battle of Aird's Moss on 22 July 1680. [Muirkirk Monument Ayrshire][Z.201]

CAMERON, ROBERT, from West Teviotdale, was imprisoned in Canongate Tolbooth, then was banished to the Plantations on 24 July 1685, was transported bound for Jamaica in August 1685, died at sea. [RPCS.XI.329]

CAMPBELL, ALEXANDER, from Calder, Mid Lothian, in Ireland by 1685. [RPCS.X.413]

CAMPBELL, ALEXANDER, an advocate, was tried for his part in Argyll's Rebellion, in 1685. [NRS.JC39.8]

CAMPBELL, ALEXANDER, of Sonachan, Argyll, was accused of participating in the Earl of Argyll's Rebellion in 1685 and tried in 1687. [NRS.JC39.88]

CAMPBELL, ARCHIBALD, Earl of Argyll, was executed on 27 May 1661 in Edinburgh. [Grayfriars Monument] [NRS.JC39.114]

CAMPBELL, ARCHIBALD, son of Lord Neil Campbell, tried for his part in the Earl of Argyll's Rebellion, in 1685. [NRS.JC39.82]; was banished from Britain and Ireland never to return, 31 August 1685. [ETR]

CAMPBELL, ARCHIBALD, from Mondrige, Kintyre, Argyll, imprisoned in Paul's Work, Edinburgh, found guilty of taking part in the Earl of Argyll's rebellion in 1685, was banished to the American Plantations on 24 July 1685, was stigmatised on 4 August 1685, landed in East New Jersey in December 1685. [NRS.JC39.72/77] [RPCS.XI.329] [NJSA. EJD.Liber A.225]

CAMPBELL, ARCHIBALD, of Danna, was warded in Edinburgh Tolbooth on 28 July 1685, [ETR]; and was tried for his part in Argyll's Rebellion, in 1685. [NRS.JC39.86]

CAMPBELL, CHARLES, from Airth, Stirlingshire, was banished to the American Plantations on 18 August 1670. [RPCS.III.207/228/258]

CAMPBELL, CHARLES, son of the Earl of Argyll, was tried for his part in Argyll's Rebellion, in 1685. [NRS.JC39.82]

CAMPBELL, CHARLES, son of Lord Neil Campbell was warded in Edinburgh Tolbooth on 21 August 1685. [ETR]

CAMPBELL, COLIN, Captain of Argyll's Regiment in Dunluce, Antrim in 1642. [SCIC]

CAMPBELL, COLIN, of Blairintibbert, was warded in Edinburgh Tolbooth on 28 July 1685, [ETR] and was tried for his part in Argyll's Rebellion, in 1685. [NRS.JC39.86]

CAMPBELL, Sir COLIN, of Ardkinglass, a prisoner in Edinburgh Tolbooth, was transferred to Blackness Castle on 16 September 1684, later was brought from Blackness Castle to Edinburgh Tolbooth on 30 April 1685. [ETR]

CAMPBELL, COLIN, for participating in Argyll's Rebellion of Spring 1685, he was banished to the American Plantations on 30 July

1685, then stigmatised and transported via Leith to East New Jersey in July 1685. [RPCS.XI.329]

CAMPBELL, COLIN, brother german to Walter Campbell of Skipness, Argyll, was hanged for his part in the Earl of Argyll's Rebellion in 1685. [Inveraray Covenanters Memorial, Argyll]

CAMPBELL, DAVID, from Falkirk, Stirlingshire, was banished to the American Plantations on 11 August 1685, then transported via Leith aboard the Henry and Francis bound for East New Jersey on 11 August 1685, landed there on 7 December 1685. [RPCS.XI.145/159/321] [NWI.I.422]

CAMPBELL, DONALD, of Ob, was tried for his part in Argyll's Rebellion of 1685, in 1686. [NRS.JC39.86]

CAMPBELL, DONALD, of Belnabie, was tried for his part in Argyll's Rebellion, in 1685. [NRS.JC39.86]

CAMPBELL, DONALD, of Barbreck, was tried for his part in Argyll's Rebellion, in 1685. [NRS.JC39.83]

CAMPBELL, Sir DONALD, of Auchinbreck, was tried for his part in Argyll's Rebellion, in 1685. [NRS.JC39.83]

CAMPBELL, DONALD, was banished to the Plantations and transported via Leith to Jamaica in August 1685. [RPCS.XI.330]

CAMPBELL, DOUGLAS, of Kilberry, Argyll, was tried for his part in Argyll's Rebellion, in 1685. [NRS.JC39.83]

CAMPBELL, Sir DUNCAN, of Auchinbreck, Lieutenant Colonel of Argyll's Regiment in Dunluce, County Antrim, in 1642. [SCIC]

CAMPBELL, DUNCAN, of Inverliver, Captain of Argyll's Regiment, Captain of Argyll's Regiment in Dunluce, County Antrim, in 1642. [SCIC]

CAMPBELL, DUNCAN, of Dunans, Captain of Argyll's Regiment in Dunluce, Antrim, in 1642. [SCIC]

CAMPBELL, DUNCAN, son of Colin Campbell of Blairtibert, was warded in Edinburgh Tolbooth on 28 July 1685, suspected of being in Argyll's Rebellion. [ETR]

CAMPBELL, DUNCAN, of Drumsire, was tried for his part in Argyll's Rebellion, in 1685. [NRS.JC39.86]

CAMPBELL, DUNCAN, of Carradale, was tried for his part in Argyll's Rebellion, in 1685. [NRS.JC39.83]

CAMPBELL, DUNCAN, a tenant of the Earl of Breadalbane, suspected of being a rebel, was released on 23 September 1685. [ETR]

CAMPBELL, EWAN, in Craignis, was warded in Edinburgh Tolbooth on 28 July 1685, accused of being in Argyll's Rebellion. [ETR]

CAMPBELL, GEORGE, from Irvine, Ayrshire, was transported via Leith aboard the Crown of London bound for Barbados on 27 November 1679, was shipwrecked and drowned off Orkney on 10 December 1679. [RBM] [Irvine gravestone]

CAMPBELL, Sir GEORGE, son of Sir Hugh Campbell of Cessnock, imprisoned in Edinburgh Tolbooth for treason, was released on 4 August 1685. [ETR]

CAMPBELL, HUGH, born 1626, was educated at the University of Glasgow, minister a Riccarton, Ayrshire, from 1650 until deprived in 1662, he returned in 1687 and died after 7 October 1690. [F.III.64]

CAMPBELL, Sir HUGH, of Cessnock, imprisoned in Edinburgh Tolbooth for treason, was released on 4 August 1685. [ETR]

CAMPBELL, JAMES, was captured at the Siege of Worcester in September 1651, and transported via Gravesend, London, aboard the John and Sarah bound for New England in December 1651, landed in Boston in February 1652. [SD.1.5-6]

CAMPBELL, JAMES, of Glendarell, subscribed in Inveraray, Argyll, to a bond undertaking that he will not assist the Earl of Argyll or any other rebel under a penalty of 4,000 pounds Scots, dated 27 August 1684. [RPCS.IX.318]

CAMPBELL, JAMES, of Treesbanks, Ayrshire, imprisoned in Edinburgh Tolbooth, having taken the Test Act, was released on 17 December 1684. [ETR]

CAMPBELL, JANET, a prisoner in Edinburgh Tolbooth, was transported via Greenock bound for New York on 21 October 1682. [ETR.221]

CAMPBELL, JOHN, Captain of Argyll's Regiment in Ballycastle, Ulster, in 1642. [SCIC]

CAMPBELL, JOHN, was captured at the Siege of Worcester in September 1651, and transported via Gravesend, London, aboard the John and Sarah bound for New England in December 1651, landed in Boston in February 1652. [SD.1.5-6]

CAMPBELL, JOHN, was educated a Glasgow University, minister at Sorn, Ayrshire, from 1658 until deprived in 1662, then preached at conventicles, imprisoned in 1684. [F.III.68]

CAMPBELL, JOHN, a prisoner in Edinburgh Tolbooth, was transported via Leith aboard the Phoenix of Leith bound for Virginia in April 1666. [ETR]

CAMPBELL, JOHN, from Muirkirk, Ayrshire, was transported via Leith aboard the Crown of London bound for Barbados on 27 November 1679, was shipwrecked and drowned off Orkney on 10 December 1679. [RBM]

CAMPBELL, JOHN, from Muirkirk, Ayrshire, a rebel imprisoned in Canongait Tolbooth, was released in September 1684. [RPCS.IX.170]

CAMPBELL, JOHN, late minister of Dalgean, a prisoner in Edinburgh Tolbooth, was released on condition he did not keep conventicles or marry or baptise, on 24 January 1684. [ETR]

CAMPBELL, JOHN, a gentleman, was warded in Edinburgh Tolbooth, accused of in Argyll's Rebellion, on 28 July 1685. [ETR]

CAMPBELL, JOHN, son of the Earl of Argyll, was tried for his part in Argyll's Rebellion, in 1685. [NRS.JC39.82]; was warded in Edinburgh Tolbooth on 22 August 1685, was transported to Stirling Castle on 1 September 1685. [ETR]

CAMPBELL, alias BEUTIE, JOHN, was warded in Edinburgh Tolbooth on 26 May 1685. [ETR]

CAMPBELL, JOHN, of Artarich, was accused of participating in the Earl of Argyll's Rebellion of 1685 and was tried in 1687. [NRS.JC39.88]

CAMPBELL, JOHN, the younger of Melfort, Argyll, was tried for his part in Argyll's Rebellion, in 1685. [NRS.JC39.83]

CAMPBELL, JOHN, of Knap, was tried for his part in Argyll's Rebellion, in 1685. [NRS.JC39.83]

CAMPBELL, JOHN, of Ulva, Argyll, was tried for his part in Argyll's Rebellion, in 1685. [NRS.JC39.86]

CAMPBELL, JOHN, son of Donald Campbell in Auchenchrydie, Cowal, Argyll, a prisoner in Paul's Work, Edinburgh, was banished to the Plantations on 24 July 1685 and transported to Jamaica on 7 August 1685. [RPCS.XI.329]

CAMPBELL, JOHN, son of Walter Campbell in Dunalter, Kintyre, Argyll, a prisoner in Paul's Work, Edinburgh, was banished to the Plantations on 24 July 1685 and transported to Jamaica on 7 August 1685. [RPCS.XI.329]

CAMPBELL, JOHN, son of Robert Campbell at Lochwoar, Lorne, Argyll, a prisoner in Paul's Work, Edinburgh, was banished to the Plantations on 24 July 1685 and transported to Jamaica on 7 August 1685. [RPCS.XI.329]

CAMPBELL, JOHN, in Lochfyneside, Argyll, a prisoner in Paul's Work, Edinburgh, was banished to the Plantations on 24 July 1685 and transported to East New Jersey in July 1685, landed there in December 1685. [RPCS.XI.329] [EJD.Liber.A.225]

CAMPBELL, JOHN, born 1642, from Wellwood, was banished to the Plantations in 1683, returned from Jamaica in 1685, died in 1721. [Barr gravestone, Ayrshire]

CAMPBELL, JOHN, in Kirkcudbright, was accused, in Kirkcudbright in October 1684, of conversing with rebels, John Coultart and William Campbell. [RPCS.IX.374]

CAMPBELL, JOHN, from Over Wellwood, a rebel imprisoned in Canongait Tolbooth, was released in September 1684. [RPCS.IX.170]

CAMPBELL, JOHN, of Duntroon, imprisoned in Edinburgh Tolbooth for his part in Argyll's Rebellion, was released on 19 March 1686. [ETR]

CAMPBELL, JOHN, of Moy, a Captain of Lord Angus's Regiment, [the Cameronians], who fought at the Battle of Killiecrankie in 1689. [BK]

CAMPBELL, JOHN, of Moy, the younger, a Captain of Lord Angus's Regiment, [the Cameronians], who fought at the Battle of Killiecrankie in 1689. [BK]

CAMPBELL, MATTHEW, Captain of Argyll's Regiment in Ballymoney, Ulster, in 1642. [SCIC]

CAMPBELL, NEIL, was captured at the Siege of Worcester in 1651, was transported via Gravesend, London, aboard the John and Sarah bound for New England, landed in Boston in February 1652. [SD.I.5-6]

CAMPBELL, NEIL, from Argyll, was taken from Blackness Castle to Edinburgh Tolbooth on 25 May 1685; [ETR]; for his part in Argyll's Rebellion of 1685, was transported via Leith bound for East New Jersey in August 1685. [RPCS.XI,136]

CAMPBELL, PATRICK, of Torblaren, born 1633, son of Donald Campbell, was educated at the University of Glasgow, minister of Glenaray, Argyll, from 1657 until deprived in 1662, he was arrested in 1681 but released in 1685 on condition that he left the kingdom, he returned in 1687 and died in March 1700, his son born 13 March 1673 was Colonel John Campbell of Black River, Jamaica, who died there on 29 January 1740. [F.IV.9]

CAMPBELL, ROBERT, then in Edinburgh Tolbooth, put in irons and imprisoned in Canongait Tolbooth on 29 July 1685. [ETR]

CAMPBELL, ROBERT, a prisoner in Canongait and in Leith Tolbooths, was banished to the Plantations in August 1685, and transported via Leith aboard the <u>Henry and Francis</u> bound for East New Jersey in August 1685, landed there on 7 December 1685. [RPCS.XI.115/145/159/329] [NJSA.EJD.Liber A.225]

CAMPBELL, WILLIAM, Major of Argyll's Regiment in Ballycastle, Ulster, in 1642. [SCIC]

CAMPBELL, WILLIAM, a rebel imprisoned in Edinburgh Tolbooth, was released in September 1684. [RPCS.IX.170]

CAMPBELL, WILLIAM, from Arras, was warded in Edinburgh Tolbooth on 28 July 1685, accused of his part in Argyll's Rebellion. [ETR]

CAMPBELL, WILLIAM, a prisoner in Leith Tolbooths, was banished to the Plantations in August 1685, and transported via Leith aboard the <u>Henry and Francis</u> bound for East New Jersey in August 1685, landed there on 7 December 1685. [RPCS.XI.115/145/159/329] [NWI.I.422]

CAMPBELL, WILLIAM, an Ensign of Lord Angus's Regiment, [The Cameronians], fought at the Battle of Killiecrankie and the Siege of Dunkeld in August 1689. [BK]

CAMPBELL, WILLIAM, at Blatts Mill, was accused in Kirkcudbright of conversing with Alexander Campbell and other rebels, in 1684. [RPCS.IX.374]

CAMPBELL, Major, was hanged for his part in the Earl of Argyll's Rebellion in 1685. [Inveraray Covenanters Memorial, Argyll]

CANNON, GILBERT, in Miltoun of Dalry, a rebel sought in 1667. [RPCS.II.345]

CANNON, JAMES, of Barnshalloch, the younger, was sought by the Justice Court in August 1667 for his part in the late rebellion. [GC.123] [RPCS.II.345]

CANNON, ......, of Barley, a rebel, was sought in 1667. [RPCS.II.345]

CANNON, JOHN, of Barley, Dumfries-shire, was indicted for 'hearing and recepting rebellious preachers', in 1684. [RPCS.IX.555]

CANNON, ROBERT, in Middleton of Dalry, Kirkcudbrightshire, was sought by the Justice Court in August 1667 for his part in the late rebellion. [GC.123] [RPCS.II.345]

CANNON, ROBERT, of Mardrochat [Mondrogat?], the younger, was sought by the Justice Court in August 1667 for his part in the late rebellion. [GC.123] [RPCS.II.345]; a prisoner in September 1668. [RPCS.II.542/547]

CANNON, JOHN, of Phirmastoun, Dumfries-shire, was indicted at Dumfries for harbouring his brother David Cannon, ..... Gilchrist, and Patrick Vernour, preachers and traitors in 1684. [RPCS.IX.555]

CANNON, SAMUEL, from Banscalloch, Kirkcudbrightshire, was imprisoned in Kirkcudbright Tolbooth, was banished to the Plantations on 13 October 1684, then taken via Dumfries to Edinburgh where he was imprisoned in Canongait Tolbooth on 16 February 1685. [RPCS.X.258/377/604]

CANT, JOHN, a minister in Galloway, was accused of holding conventicles within the Presbytery in 1666. [GC.107]

CARGILL, DONALD, born 1621, a field preacher, 1679. [NRS.JC39/20]; joint author of the Sanquhar Declaration, a minister in exile in Rotterdam, Holland, in 1679, was captured in Queensferry on 3 June 1680 and imprisoned in Canongait Tolbooth; trial papers. [NRS.JC39.115], was beheaded in Edinburgh on 27 July 1681. [SEC]

CARLISLE, ROBERT, of Locharture, was indicted in Dumfries for harbouring Robert McInstrae in Halmyre, a declared traitor, in 1684. [RPCS.IX.555]

CARMICHAEL, DANIEL, a rebel in 1684. [RPCS.IX.363]

CARMICHAEL, JOHN, was captured at the Siege of Worcester, then transported via Gravesend, London, aboard the John and Sarah bound for New England in December 1651, landed in Boston in February 1652. [SD.I.5-6]

CARMICHAEL, WILLIAM, was captured at the Siege of Worcester, then transported via Gravesend, London, aboard the John and Sarah bound for New England in December 1651, landed in Boston in February 1652. [SD.I.5-6]

CARMONT, SAMUEL, a burgess of Kirkcudbright, was imprisoned in Edinburgh Tolbooth, for his wife's part in the tumult in Kirkcudbright, was released after guaranteeing his wife's future attitude toward bishops, the Church and the State in 1663. [RPCS.I.377]

CARNOCHAN, EDMOND, a prisoner in Canongait Tolbooth, who refused to take an Oath of Allegiance, was banished to the American Plantations on 17 December 1685. [ETR], was transported via Leith aboard the John and Nicholas bound for Barbados on 17 December 1685. [RPCS.IX.389] [ETR]

CARNOCK, MARGARET, from Dalkeith, Midlothian, imprisoned in Edinburgh Tolbooth for conversing with rebels, was liberated on 28 January 1684. [ETR]

CARSE, MARGARET, in West Calder, Mid Lothian, a rebel and rioter, was banished and transported to Virginia, on 30 July 1668. [RPCS.II.503]

CARSEHILL, JAMES, having attended conventicles he was tried for treason in 1687. [NRS.JC39.100]

CARSAN, JOHN, of Senwick, was accused of rioting in Kirkcudbright in the parish of Irongray, in 1663. [RPCS.I.373]

CARSAN, THOMAS, and his spouse Margaret Gibson, in Kirkcudbright, were accused of rioting in Kirkcudbright in the parish of Irongray, in 1663. [RPCS.I.373]

CARSTAIRS, JOHN, fought at the Battle of Rullion Green, was sought by the Justice Court in August 1667 for his part in the late rebellion. [GC.123]

CARSTAIRS, WILLIAM, was imprisoned in Edinburgh Tolbooth, where he was tortured to reveal what he knew of the Earl of Argyll's plots, in September 1684, but refused to provide answers. [RPCS.IX.144]; was tortured and undertook to provide limited information, 6 September 1684, then was transferred to Dunbarton Castle in September 1684. [RPCS.IX.179/344][ETR]

CARTER, NEIL, was captured at the Siege of Worcester in September 1651, and transported vis Gravesend, London, aboard the John and Sarah bound for New England in December 1651, landed at Boston in February 1652. [SD.1.5-6]

CASSILLS, JEAN, servant of John Russell in Easter Lenzie, Dunbartonshire, was tried in Glasgow, imprisoned and banished to the Plantations on 6 October 1684. [RPCS.IX.292/709]

CATHCART, ROBERT, in Docherneill, born 1654, admitted having been at conventicles, was fined and subscribed to a bond, in 1684. [RPCS.IX.517]

CAVERS, JOHN, a prisoner in Edinburgh Tolbooth, was transported via Leith aboard the St Michael of Scarborough bound for the West Indies on 12 December 1678. [RPCS.VI.76]

CAVIE, CHRISTIAN, was imprisoned in Dunnottar Castle, then in Leith and Edinburgh Tolbooths, before being banished to the Plantations on 11 October 1684, was was taken from Leith Tolbooth, put in irons and imprisoned in Edinburgh Tolbooth, [ETR], then transported via Leith aboard the Henry and Francis bound for East New Jersey in August 1685, landed there on 7 December 1685.

CHALMERS, JAMES, of Waterside, in the parish of Kells, Kirkcudbrightshire, a suspected Covenanter in 1665. [GC.111]

CHALMERS, ROBERT, brother of ... Chalmers of Gadgirth, was sought by the Justice Court in August 1667 for his part in the late rebellion. [GC.123] [RPCS.II.345]; his banishment to Tangiers was postponed in 1669. [RPCS.II.611]

CHALMERS, ROBERT, from Shotts, Lanarkshire, was transported via Leith aboard the Crown of London bound for Barbados on 27 November 1679, was shipwrecked and drowned off Orkney on 10 December 1679. [RBM]

CHANCELLOR, JAMES, of Shillhill, was warded in Edinburgh Tolbooth on 13 November 1684, having taken the Oath of Allegiance was released on 6 December 1684. [ETR]

CHEYNE, JOHN, was captured at the Siege of Worcester in 1651, and was transported via Gravesend, London, aboard the John and Sarah bound for New England in December 1651, landed in Boston in February 1652. [SD.1.5-6]

CHISHOLM, ADAM, in Mossdaill, to be tried accused of rebellion, 3 June 1684. [RPCS.IX.205]

CHRISTIE, ROBERT, in Blairstrowie, for attending conventicles, was outlawed on 29 August 1672. [RPCS.III.583]

CHRISTISON, JOHN, from Kilmadock, Perthshire, was transported via Leith aboard the Crown of London bound for Barbados on 27 November 1679, was shipwrecked and drowned off Orkney on 10 December 1679. [RBM]

CLERK, ANDREW, from Lochruttan, Galloway, fought at the Battle of Bothwell Bridge, was transported via Leith aboard the Crown of London bound for Barbados on 27 November 1679, was shipwrecked and drowned off Orkney on 10 December 1679. [RBM]

CLARK, DAVID, in Beckbie, was accused of conversing with rebel John Corsan in May 1684. [RPCS.IX.376]

CLERK, DOUGALD, a farmer at Otter Gallachie, Argyll, a prisoner to be returned to the ship at Leith bound for Jamaica on 12 August 1685. [ETR][RPCS.II.330]

CLARK, JAMES, from Kilbride, Lanarkshire, was transported via Leith aboard the Crown of London bound for Barbados on 27 November 1679, was shipwrecked and drowned off Orkney on 10 December 1679. [RBM]

CLARK, JOHN, was captured at the Battle of Dunbar in 1650, and transported via London aboard the Unity of Boston bound for Boston in November 1650. [SCF.1226]

CLARK, JOHN, a writer in Edinburgh, a prisoner in Edinburgh Tolbooth, was banished to the Plantations on 12 December 1678, and transported via Leith aboard the St Michael of Scarborough [RPCS.VI.76]

CLARK, JOHN, from Kilbride, Lanarkshire, was transported via Leith aboard the Crown of London bound for Barbados on 27 November 1679, was shipwrecked and drowned off Orkney on 10 December 1679. [RBM]

CLERK, MARY, from Kirkcudbright, was transported via Leith bound for Jamaica in August 1685, landed at Port Royal in November 1685. [RPCS.IX.573; XI.329][LJ.30]

CLARKSON, JAMES, from Linlithgow, West Lothian, imprisoned in Edinburgh Tolbooth, was transported to Carolina in 1684. [RPCS.VIII.527]

CLEGHORN, JAMES, a prisoner of war, was transported to New England around 1650. [NWI.I.159]

CLELAND, JAMES, in Stains, a fugitive, was warded in Edinburgh Tolbooth on 2 July 1684, then released on 14 August 1684. [ETR]

CLELAND, JOHN, son of George Cleland of Durisdeer, was educated at Edinburgh University, minister at Stow from 1640, 'he joined the Protesters in 1651', and died in August 1665. [F.II.163]

CLELAND, WILLIAM, born 1661, led the Covenanters at the Battle of Drumclog in June 1679, later, as Lieutenant Colonel he commanded the Earl of Angus's Regiment, [The Cameronians], against the Jacobite Highlanders at the Battle of Killiecrankie, was killed at the Siege of Dunkeld in 1689. [BK][Z.185]

CLEMENT, JAMES, was killed on Kirkconnell Moor, Kirkcudbrightshire, in 1685. [Kirkconnell Moor Monument]

CLERK, DOUGAL, from Otter, Argyll, a tenant farmer of the laird of Gallachie, a participant in Argyll's Rebellion, was imprisoned in Edinburgh Tolbooth, then transported via Leith to Jamaica on 12 August 1685. [ETR.373][RPCS.II.330]

CLERK, JOHN, in Meikle Careltoune, was accused, in October 1684 in Kirkcudbright, of conversing with rebel John Clinton. [RPCS.IX.374]

CLERK, JOHN, participated in Argyll's Rebellion, and was transported via Leith to New England on 9 July 1685. [RPCS.XI.94]

CLERK, MARY, was banished to the Plantations on 28 July 1685, then transported via Leith to Jamaica in August 1685, landed at Port Royal, Jamaica, in November 1685. [RPCS.XI.329][LC.30]

CLOUSTON, WILLIAM, was captured at the Siege of Worcester in 1651, then transported via London aboard the John and Sarah bound for New England in December 1651, landed in Boston in February 1652. [SD.15-6]

CLYDE, JOHN, from Kilbryde, one of the assassins of Archbishop Sharp on Magus Moor, Fife, on 3 May 1679, was executed on 25 November 1679. [Magus Moor memorial][Z.203]

CLYDE, WILLIAM, chaplain of Drummond's Horse Regiment, was captured at the Siege of Worcester in September 1651. [RHCA.369]

COCHRANE, GAVIN, of Craigmuir, a Captain of Lord Angus's Regiment, [the Cameronians], who fought at the Battle of Killiecrankie in 1689. [BK]

COCHRAN, JOHN, from Avondale, Lanarkshire, was transported via Leith aboard the Crown of London bound for Barbados on 27

November 1679 was shipwrecked and drowned off Orkney on 10 December 1679. [RBM]

COCHRANE, Sir JOHN, and his son John Cochrane, prisoners, were brought from Hamilton to be warded in Edinburgh Tolbooth on 3 July 1685. [ETR]

COCHRANE, MUNGO, a merchant burgess of Glasgow, a Covenanter in Edinburgh Tolbooth, was transported via Leith aboard the St Michael of Scarborough bound for the West Indies on 12 December 1678. [RPCS.VI.76]

COCHRANE, MUNGO, then in Edinburgh Tolbooth, was transferred to Dunnottar Castle, Kincardineshire, on 29 July 1685. [ETR]

COCHRANE, NICOL, born 1645, portioner of Newtown, died on 20 January 1703. [Melrose Abbey gravestone, Roxburghshire]. [Kirkton gravestone, Bathgate, West Lothian]

COGAN, ROBERT, schoolmaster in Glencairn, and his wife Isobel Kirko, for aiding rebels Alexander McCubbin, James MacMichael, and two others, were declared to be rebels and fugitives in October 1684. [RPCS.IX.367]

COLLIE, JOHN, a prisoner in Edinburgh Tolbooth, was transferred to Dunnottar Castle in Kincardineshire, on 29 July 1685. [ETR]

COLQUHOUN, JOHN, was captured at the Siege of Worcester in 1651, and transported via London aboard the John and Sarah bound for New England in December 1651, landed in Boston in February 1652. [SD.1.5-6]

COLQUHOUN, JOHN, of Kenmure, fled to Ireland during 1680. [NRS.GD61.71]

COLQUHOUN, JOHN, a prisoner in Edinburgh Tolbooth in May 1685. [ETR]

COLVILL, HENDRY, in Orr, imprisoned in Canongait Tolbooth suspected of being a rebel, having taken the Oath of Allegiance, was released on 18 July 1667. [RPCS.II.399]

COLVILL, JAMES, from Glencairn, Nithsdale, Dumfries-shire, was transported via Leith aboard the Crown of London bound for Barbados on 27 November 1679, was shipwrecked and drowned off Orkney on 10 December 1679. [RBM]

COLVIN, JAMES, was killed at Scarvating in 1679. [Nithsdale Martyrs Cross, Dumfries]

CONGILTON, JOHN, from Edinburgh, was transported via Leith aboard the Mary bound for Barbados on 8 May 1663. [EBR.186.13.4]

CONNELL, JOHN, was captured at the Siege of Worcester in 1651, and transported via London aboard the John and Sarah bound for New England, in December 1651, landed in Boston in February 1652. [SD.1.5-6]

CONANE, JOHN, in Crofthead Tynwald, for harbouring a rebel's wife, was 'committed to the castle' in 1684. [RPCS.IX.703]

CONDY, JOHN, in Cothill, for attending conventicles, was outlawed on 29 August 1672. [RPCS.III.583]

CONYNGHAM, GEORGE, was t the Siege of Worcester in September 1651, a lease in the parish of Raphoe, County Donegal, by 1654. [CS]

COOK, ANDREW, from Melrose, Roxburghshire, was transported via Leith aboard the Crown of London bound for Barbados on 27 November 1679, was shipwrecked and drowned off Orkney on 10 December 1679. [RBM]

COOKE, THOMAS, was killed at the Loan of Balmadie on 11 May 1685. [Cathcart gravestone, Glasgow]

COOPER, ALEXANDER, was captured at the Battle of Dunbar in September 1650, and transported via London aboard the Unity bound for Boston, New England, in November 1650, probate 1684, Maine.

COPLAND, JOHN, sometime in Drumcork, a rebel, accused of aiding in the ambush at Enterkin, his wife Agnes Rosper and their daughter were also declared rebels in 1684. [RPCS.IX.359]

CORBETT, ANDREW, was banished to the Plantations on 13 August 1685, transported via Leith aboard the Henry and Francis bound for East New Jersey in August 1685. [RPCS.XI.154][NWI.I.422]

CORBETT, JOHN, was banished to the Plantations on 13 August 1685, transported via Leith aboard the Henry and Francis bound for East New Jersey in August 1685. [RPCS..XI.154][NWI.I.422]

CORHEAD, AGNES, was banished to the Plantations on 13 August 1685, transported via Leith aboard the Henry and Francis bound for East New Jersey in August 1685. [RPCS..XI.154][NWI.I.422]

CORSAN, GEORGE, was killed at New Cumnock, Ayrshire, in 1685. [Nithsdale Martyrs Cross, Dumfries]

CORSAN, JAMES, from Kirkcudbrightshire, a prisoner in Edinburgh Tolbooth, was transported via Leith aboard the Crown of London bound for Barbados on 27 November 1679, was shipwrecked and drowned off Orkney on 10 December 1679. [RBM][ETR]

CORSAN, JAMES, from Jedburgh, Roxburghshire, a rebel in Dumfries-shire in 1684. [RPCS.IX.265]

CORSAN, JOHN, in Gleanzean, for aiding rebels John Smith son of John Smith in Camonell, and one other, was declared to be a rebel and fugitive in October 1684. [RPCS.IX.367], refused to take the Test in October 1684, [RPCS.IX.700]; was banished to the American Plantations on 18 August 1685, then was transported via Leith aboard the Henry and Francis bound for East New Jersey in August 1685. [RPCS.XI.154][NWI.1.422] [Nithsdale Martyrs Cross, Dumfries]

CORSAN, JOHN, in Pluntoun, was accused, in Kirkcudbright on 4 October 1684, of aiding fugitive William Campbell. [RPCS.IX.375]

CORSAN, JOHN, in Craigturron, Dunscore, and his wife Janet Pathieson, for aiding rebels, Walter Smith, Thomas Hunter in

Breckinside, and John MacCall in Poundland, were declared rebels and fugitives in October 1684. [RPCS.IX.369]

CORSAN, LAURENCE, at Twomerkland Mill, Glencairn, for aiding his brother John Corsan a rebel, was declared to be a rebel and fugitive in October 1684. [RPCS.IX.367]; was transported in October 1684. [RPCS.X.311]

CORSAN, MARION, in Poundland, Tynron, for aiding rebels, her brothers James and William Corsan, John MacCall in Poundland, and John Gibson in Poundland, was declared to be a rebel and fugitive in October 1684. [RPCS.IX.368]

CORSBIE, JAMES, was transported via Leith to Jamaica in 1685. [RPCS.IX.329]

CORSE, ELIZABETH, was banished to the Plantations on 11 October 1684, was taken from Leith Tolbooth, put in irons and imprisoned in Edinburgh Tolbooth, in 1685, [ETR], was transported via Leith aboard the Henry and Francis bound for East New Jersey in August 1685. [RPCS.X.251/ RPCS.XI.166]

COSTINE, DAVID, in Minblie, was accused, in Kirkcudbright on 4 October 1684, of aiding the declared traitor Andrew Brig in Minblie. [RPCS.IX.378]

COUPAR, JAMES, from Carnwath, Lanarkshire, was transported via Leith aboard the Crown of London bound for Barbados on 27 November 1679, was shipwrecked and drowned off Orkney on 10 December 1679. [RBM]

COUSTON, JAMES, frm Southdean, Roxburghshire, was transported via Leith aboard the Crown of London bound for Barbados on 27 November 1679, was shipwrecked and drowned off Orkney on 10 December 1679. [RBM]

COWAN, BARBARA, was banished to the Plantations on 18 August 1685, was transported via Leith aboard the Henry and Francis bound for East New Jersey in August 1685. [RPCS.XI.154] [NWI.I.422]

COWAN, JAMES, was warded in Edinburgh Tolbooth, on 15 October 1684. [ETR]

COWAN, JOHN, was captured at the Siege of Worcester in 1651 and was transported via London aboard the <u>John and Sarah</u> bound for New England in December 1651, landed in Boston in February 1652. [SD.1.5-6]

COWAN, JOHN, in Crofthead, for aiding the rebel Robert Cowan, whose wife died there, was declared a rebel and fugitive in October 1684. [RPCS.IX.372]

COWAN, MARJORY, was banished to the Plantations on 18 August 1685, was transported via Leith aboard the <u>Henry and Francis</u> bound for East New Jersey in August 1685. [RPCS.XI.154] [NWI.I.422]

COWAN, ROBERT, a rebel and fugitive in 1684. [RPCS.IX.360]

COWAND, NINIAN, a gardener in Bardarroch, was accused, in Kirkcudbright in 1684, of conversing with rebel Gilbert McGie in August 1684. [RPCS.IX.376]

COWDEN, PETER, a fugitive, in Tynwald parish in July 1684. [RPCS.IX.216/357]

COWE, ALESTAR, was captured at the Siege of Worcester in 1651 and was transported via London aboard the <u>John and Sarah</u> bound for New England in December 1651, landed in Boston in February 1652. [SD.1.5-6]

CRAICHLEY, ....., a rebel who fled to Ireland on 7 October 1680. [RPCS.V.560]

CRAIG, JAMES, from Glasford, Lanarkshire, was transported via Leith aboard the <u>Crown of London</u> bound for Barbados on 27 November 1679, was shipwrecked and drowned off Orkney on 10 December 1679. [RBM]

CRAIG, JOHN, was captured at the Siege of Worcester in 1651 and was transported via London aboard the <u>John and Sarah</u> bound for

New England in December 1651, landed in Boston in February 1652. [SD.1.5-6]

CRAIGAN, JOHN, was captured at the Siege of Worcester in 1651 and was transported via London aboard the <u>John and Sarah</u> bound for New England in December 1651, landed in Boston in February 1652. [SD.1.5-6]

CRAIKIN, HELEN, in Kirkcudbright, was accused of rioting in Kirkcudbright in the parish of Irongray, in 1663. [RPCS.I.373]

CRAWFORD, DUNCAN, a prisoner in Edinburgh Tolbooth, was banished to the Plantations on 11 August 1685, was transported via Leith to Jamaica on 12 August 1685. [ETR]

CRAWFORD, GIDEON, from Lanark, a rebel, was brought as a prisoner from Fife and warded in Edinburgh Tolbooth on 20 June 1684, [ETR]; a prisoner in Edinburgh Tolbooth, was banished to the Plantations on 2 July 1684, then transported via Leith to Carolina in August 1684. [ETR] [RPCS.IX.28]

CRAUFORD, HUGH, born 1628, son of Patrick Crauford of Auchenames, born 1628, was educated at Glasgow University, minister at New Cumnock, Ayrshire, from 1653 until he was deprived in 1662, later was a minister in Glenarm, Ireland, from 1685 to 1688, returned to Scotland died in May 1692. [F.III.27][FI.60][F.VII.528]

CRAWFORD, JAMES, from Crail, Fife, 'a notorious rebel', imprisoned in Edinburgh Tolbooth in 1684. [RPCS.XI.13]

CRAWFORD, JOHN, a messenger, a rebel, was banished and transported to Virginia, on 30 July 1668. [RPCS.II.503]

CRAWFORD, JOHN, from Otter, Argyll, for his part in Argyll's Rebellion, was banished to the Plantations on 31 July 1685 and transported via Leith to Jamaica on 12 August 1685. [RPCS.XI.136] [ETR]

CRAWFORD, JOHN, the younger of Crawfordland, a prisoner in Edinburgh Tolbooth, was released on 9 July 1685. [ETR]

CRAWFORD, JOHN, of Castle Cavell, was accused of attending conventicles, trial papers in 1687. [NRS.JC39.102]

CRAWFORD, MALCOLM, in West Calder, a rebel and rioter, was banished and transported to Virginia, on 30 July 1668. [RPCS.II.503]

CRAWFORD, WILLIAM, was transported via Leith to Jamaica on 12 December 1685. [RPCS.XI.148] [ETR.373]

CRAWFORD, Mrs, wife of Malcolm Crawford a rioter in Calder and now a fugitive, to be imprisoned in Edinburgh Tolbooth in June 1668. [RPCS.II.470]

CREICHTOUN, HUGH, in Breckinside, Tynron, for aiding rebel James Corsan from Jedburgh, was declared to be a rebel and fugitive in October 1684. [RPCS.IX.368]

CRICHTON, JOHN, from Kilpatrick on the Muir, Dunbartonshire, a prisoner in Canongait Tolbooth, was banished to the Plantations in Carolina in 1685. [RPCS.XI.16]

CRICHTON, JOHN, from Dalry, Ayrshire, a prisoner in the tolbooth of Burntisland, Fife, in Dunottar Catle, Kincardineshire, and Leith Tolbooth, was banished to the Plantations on 18 August 1685, then shipped via Leith aboard the Henry and Francis on 5 September 1685, landed in East New Jersey on 7 December 1685. [RPCS.XI.154/292] [NWI.I.422]

CREIGHTOUN, ROBERT, in Finglain, Dalry, a rebel in 1666, imprisoned in Edinburgh Tolbooth or Canongait Tolbooth, having taken the Oath of Allegiance, was released on 11 July 1667. [RPCS.II.308]

CRICHTON, ROBERT, an Ensign of Lord Angus's Regiment, [The Cameronians], fought at the Battle of Dunkeld in August 1679. [BK]

CRIGHTON, THOMAS, from Carnwath, Lanarkshire, was transported via Leith aboard the Crown of London bound for Barbados on 27 November 1679, was shipwrecked and drowned off Orkney on 10 December 1679. [RBM] [ETR]

CROCKFORD, JAMES, was captured at the Siege of Worcester in September 1651, then transported via London on the <u>John and Sarah</u> bound for New England in December 1651, landed in Boston in February 1652. [SD.1.5-6]

CROOKSHANKS, JOHN, born 1630, from Redgorton, Perthshire, was educated at Edinburgh University, a minister from Convoy, Raphoe, Ulster, in 1657, was ejected from his parish in 1661, returned to Scotland, was accused of sedition and was ordered to appear before the Privy Council on 23 June 1664, [RPCS.I.551]; a former minister in Galloway was accused of holding conventicles, in 1666. [GC.114]; was killed at the Battle of Rullion Green on 28 November 1666. [Z.194]

CROSBIE, DAVID, from Carmunnock, Lanarkshire, a prisoner in Edinburgh Tolbooth, was transported via Leith aboard the <u>St Michael of Scarborough</u> bound for the West Indies on 12 December 1678. [RPCS.VI.76]

CROSSHONE, PATRICK, was captured at the Siege of Worcester in September 1651, then transported via London on the <u>John and Sarah</u> bound for New England in December 1651, landed in Boston in February 1652. [SD.1.5-6]

CUBBISON, JAMES, in Glenmuck, to be tried accused of rebellion, 3 June 1684. [RPCS.IX.205]

CULLEN, ANDREW, from Ireland, was warded in Edinburgh Tolbooth on 20 May 1685, but having sworn an Oath of Allegiance, was released on 28 May 1685. [ETR]

CUMIN, JOHN, a weaver from the Brigend of Glasgow, a prisoner in Canongait Tolbooth, was banished to the Plantations on 1 August 1678, was shipped via Leith aboard the <u>St Michael of Scarborough</u> bound for the West Indies on 12 December 1678. [RPCS.VI.76]

CUMIN, MARGARET, spouse of Robert Foules in Buittle, Kirkcudbrightshire, a fugitive and fanatica in 1684. [RPCS.IX.571]

CUMING, JOHN, a weaver in the Gorbals, Glasgow, a prisoner in Canongait Tolbooth, having signed a bond was released on 23 August 1684. [RPCS.IX.315]

CUNNINGHAM, ALEXANDER, of Hyndhope, was educated at St Andrews University, minister of Ettrick and Buccleugh, from 1641, refused to conform to Episcopacy. [F.II.174]

CUNNINGHAM, ALEXANDER, of Craigans, was warded in Edinburgh Tolbooth on 13 November 1684. [ETR]

CUNNINGHAM, ALEXANDER, the younger, was warded in Edinburgh Tolbooth on 13 November 1684. [ETR]

CUNNINGHAM, ARTHUR, in Paisley, a rebel in Glasgow Tolbooth, was banished to the Plantations in June 1684, and transported via Glasgow aboard the Pelican of Glasgow bound for Carolina, bond by Walter Gibson, a merchant in Glasgow, dated 20 June 1684. [RPCS.IX.208]

CUNNINGHAM, DANIEL, from Drummond, Stirlingshire, was transported via Leith aboard the Crown of London bound for Barbados on 27 November 1679, was shipwrecked and drowned off Orkney on 10 December 1679. [RBM]

CUNNINGHAM, DAVID, a prisoner in Edinburgh Tolbooth, was shipped from Leith in November 1679. [ETR]

CUNNINGHAM, GABRIEL, born 1622, was educated at the University of Glasgow, minister at Dunlop, Ayrshire, from 1648 until deprived in 1664 for not conforming to Episcopacy, was a preacher at conventicles in 1674, and in 1683 was accused of harbouring rebels, he returned to the parish in 1687, and died in May 1691. [F.III.91]

CUNNINGHAM, GEORGE, a prisoner in Edinburgh Tolbooth, was banished to the Plantations on 24 July 1685. [RPCS.XI.114]

CUNNINGHAM, JAMES, was transported via Leith to Jamaica on 17 December 1685, landed at Port Royal, Jamaica, died there. [ETR] [LJ.35]

CUNNINGHAM, JAMES, transported via Leith aboard the John and Nicholas bound for Barbados on 12 December 1685. [ETR]

CUNYNGHAME, JOHN, of Blook, minister at Cumnock, Ayrshire, from 1647, refused to confirm to Episcopacy in 1662, he died in October 1668. [F.III.25]

CUNNINGHAM, JOHN, of Bedland, a rebel in 1666, was sought by the Justice Court in August 1667 for his part in the late rebellion. [GC.123]; was captured in Ireland and returned to Scotland, then imprisoned in Dunbarton Castle on 4 February 1669. [RPCS.II.595]

CUNNINGHAM, JOHN, a prisoner in Edinburgh Tolbooth, to be transported via Leith bound for Jamaica on 11 August 1685. [ETR] [RPCS.XI.329]

CUNNINGHAM, PATRICK, was warded in Edinburgh Tolbooth on 2 July 1684, was transferred to Dunnottar Castle, Kincardineshire, on 29 July 1685. [ETR]; was banished to the Plantations on 18 August 1685, was taken from Leith Tolbooth, put in irons and imprisoned in Edinburgh Tolbooth, [ETR], then shipped from Leith aboard the Henry and Francis bound for East New Jersey on 5 September 1685, landed there on 7 December 1685. [RPCS.XI.114/289] [NWI.I.422]

CUNNINGHAME, ROBERT, was educated at the University of Glasgow, minister at Hawick, Roxburghshire, from 1635 until 1656, his signature appears on the copy of the National Covenant preserved at Cavers. [F.III.113]

CUNNINGHAM, WILLIAM, born 1629, son of Alexander Cunningham of Collellan, minister at West Kilbride, Ayrshire, from 1658 until deprived in 1662, he died in January 1669. [F.III.128]

CUNNINGHAM, WILLIAM, from Ashinyards, Ayrshire, was warded in Edinburgh Tolbooth on 25 October 1684, was transported via Leith aboard the Henry and Francis bound for East New Jersey in August 1685. [RPCS.XI.159] [ETR]

CUNNINGHAM, WILLIAM, of Enterkin, Lanarkshire, was warded in Edinburgh Tolbooth on 20 November 1684, was released on 28 December 1684. [ETR]

CURRIE, DAVID, from Fenwick, Ayrshire, was transported via Leith aboard the Crown of London bound for Barbados on 27 November 1679, was shipwrecked and drowned off Orkney on 10 December 1679. [RBM]

CURRIE, JAMES, minister at Kirk o' Shotts, Lanarkshire, was warded in Edinburgh Tolbooth, on 15 October 1684. [ETR]

CURRY, ROBERT, a miller at Hemisfieldtoun, Tynwald, in July 1684 and not reporting it, was declared to be a rebel and fugitive in October 1684. [RPCS.IX.370]

CUTHBERTSON, JOHN, from Kilmarnock, Ayrshire, was transported via Leith aboard the Crown of London bound for Barbados on 27 November 1679, was shipwrecked and drowned off Orkney on 10 December 1679. [RBM]

CUTHBERTSON, THOMAS, tenant of Lord Boyd, a rebel in 1666, imprisoned in Edinburgh Tolbooth or Canongait Tolbooth, having taken the Oath of Allegiance, was released on 11 July 1667. [RPCS.II.308]

CUTHBERTSON, WILLIAM, was imprisoned in Edinburgh Tolbooth in 1666, was banished to Virginia on 10 June 1669. [RPCS.III.22]

DALGLEISH, ALEXANDER, from Kilbryde, was banished to the Plantationson18 August 1685, transported via Leith aboard the Henry and Francis bound for East New Jersey in August 1685, landed there on 7 December 1685. [RPCS.XI.154/291]

DALRYMPLE, ANDREW, minister at Auchinleck, Ayrshire, from 1651 until deprived in 1662, in 1669 he was accused of conducting a conventicle. [F.III.3]

DALRYMPLE, Sir JAMES, of Stair, was tried for treason as an accessory to the Rebellion of 1679, in 1686. [NRS.JC39.66]

DALRYMPLE, NICOLA, wife of John Osburne in Penfilland, parish of Keir, Dumfries-shire, a fugitive in May 1683. [RPCS.VIII.609]

DALYELL, ANDREW, for conversing with rebels Thomas Hunter in Dinduff, Thomas Hunter in Breckinside, and Gilbert Gilchrist, also Robert Greir a chapman, and John MacCall, was declared a rebel and fugitive in October 1684. [RPCS.IX.363]

DALZELL, CHARLES, a Lieutenant of Lord Angus's Regiment, [The Cameronians], fought at the Battle of Dunkeld in August 1679. [BK]

DALYELL, JAMES, in Hallcleughside, Kilbride, to be imprisoned in Edinburgh Tolbooth in August 1684. [RPCS.IX.126]

DALZELL, JAMES, in Gategill, was accused, in Kirkcudbright in October 1684, of conversing with rebel Gilbert McGie. [RPCS.IX.374]

DALYELL, JOHN, in Blairfoot, was declared a rebel and fugitive in 1684. [RPCS.IX.359]

DARLING, GEORGE, was captured at the Battle of Dunbar in September 1650, was transported via London aboard the Unity bound for Boston, New England, in November 1650. [SCF.1226]

DARROCH, JOHN, was educated at Glasgow University, minister on Jura, Argyll, from 1635 until 1646 when he was deposed 'for preaching to and gross compliance with the rebels', he died before 9 May 1649. [F.IV.70]

DAVIDSON, JOHN, was educated at St Andrews University, minister of Southdean, [alias Charteris], from 1635 until 1666 when he was deprived for not converting to Episcopacy. [F.II.138]

DAVIE, JAMES, a conventlicer who was killed at Black Dub in April 1673.

DEANS, JOHN, from Nenthorn, Berwickshire, was transported via Leith aboard the Crown of London bound for Barbados on 27 November 1679, was shipwrecked and drowned off Orkney on 10 December 1679. [RBM]

DELL, WILLIAM, was captured at the Siege of Worcester in 1651, then transported via Gravesend, London, aboard the John and Sarah bound for Boston, New England, in December 1651. [SD.1/5-6]

DEMPSTER, ANDREW, of Carradow, was sought by the Justice Court in August 1667 for his part in the late rebellion. [GC.123] [RPCS.II.345]

DEMPSTER, JOHN, a tailor in Garrieyard, Dalry, Kirkcudbrightshire, fought at the Battle of Bothwell Bridge, Lanarkshire, on 22 June 1679, was killed at Muill Hill. [GC.372]

DENHOLM, WILLIAM, of Westshiells, having participated in the Earl of Argyll's Rebellion was tried for treason in 1685. [NRS.JC39.71]

DENISTOUN, JANET, a widow, was accused of rioting in Kirkcudbright in the parish of Irongray, in 1663. [RPCS.I.373]

DICK, JOHN, a student of theology, son of David Dick, a writer, a rebel, was banished and transported to Virginia, on 30 July 1668. [RPCS.II.503]; was warded in Edinburgh Tolbooth on 4 March 1684 and executed for treason at the Grassmarket of Edinburgh on 5 March 1684. [ETR]

DICK, or KID, JOHN, in Livingstone, West Lothian, a rebel in Glasgow Tolbooth, was banished to the Plantations in June 1684, and transported via Glasgow aboard the Pelican bound for Carolina, bond by Walter Gibson, a merchant in Glasgow, dated 20 June 1684. [RPCS.IX.208]

DICK, QUENTIN, from Dalmellington, was warded in Edinburgh Tolbooth on 28 October 1684, transferred to Dunnottar Castle, Kincardineshire, on 29 July 1685. [ETR]; was banished to the Plantations on 20 May 1685. [RPCS.XI.289]

DICK, ROBERT, was killed at the Battle of Aird's Moss on 22 July 1680. [Muirkirk Monument, Ayrshire]

DICKS, ROBERT, a prisoner in Edinburgh Tolbooth, was transported via Leith aboard the St Michael of Scarborough bound for the West Indies on 12 December 1678. [RPCS.IV.76]

DICKSON, JOHN, a preacher at a conventicle at Beath Hill, Dunfermline, Fife, in 1670. [Z.199]

DINN, DAVID, in Laicht, to be tried accused of rebellion, 3 June 1684. [RPCS.IX.205]

DINN, JAMES, was warded in Edinburgh Tolbooth on 28 May 1685, but, having subscribed to the Test Act was released on 28 May 1685. [ETR]

DINWIDDIE, THOMAS, was killed at the Battle of Bothwell Bridge, Lanarkshire, on 22 June 1679. [Nithsdale Martyrs Cross, Dumfries]

DONALD, ROBERT, was warded in Edinburgh Tolbooth on 28 May 1685. [ETR]

DONALDSON, ANDREW, was educated at the University of St Andrews, minister at Dalgety, Fife from 1644 until deposed in 1664 for his opposition to Episcopacy, he was chaplain to Lord Dunfermline's Regiment when in England 1645-1646, he preached at conventicles around 1676 but was imprisoned in Linlithgow until 1679, he died after 1693. [F.V.22]

DONALDSON, ANDREW, from Girthorn, Kirkcudbrightshire, was transported via Leith aboard the Crown of London bound for Barbados on 27 November 1679, was shipwrecked and drowned off Orkney on 10 December 1679. [RBM]

DONALDSON, JAMES, was captured at the Battle of Dunbar in 1650, was transported via London aboard the Unity bound for Boston, New England, in 1650. [SCF.1226]

DONALDSON, JAMES, from Kelton, Kirkcudbrightshire, was transported via Leith aboard the Crown of London bound for Barbados on 27 November 1679, was shipwrecked and drowned off Orkney on 10 December 1679. [RBM]

DONALDSON, JOHN, from Kincardine, Perthshire, was transported via Leith aboard the Crown of London bound for Barbados on 27 November 1679, was shipwrecked and drowned off Orkney on 10 December 1679. [RBM]

DONALDSON, JOHN, miller at Balmagie, was accused in Kirkcudbright of conversing with fugitives John Graham and Thomas Graham, in 1684. [RPCS.IX.374]

DONALDSON, THOMAS, was educated at Edinburgh University, minister at Smailholm from 1640, chaplain to Cranstoun's Regiment during the invasion of England in 1644, died in 1671. [F.II.161]

DOUGALL, ALEXANDER, was captured at the Battle of Dunbar in 1650, was transported via London aboard the Unity bound for Boston, New England, in 1650. [SCF.1226]

DOUGALL, ARTHUR, a wright in Glasgow, was transported via Leith aboard the St Michael of Scarborough bound for the West Indies on 13 June 1678. [RPCS.VI.76]

DOUGALL, EDWARD, was captured at the Siege of Worcester in 1651, then transported via Gravesend, London, aboard the John and Sarah bound for Boston, New England, in December 1651. [SD.1/5-6]

DOUGALL, WILLIAM, was captured at the Siege of Worcester in 1651, then transported via Gravesend, London, aboard the John and Sarah bound for Boston, New England, in December 1651. [SD.1/5-6]

DOUGLAS, ALEXANDER, in Auchinhestning, for conversing with rebel Thomas Hunter the younger in Dinduff, was declared to be a rebel and fugitive in October 1684. [RPCS.IX.367]

DOUGLAS, CHARLES, was transported via Leith aboard the Henry and Francis bound for East New Jersey in August 1685, landed there on 7 December 1685.
[RPCS.XI.154/290/292] [NWI.I.422]

DOUGLAS, DANIEL, born 1619, from Hilton, Berwickshire, a minister in exile in the Netherlands. [SEC]

DOUGLAS, DAVID, was transported via Leith aboard the Phoenix of Leith bound for Virginia in April 1666. [ETR]

DOUGLAS, GEORGE, a rebel, formerly prisoner in Dunnottar Castle, Kincardineshire, who had been transferred to Edinburgh Tolbooth, died there on 3 January 1685. [ETR]

DOUGLAS, JAMES, was transported via Leith aboard the Phoenix of Leith bound for Virginia in April 1666. [ETR]

DOUGLAS, JAMES, a rebel in 1684. [RPCS.IX.363]

DOUGLAS, JOHN, a former minister in Galloway was accused of holding conventicles, in 1666. [GC.114]

DOUGLAS, JOHN, from Kirkmichael, Ayrshire, was transported via Leith aboard the Crown of London bound for Barbados on 27 November 1679, was shipwrecked and drowned off Orkney on 10 December 1679. [RBM]

DOUGLAS, JOHN, of Timpindean, and his wife Euphan Turnbull, were fined for withdrawing from the parish church in 1684. [RPCS.IX.713]

DOUGLAS, JOHN, a servant of John Milligan a weaver in Lascairn, having seen rebels and failed to report them, was declared to be a fugitive in October 1684. [RPCS.IX.360]

DOUGLAS, JOHN, in Ferdinallan, for aiding rebels James Douglas, and Gilbert Gilchrist at Glen Gar, and failing to report it was declared to be a rebel and fugitive in October 1684. [RPCS.IX.365]

DOUGLAS, JOHN, of Stonehouse, Lanarkshire, was a prisoner in Edinburgh on 19 December 1685.

DOUGLAS, ROBERT, in Whytfall Dumfries-shire, for seeing rebel William Milligan since he broke prison in Dumfries, and not reported it, was declared to be a rebel and fugitive in October 1684. [RPCS.IX.373]

DOUGLAS, SAMUEL, from Cavers, Roxburghshire, was transported via Leith aboard the Crown of London bound for Barbados on 27 November 1679, was shipwrecked and drowned off Orkney on 10 December 1679. [RBM]

DOUGLAS, THOMAS, was educated at Edinburgh University, he was accused of holding conventicles in 1671, and denounced as a rebel in 1674, he was at the Battle of Drumclog on 1 June 1679, and was minister later in London and at Wamphrey from 1690 until his death in 1695. [F.II.225]

DOUGLAS, THOMAS, a prisoner in Edinburgh Tolbooth, willing to go to America [sic] was released to go there on 17 December 1685. [ETR]

DOUGLAS, WILLIAM, from the Bridge of Ken, was was taken from Leith Tolbooth, put in irons and imprisoned in Edinburgh Tolbooth, [ETR], then transported via Leith aboard the Henry and Francis bound for East New Jersey in August 1685, landed there on 7 December 1685. [ETR]
[RPCS.XI.154/290/292] [NWI.I.422]

DOWNIE, JOHN, took part in Argyll's Rebellion, was banished on 7 August 1685, then stigmatised, and transported via Leith bound for Jamaica in August 1685. [RPCS.XI.130]

DOWNING, MALCOLM, was captured at the Battle of Dunbar, and transported via London aboard the Unity bound for Boston, New England, in November 1650. [SCF.1226]

DRAFIN, GEORGE, from Lesmahagow, Lanarkshire, fought at the Battle of Bothwell Bridge in 1679, was transported via Leith aboard the Crown of London bound for Barbados on 27 November 1679, was shipwrecked and drowned off Orkney on 10 December 1679. [RBM]

DRENNAN, WILLIAM, was banished to the Plantations on 29 July 1685, stigmatised, then transported via Leith bound for Jamaica in August 1685. [RPCS.XI.329] [ETR]

DREW, JOHN, portioner of Calder, Mid Lothian, a prisoner in 1683. [RPCS.VIII.643]

DRIPS, WILLIAM, from Mauchline, Ayrshire, was transported via Leith aboard the Crown of London bound for Barbados on 27 November 1679, was shipwrecked and drowned off Orkney on 10 December 1679. [RBM]

DRUMMOND, JEAN, was warded in Edinburgh Tolbooth, on 3 December 1684. [ETR]

DRUMMOND, THOMAS, a non-conformist minister who was imprisoned in Lifford, Ireland, in 1669. [Cal.SP.Ire]

DRYSDALE, JOHN, was educated at Glasgow University, probably ordained in Ireland, minister in Paisley, Renfrewshire, from 1650 until outed in 1661 on the establishment of Episcopacy, [RPCS.III.154]; was banished to the Plantations in the [West] Indies on 11 October 1681. [RPCS.VII.219]

DUFF, JAMES, imprisoned in Edinburgh Tolbooth for being in Argyll's Rebellion, was released on 25 March 1686. [ETR]

DULLEN, EDWARD, was captured at the Siege of Worcester in 1651, then transported via London aboard the John and Sarah bound for New England landed in Boston in February 1652. [SD.1/5-6]

DUN, JAMES, was killed at Caldons, Loch Trool, on 23 January 1685. [Newton Stewart gravestone, Kirkcudbrightshire]

DUN, ROBERT, was killed at Caldons, Loch Trool, on 23 January 1685. [Newton Stewart gravestone, Kirkcudbrightshire]

DUN, ROGER, born 1659 at Benquhat near Dalmellington, Ayrshire, was killed at Brocklock farm in June 1689. [Carsphairn gravestone, Kirkcudbrightshire]

DUNBAR, ALEXANDER, was warded in Edinburgh Tolbooth on 3 February 1686. [ETR]

DUNBAR, GEORGE, from Craigie, Ayrshire, fought at the Battle of Bothwell Bridge in 1679, was transported via Leith aboard the Crown of London bound for Barbados on 27 November 1679, was shipwrecked and drowned off Orkney on 10 December 1679. [RBM]

DUNBAR, ROBERT, born 1634, son of Ninian Dunbar of Georgehill, a prisoner of war who was transported to Boston, Massachusetts, in 1650, died on 19 September 1693. [FEAF] [AncH-NE][SH.13]

DUNCAN, JAMES, from Grange, was transported to the colonies in August 1670. [RPCS.III.206]

DUNCAN, WILLIAM, in Luffilaw, for attending conventicles, was outlawed on 29 August 1672. [RPCS.III.583]

DUNCANSON, ANDREW, son of Reverend Andrew Duncanson in St Boswells, was educated at Edinburgh University, minister of Maxton and Rutherford from 1640, he refused to conform with Episcopacy in 1662, and died by 1672. [F.II.185]

DUNCANSON, ROBERT, former minister in Campbeltown, Argyll, a prisoner in Edinburgh Tolbooth, was released on parole on 26 March 1685. [ETR]

DUNDAS, JAMES, son of the laird of Dundas, was banished to the Plantations on 11 August 1670, sentence cancelled on 18 August 1670, later went to East New Jersey. [RPCS.III.204/207]

DUNGALSTONE, NICOLL, in Larg, was accused, in Kirkcudbright in October 1684, of conversing with rebel John Carsan in June 1684. [RPCS.IX.376]

DUNLOP, ALEXANDER, born 1621, was educated at Glasgow University, a minister in Paisley, Renfrewshire, from 1644 until deprived in 1661 on the establishment of Episcopacy, died in Bo'ness, West Lothian, on 13 March 1667. [F.III.164]

DUNN, QUENTIN, a prisoner in Edinburgh Tolbooth was banished to the Plantations on 29 July 1685, was transported via Leith to Jamaica on 11 August 1685. [ETR][RPCS.XI.329]

DUNSMORE, JAMES, was captured at the Battle of Dunbar in 1650, was transported via London aboard the Unity bound for New England in 1650. [SCF.1226][SH.14][IWP]

DURHAM, ALEXANDER, of Duntarvie, was warded in Edinburgh Tolbooth on 21 May 1685, was released on 7 July 1685. [ETR]

DURIE, ISOBEL, was banished to the Plantations on 18 August 1685, was transported via Leith aboard the Henry and Francis bound for East New Jersey in August 1685, landed there on 7 December 1685. [RPCS.XI.154][NWI.I.422]

DURY, MARGARET, widow of James Kello a merchant in Edinburgh, having refused to identify those who attempted to assassinate the Archbishop of St Andrews and the Bishop of Orkney in Edinburgh, was banished to the Plantations on 29 July 1668. [RPCS.II.500]

DYKES, ANDREW, from St Bride's Chapel, was banished to the Plantations on 17 October 1684. [RPCS.X.275]

EATON, ALEXANDER, was captured at the Battle of Dunbar in 1650, was transported via London aboard the Unity bound for New England in November 1650. [SCF.1226][SH.14]

EASTON, ANDREW, from Torpichen, West Lothian, was transported via Leith aboard the Crown of London bound for Barbados on 27 November 1679, was shipwrecked and drowned off Orkney on 10 December 1679. [RBM]

EASTON, JAMES, from Torpichen, West Lothian, was transported via Leith aboard the Crown of London bound for Barbados on 27 November 1679, was shipwrecked and drowned off Orkney on 10 December 1679. [RBM]

EASTON, JOHN, from Torpichen, West Lothian, was transported via Leith aboard the Crown of London bound for Barbados on 27 November 1679, was shipwrecked and drowned off Orkney on 10 December 1679. [RBM]

ECCLES, MUNGO, from Maybole, Ayrshire, was transported via Leith aboard the Crown of London bound for Barbados on 27

November 1679, was shipwrecked and drowned off Orkney on 10 December 1679. [RBM]

EDGAR, JOHN, from Balmaclellan, Galloway, fought t the Battle of Bothwell Bridge in 1679, was transported via Leith aboard the Crown of London bound for Barbados on 27 November 1679, was shipwrecked and drowned off Orkney on 10 December 1679. [RBM]

EDMINSTONE, JOHN, was captured at the Siege of Worcester in 1651, then transported via London aboard the John and Sarah bound for New England, landed in Boston in February 1652. [SD.1.5-6]

EDWARD, JAMES, in Greenock, Renfrewshire, a rebel, was warded in Edinburgh Tolbooth, then banished to the Plantations on 2 July 1684, was transported via Leith to Carolina in August 1684. [RPCS.IX.28] [ETR]

EDWARD, JOHN, in Dalgain, a rebel in Glasgow Tolbooth, was banished to the Plantations in June 1684, and transported via Glasgow aboard the Pelican bound for Carolina, bond by Walter Gibson, a merchant in Glasgow, dated 20 June 1684. [RPCS.IX.208]

EDWARD, ROBERT, from Cumnock, Ayrshire, participated in Argyll's Rebellion, was banished to the Plantations on 30 July 1685, was stigmatised then transported via Leith bound for Jamaica in August 1685. [RPCS.XI.136]

ELDER, ALEXANDER, in Hedderwick, for attending conventicles, was outlawed on 29 August 1672. [RPCS.III.583]

ELDER, JAMES, the younger, in Burnside, for attending conventicles, was outlawed on 29 August 1672. [RPCS.III.583]

ELDER, JOHN, in Burnside, for attending conventicles, was outlawed on 29 August 1672. [RPCS.III.583]

ELLIOT, GILBERT, a writer in Edinburgh, having participated in the Earl of Argyll's Rebellion in 1685 was tried for treason in 1685. [NRS.JC39.66/71]

ELLIOT, JOHN, from Southdean, Roxburghshire, was transported via Leith aboard the Crown of London bound for Barbados on 27 November 1679, was shipwrecked and drowned off Orkney on 10 December 1679. [RBM]

ELLIOT, JOHN, from Teviotdale, imprisoned in Canongait Tolbooth, was banished to the Plantations on 24 July 1685, then transported via Leith bound for Jamaica in August 1685, landed at Port Royal. [RPCS.XI.329] [LJ.44]

ELLIOT, ROBERT, from Cavers, Roxburghshire, was warded in Edinburgh Tolbooth on 28 May 1685, having subscribed to the Test Act was released on 21 July 1685. [ETR]

ERSKINE, Reverend HENRY, born 1624, was a prisoner on the Bass Rock in the Firth of Forth, died in 1696. [Chirnside, gravestone, Berwickshire]

ERSKINE, HENRY, Lord Cardross, born 1650, co-founder of the Scots colony at Stuartstown, Carolina, in 1684, driven out by the Spanish he settled in Den Haag, Holland, in 1686, he accompanied William and Mary to England in 1688, he died in Edinburgh during 1693. [NRS.NA.21647]

EWART, HELEN, spouse of John Thomson, was accused of rioting in Kirkcudbright in the parish of Irongray, in 1663. [RPCS.I.373]

EWART, JANET, sister in law of John Thomson, was accused of rioting in Kirkcudbright in the parish of Irongray, in 1663. [RPCS.I.373]

EWART, JOHN, late provost of Kirkcudbright, was accused of rioting in Kirkcudbright in the parish of Irongray, in 1663. [RPCS.I.373]

FAIRBAIRN, JOHN, from Kirkliston, West Lothian, was transported via Leith aboard the St Michael of Scarborough bound for the West Indies on 12 December 1678. [RPCS.VI.76]

FALA, JOHN, a shoemaker from Kelso, Roxburghshire, imprisoned in Edinburgh Tolbooth, was transported to the colonies on 16 October 1684. [RPCS.IX.449]

FENWICK, JAMES, a prisoner in Leith Tolbooth, was transported via Leith aboard the Henry and Francis bound for East New Jersey in August 1685, landed there on 7 December 1685. [RPCS.XI.154][NWI.I.423]

FERGUSON, ALEXANDER, born 1628, was educated at Glasgow University, was minister at Sorbie, Wigtownshire, later in Killyleagh, County Down, from 1670 to his death on 6 November 1684. [Killyleagh gravestone] [FI.61] [RPCS.VI.657]

FERGUSON, ALEXANDER, servant to Master Archibald McGauchin, for being in arms at the Battle of Bothwell Bridge, Lanarkshire, in 1679, was declared to be a rebel and fugitive, in September 1684. [RPCS.IX.373]

FERGUSON, ANDREW, was killed in Glasgow in 1685. [Nithsdale Martyrs Cross, Dumfries]

FERGUSON, ANGUS, was transported via Leith to Jamaica in August 1685. [RPCS.XI.149]

FERGUSON, DANIEL, was captured at the Battle of Dunbar in 1650, transported via London aboard the Unity bound for New England in November 1650, settled in Kittery, Maine, by 1656. [CEB]

FERGUSON, DAVID, from Bridgend, Glasgow, was transported via Leith aboard the St Michael of Scarborough bound for the West Indies on 12 December 1678. [RPCS.VI.76]

FERGUSON, DONALD, from Ruchard, was transported via Leith bound for Jamaica in August 1685. [RPCS.XI.136]

FERGUSON, DUNCAN, a prisoner in Edinburgh or Canongait Tolbooth, a rebel, was banished to the Plantations in Carolina on 8 August 1684. [RPCS.IX.95] [ETR]

FERGUSON, DUNCAN, a farmer from Polmaise, Stirlingshire, was transported via Leith to Jamaica in August 1685. [RPCS.XI.138] [ETR]

FERGUSON, ELIZABETH HUNT, in Holland. [no date], [Nithsdale Martyrs Cross, Dumfries]

FERGUSON, ELSPETH, in Leith Tolbooth, was banished to the Plantations on 18 August 1685, was transported via Leith aboard the Henry and Francis of Newcastle bound for East New Jersey on 5 September 1685, landed there on 7 December 1685. [RPCS.XI.154/155/292] [NWI.I.422]

FERGUSON, GILBERT, took part in Argyll's Rebellion, and was transported via Leith to Virginia in August 1685. [RPCS.XI.329]

FERGUSON, HUGH, an Ensign of Lord Angus's Regiment, [The Cameronians], fought at the Battle of Dunkeld in August 1679. [BK]

FERGUSON, JAMES, of Cairoch, Dumfries-shire, was indicted for 'hearing and recepting rebellious preachers', in 1684. [RPCS.IX.555]

FERGUSON, JAMES, of Fourmerkland, Holywood, for seeing rebel John Weir in Kilroy in August 1684 and failed to report it, was declared to be a rebel and fugitive in October 1684. [RPCS.IX.370]

FERGUSON, JAMES, was warded in Edinburgh Tolbooth on 28 May 1685. [ETR]

FERGUSON, JANET, in Leith Tolbooth, was banished to the Plantations on 18 August 1685, was transported via Leith aboard the Henry and Francis of Newcastle bound for East New Jersey on 5 September 1685, landed there on 7 December 1685. [RPCS.XI.155/292] [NWI.I.422]

FERGUSON, JOHN, from Glencairn, Dumfriesshire, was transported via Leith aboard the Crown of London bound for Barbados on 27 November 1679, was shipwrecked and drowned off Orkney on 10 December 1679. [RBM]

FERGUSON, JOHN, in Enterkin Mains, Lanarkshire, a rebel in 1679, was tried in 1685. [NRS.JC39.75]

FERGUSON, MARY, spouse to John MacCall in Laight, for aiding rebels, William Milligan in Floors, Thomas Hunter in Dinduff, and Walter Smith, was declared a rebel and a fugitive in October 1684. [RPCS.IX.369]

FERGUSON, ROBERT, chaplain to the Earl of Shaftesbury, was tried for treason as an accessory to the Rebellion of 1679, in 1666. [NRS.JC39.66]

FERGUSON, ROBERT, was killed on Auchencloy Moor on 18 December 1685. [Auchencloy Martyrs Monument, Kirkcudbrightshire] [Nithsdale Martyrs Cross, Dumfries]

FERGUSON, WILLIAM, a weaver from Lanark, who was in the rebellion of 1666, was imprisoned in Edinburgh Tolbooth, was banished to the Plantations in Virginia on 18 June 1668, was transported via Leith aboard the Convertin bound for Virginia on 3 September 1668. [RPCS.II.470/507/534]

FERGUSON, WILLIAM, from Glencairn, Dumfriesshire, fought at the Battle of Bothwell Bridge in 1679, was transported via Leith aboard the Crown of London bound for Barbados on 27 November 1679, was shipwrecked off Orkney on 10 December 1679, later transported to Jamaica. [RBM][CEC.212/5][SW.202]

FIMMERTON, JANET, then in Edinburgh Tolbooth, was transferred to Dunnottar Castle, Kincardineshire, on 29 July 1685. [ETR]

FINDLAY, THOMAS, from Kilmarnock, Ayrshire, fought at the Battle of Bothwell Bridge in 1679, was transported via Leith aboard the Crown of London bound for Barbados on 27 November 1679, was shipwrecked and drowned off Orkney on 10 December 1679. [RBM][Kilmarnock gravestone]

FINLATOR, THOMAS, was transported via Leith aboard the Henry and Francis bound for East New Jersey on 5 September 1685, died at sea.
[NWI.I.422]

FINDLAY, ALEXANDER, from Buchlyvie, Stirlingshire, imprisoned in Canongait Tolbooth, was transported via Leith aboard the St

Michael of Scarborough bound for the West Indies on 12 December 1678. [RPCS.VI.76]

FINLAY, DAVID, of Newmilns, Ayrshire, was tortured then executed in 1666. [Z.196]

FINLAY, MARGARET, servant of Alexander Clachton, was accused of rioting in Kirkcudbright in the parish of Irongray, in 1663. [RPCS.I.373]

FINLAY, THOMAS, a notary in West Calder, Mid Lothian, a rebel and rioter, was banished and transported to Virginia, on 30 July 1668. [RPCS.II.503]

FINLAY, Mrs, wife of Thomas Finlay a rioter in Calder and now a fugitive, to be imprisoned in Edinburgh Tolbooth in June 1668. [RPCS.II.470]

FINLAYSON, JAMES, from New Kilpatrick, Dunbartonshire, fought at the Battle of Bothwell Bridge in 1679, was transported via Leith aboard the Crown of London bound for Barbados on 27 November 1679, was shipwrecked and drowned off Orkney on 10 December 1679. [RBM]

FINNISON, JOHN, a prisoner in Canongait Tolbooth was banished to the Plantations on 28 July 1685, was stigmatised and transported via Leith bound for Jamaica in August 1685. [RPCS.XI.329]

FINNISON, PETER, was banished to the Plantations on 11 October 1684. [RPCS.II.251]

FISHER, JAMES, a weaver from Bridgend, Glasgow, was banished to the [West] Indies on 13 June 1678. [RPCS.V.474]

FLEMING, GEORGE, an alleged assassin of Archbishop Sharp, fled to Ireland on 7 October 1680. [RPCS.VI.560]

FLEMING, JOHN, in Stonehouse, Stirlingshire, son of Robert Fleming a tenant in the Stanhopes, a rebel, a prisoner in Edinburgh or Canongait Tolbooth, was banished to the Plantations on 2 July 1684. [RPCS.IX.28]; successfully petitioned, on the condition that he lived regularly, and attended his parish church, was liberated on 6 August 1684. [RPCS.IX.95/97]

FLEMING, JOHN, from Glasford in Clydesdale, was warded in Edinburgh Tolbooth on 20 May 1685, but, having sworn an Oath of Allegiance was released on 28 May 1685. [ETR]

FLEMING, MATTHEW, was educated at Glasgow University, minister at Culross, Fife, from 1656 until 1675, was confined to his parish for non-conformity to Episcopacy. [F.V.15]

FLEMING, ROBERT, born 1630 in Yester, was educated at Edinburgh University, and at St Andrews, minister at Cambuslang from 1653 until deprived in 1662, in 1677 he was with the Scots Kirk in Rotterdam, the Netherlands, in 1678 he was preaching at conventicles in Scotland until imprisoned in Edinburgh Tolbooth and released on 9 July 1684, later returned to Rotterdam, he died in London on 25 July 1694. [F.III.237][ETR]

FLETCHER, ADAM, was warded in Edinburgh Tolbooth on 20 May 1685, but, having subscribed to the Test Act was released on 28 May 1685. [ETR]

FLETCHER, DUNCAN, was in Argyll's Rebellion, was imprisoned in Paul's Work, Edinburgh, was banished to the Plantations on 30 July 1685, transported via Leith to Jamaica in August 1685. [RPCS.XI.136]

FLETCHER, HARRY, was liberated from Edinburgh Tolbooth on 9 July 1685. [ETR]

FLETCHER, JOHN, was in Argyll's Rebellion, was imprisoned in Paul's Work, Edinburgh, was banished to the Plantations on 30 July 1685, transported via Leith to Jamaica in August 1685. [RPCS.XI.329]

FLEUCKHARD, JOHN, in Tamenen, for attending conventicles, was outlawed on 29 August 1672. [RPCS.III.583]

FLINT, JOHN, a minister in exile in Groningen in the Netherlands from 1682 until 1683. [SEC]

FORBES, ARTHUR, son of John Forbes minister at Alford, Aberdeenshire, an officer of the Covenanters from 1640.

FORBES, WILLIAM, born 1630, was captured at the Battle of Dunbar in 1650, transported via London aboard the Unity bound for Boston, New England, on 11 November 1650, died in Kittery, Maine, on 21 March 1701. [SG.34.4]

FORD, JAMES, from Crichton, Midlothian, fought at the Battle of Bothwell Bridge in 1679, was transported via Leith aboard the Crown of London bound for Barbados on 27 November 1679, was shipwrecked and drowned off Orkney on 10 December 1679. [RBM]

FORD, JOHN, a prisoner banished to the Plantations on 18 August 1685, transported via Leith bound for East New Jersey in August 1685. [RPCS.XI.154/291/292]

FOREMAN, JOHN, then in Edinburgh Tolbooth, was transferred to Dunnottar Castle, Kincardineshire, on 29 July 1685. [ETR]; was banished to the Plantations on 18 August 1685, transported via Leith aboard the Henry and Francis of Newcastle bound for East New Jersey in August 1685. [RPCS.XI.154/289/292] [NWI.I.422]

FORREST, JAMES, from Cambusnethan, Lanarkshire, was banished to the Plantations on 24 July 1685 and transported via Leith to Jamaica in August 1685, landed at Port Royal on 7 December 1685. [RPCS.XI.155] [LC.17]

FORREST, MARGARET, from Cambusnethan, Lanarkshire, was banished to the Plantations on 11 October 1684 and transported via Leith to East New Jersey in August 1685, landed there on 7 December 1685. [RPCS.XI.155/292]

FORREST, WILLIAM, from Lanark, was imprisoned in Edinburgh Tolbooth as he had fought in the late rebellion, was released having signed a bond for the peace in June 1668. [RPCS.II.470]

FORRESTER, ALEXANDER, born 1611, was educated at the University of St Andrews, minister of St Mungo, Lochmaben, Dumfries-shire, from 1650 until 1662 when he refused to conform to Episcopacy, later held conventicles for which he was imprisoned on the Bass Rock in the Firth of Forth in 1677, he died in Edinburgh on 28 May 1686. [F.II.221]

FORRESTER, JOHN, born 1654, from Annan, Dumfriesshire, a minister in exile in Leiden and Utrecht in the Netherlands from 1684 until 1687. [SEC]

FORRESTER, MARION, in Kirkcudbright, was accused of rioting in Kirkcudbright in the parish of Irongray, in 1663. [RPCS.I.373]

FORRESTER, MARION, was taken from Leith Tolbooth, put in irons and imprisoned in Edinburgh Tolbooth, in 1685.[ETR]

FORRESTER, THOMAS, born around 1635, from Alva, Stirlingshire, a minister in exile in Rotterdam, Holland, from 1683 until 1685. [SEC]

FORSON, WILLIAM, 'who was exiled to Ireland for non-conformity, returned home in 1689, and settled on the farm of Holydean Mill, where he died in 1748 aged 82'. [Dryburgh Abbey gravestone, Berwickshire]

FORSYTH, JAMES, a minister in Kirkpatrick, father of James and Robert, who was banished to Ireland in 1638. [RPCS.I.215]

FORSYTH, JAMES, from Annandale, Dumfries-shire, was banished to the Plantations on 18 August 1685, then transported via Leith aboard the Henry and Francis of Newcastle bound for East New Jersey in August 1685, landed there on 7 December 1685. [RPCS.XI.154/291/292] [NWI.I.422]

FORSYTH, Mrs JAMES, a prisoner who died in Dunnottar Castle, Kincardineshire, in 1685. [Nithsdale Martyrs Cross, Dumfries]

FORSYTH, JOHN, a rebel in 1684. [RPCS.IX.357]

FORSYTH, THOMAS, the elder, in Thirstoun, a rebel and a fugitive in 1684. [RPCS.IX.358]

FORSYTH, WILLIAM, was sought by the Justice Court in August 1667 for his part in the late rebellion. [GC.123] [RPCS.II.345]

FOSSAM, MICHAEL, a prisoner of war was transported via London aboard the John and Sarah of London bound for Boston, New England, in May 1652. [SD.1.5-6]

FRAME, WILLIAM, from Calder in Clydesdale, fought in the Battle of Bothwell Bridge in 1679, was transported via Leith aboard the Crown of London bound for Barbados on 27 November 1679, was shipwrecked off Orkney on 10 December 1679, later was transported to Jamaica. [CEC.212/5][SW.198][RBM]

FRASER, ALLAN, a prisoner in Edinburgh Tolbooth, willing to go to America was released to go there on 17 December 1685, was transported via Leith bound for the Plantations in December 1685. [ETR]

FRASER, ANDREW, in Glenmade, guilty of aiding rebels, including Robert Cowan and John Frisell, was declared to be a rebel and fugitive in October 1684. [RPCS.IX.361]

FRASER, JOHN, a rebel and fugitive, suspected of participating in the attack at Enterkin in 1684. [RPCS.IX.360]

FRASER, JOHN, of Pitcalzean, born 1658, a prisoner in Edinburgh Tolbooth, was transferred to Dunnottar Castle, Kincardineshire, on 29 July 1685, was banished to the Plantations on 18 August 1685, transported via Leith aboard the Henry and Francis of Newcastle bound for East New Jersey in August 1685, returned to Scotland in 1688, died on 7 November 1711. [ETR] [F.VII/26/663] [NWI.I.422] [RPCS.XI.154/289/292]

FRASER, WILLIAM, a prisoner in Edinburgh Tolbooth in May 1685. [ETR]

FRENCH, AGNES, a widow in Barony parish, Glasgow, in 1683. [RPCS.VIII.644]

FRENCH, ANDREW, a prisoner in Edinburgh Tolbooth, willing to go to America [sic] was released to go there on 17 December 1685, [ETR]; was transported via Leith aboard the John and Nicholas bound for Barbados in December 1685. [RPCS.XI.232]

FRENCH, WILLIAM, from Cambusnethan, Lanarkshire, a prisoner in Edinburgh Tolbooth, who refused to take an Oath of

Allegiance, was banished to the American Plantations on 17 December 1685. [ETR], was transported via Leith aboard the <u>John and Nicholas</u> bound for Barbados in December 1685. [RPCS.XI.232]

FRISELL, EDWARD, was captured at the Siege of Worcester in 1651, transported via London aboard the <u>John and Sarah</u> bound for Boston, New England in December 1651, lander there in February 1652. [SD.1.6-6]

FRISELL, JOHN, son of Thomas Frisell in Auchincairn, a rebel and fugitive in 1684. [RPCS.IX.360]

FRISELL, or HARKNESS, MARGARET, in Mitchellslacks, was accused of harbouring and aiding her son Thomas Harkness at her home in July 1684, was declared a fugitive in 1684. [RPCS.IX.359]

FRISELL, THOMAS, a chapman, guilty of aiding Robert Cowan a rebel, was declared to be a rebel and fugitive in October 1684. [RPCS.IX.360]

FRISELL, WILLIAM, was captured at the Siege of Worcester in 1651, transported via London aboard the <u>John and Sarah</u> bound for Boston, New England in December 1651, lander there in February 1652. [SD.1.6-6]

FULLER, Captain JOHN, was killed at the Battle of Aird's Moss on 22 July 1680. [Muirkirk Monument, Ayrshire]

FULLARTOUN, MARGARET, a widow, was accused of rioting in Kirkcudbright in the parish of Irongray, in 1663. [RPCS.I.373]

FULLARTON, WILLIAM, of Craighall, son of James Fullarton of that Ilk, was educated at Glasgow University, minister of St Quivox, Ayrshire, from 1642 until he was dismissed for not conforming to Episcopacy, later minister at Coylton, Ayrshire. [F.III.20]

FYFFE, CHRISTIAN, then in Edinburgh Tolbooth, was transferred to Dunnottar Castle, Kincardineshire, on 29 July 1685. [ETR]

FYFFE, JAMES, minister at Carstairs, Lanarkshire, was warded in Edinburgh Tolbooth on 21 May 1685. [ETR]

GAIRDNER, JOHN, a servant from Wester Harieburn, Monklands, Lanarkshire, was warded in Edinburgh Tolbooth on 2 July 1684, then transported via Leith to Carolina on 1 August 1684. [RPCS.VIII.516][ETR]

GALBRAITH, JAMES, from Kippen, Stirlingshire, fought at the Battle of Bothwell Bridge in 1679, was transported via Leith aboard the Crown of London bound for Barbados on 27 November 1679, was shipwrecked and drowned off Orkney on 10 December 1679. [RBM]

GALT, JOHN, a thatcher in Glasgow, a rebel in Glasgow Tolbooth, was banished to the Plantations in June 1684, and transported via Glasgow aboard the Pelican bound for Carolina, bond by Walter Gibson, a merchant in Glasgow, dated 20 June 1684. [RPCS.IX.208]

GANNOCHEN, ADAM, a burgess of Kirkcudbright, was imprisoned in Edinburgh Tolbooth, for his wife's part in the tumult in Kirkcudbright, was released after guaranteeing his wife's future attitude toward bishops, the Church and the State in 1663. [RPCS.I.377]

GANNOCHEN, JANET, spouse to John Halliday, was accused of rioting in Kirkcudbright in the parish of Irongray, in 1663. [RPCS.I.373]

GARDINER, CHRISTIAN, was taken from Leith Tolbooth, put in irons and imprisoned in Edinburgh Tolbooth, to be transported to the Plantations on 11 August 1685. [ETR]

GARDINER, JAMES, born in the 1630s, was educated at Glasgow University, minister in Saddell in Argyll, from 1654 until 1662 when on account of his 'seditious carriage' the Privy Council ordered him to leave H.M. dominions within a month, a minister in exile in Leiden and Rotterdam in the Netherlands from 1662 until 1667, secretly he returned to Glasgow where he died by 1685. [SEC] [F.IV.65]

GARDINER, JOHN, servant to James Ralston in Wester Harieburn, a rebel, a prisoner in Edinburgh or Canongait Tolbooth, was banished to the Plantations on 2 July 1684. [RPCS.IX.28]

GARDNER, JOHN, from Monklands, Lanarkshire, fought at the Battle of Bothwell Bridge in 1679, was transported via Leith aboard the Crown of London bound for Barbados on 27 November 1679, was shipwrecked and drowned off Orkney on 10 December 1679. [RBM]

GARMONY, ROBERT, from Kirkpatrick Durham, who was in the recent rebellion, to be released from prison on 11 February 1669. [RPCS.II.599]

GARMORY, ROBERT, in Meikle Drayburgh, was accused, in Kirkcudbright in October 1684, of aiding James Garmory. [RPCS.IX.377]

GAVIN, JAMES, a prisoner in Edinburgh Tolbooth, to be transported to the Plantations on 11 August 1685. [ETR]

GEMMILL, JOHN, from Cumnock, Ayrshire, fought at the Battle of Bothwell Bridge in 1679, was transported via Leith aboard the Crown of London bound for Barbados on 27 November 1679, was shipwrecked and drowned off Orkney on 10 December 1679. [RBM]

GEMMILL, JOHN, born 1617, was educated at Glasgow University, minister at Straiton, Ayrshire from 1642, was deposed in 1662 as he refused to conform to Episcopacy, restored to the parish died in 1705. [F.III.73]

GEMMEL, JOHN, was killed at the Battle of Aird's Moss on 22 July 1680. [Muirkirk Monument, Ayrshire]

GEMMELL, JOHN, a prisoner in Canongait Tolbooth, who refused to take an Oath of Allegiance, was banished to the American Plantations on 17 December 1685. [ETR]

GERMONT, THOMAS, from Kirkoswald, Ayrshire, fought at the Battle of Bothwell Bridge in 1679, was transported via Leith aboard the Crown of London bound for Barbados on 27

November 1679, was shipwrecked and drowned off Orkney on 10 December 1679. [RBM]

GERRAN, ANDREW, in Ironspie, was accused in Kirkcudbright of conversing with a rebel and fugitive, William Russell, in 1684. [RPCS.IX.374]

GIBB, JAMES, from Abercorn, West Lothian, fought at the Battle of Bothwell Bridge in 1679, was transported via Leith aboard the Crown of London bound for Barbados on 27 November 1679, was shipwrecked and drowned off Orkney on 10 December 1679. [RBM]

GIBB, JOHN, from Cavers, Roxburghshire, fought at the Battle of Bothwell Bridge in 1679, was transported via Leith aboard the Crown of London bound for Barbados on 27 November 1679, was shipwrecked and drowned off Orkney on 10 December 1679. [RBM]

GIBSON, ALEXANDER, and his wife Janet Miller in Foord, fugitives in May 1683. [RPCS.VIII.609]

GIBSON, JAMES, and JOHN GIBSON, in Blairstrowie, for attending conventicles, were outlawed on 29 August 1672. [RPCS.III.583]

GIBSON, JAMES, in Arrow, to be tried accused of rebellion, 3 June 1684. [RPCS.IX.205]

GIBSON, JANET, spouse to James Reid in Polgavine, for aiding four rebels in June 1684, was declared to be a rebel and fugitive in October 1684. [RPCS.IX.365]

GIBSON, JOHN, in Dalgaine, Ayrshire, a rebel in Glasgow Tolbooth, was banished to the Plantations in June 1684, and transported via Glasgow aboard the Pelican bound for Carolina, bond by Walter Gibson, a merchant in Glasgow, dated 20 June 1684. [RPCS.IX.208]

GIBSON, JOHN, was warded in Edinburgh Tolbooth on 20 May 1685, but having taken the Oath of Allegiance, was released on 28 May 1685. [ETR]

GIBSON, JOHN, died in Ingliston in 1685. [Nithsdale Martyrs Cross, Dumfries]

GIBSON, NICOLA, spouse of James Grierson of Craignestoun, for aiding rebels Robert Grierson a chapman, John Gibson, and others, was declared to be a rebel and fugitive in October 1684. [RPCS.IX.367]

GIBSON, ROBERT, was transported to Virginia in October 1669. [RPCS.III.22]

GILCHRIST, ANDREW, a Lieutenant of Lord Angus's Regiment, [The Cameronians], fought at the Battle of Dunkeld in August 1679.

GILCHRIST, BESSIE, in Kilroy, Dunscore, 'was committed to the castle' in 1684. [RPCS.IX.702]; imprisoned in Dumfries Tolbooth and Edinburgh Tolbooth, was banished to the Plantations on 24 October 1684. [RPCS.X.309]

GILCHRIST, JAMES, a Captain of Lord Angus's Regiment, [the Cameronians], who fought at the Battle of Killiecrankie in 1689.

GILCHRIST, JOHN, a shoemaker in West Calder, Mid Lothian, a rebel and rioter, was banished and transported to Virginia, on 30 July 1668. [RPCS.II.503]

GILCHRIST, PATRICK, from Gargunnock, Stirlingshire, fought at the Battle of Bothwell Bridge in 1679, was transported via Leith aboard the Crown of London bound for Barbados on 27 November 1679, was shipwrecked and drowned off Orkney on 10 December 1679. [RBM]

GILCHRIST, ROBERT, from Dalgarnock, Nithsdale, Dumfries-shire, was banished to the Plantations on 18 August 1685, transported via Leith aboard the Henry and Francis bound for East New Jersey on 5 September 1685. [RPCS.XI.154]

GILCHRIST, THOMAS, from Calder, Midlothian, fought at the Battle of Bothwell Bridge in 1679, was transported via Leith aboard the Crown of London bound for Barbados on 27

November 1679, was shipwrecked and drowned off Orkney on 10 December 1679. [RBM]

GILCHRIST, Mrs, wife of John Gilchrist a rioter in Calder, Mid Lothian, and now a fugitive, to be imprisoned in Edinburgh Tolbooth in June 1668. [RPCS.II.470]

GILFILLAN, JOHN, was banished to the Plantations on 18 August 1685, transported via Leith on the Henry and Francis bound for East New Jersey on 5 September 1685. [RPCS.XI.154]

GILKERSON, GAVIN, from Monklands, Lanarkshire, a prisoner in Edinburgh Tolbooth, was banished to the Plantations on 5 May 1684, transported via Leith to New York on 16 May 1684. [RPCS.VIII.516]

GILKERSON, WILLIAM, for his part in the recent rebellion was imprisoned in Edinburgh Tolbooth, having subscribed to a bond was released on 18 February 1669. [RPCS.II.602]

GILLAN, JAMES, born 1629, was educated at Edinburgh University, minister at Cavers, Roxburghshire, from 1658 until deprived in 1662, he was arrested in 1668 and died on 5 August 1668. [F.II.105]

GILLESPIE, AGNES, spouse of John Broun in Gubhill, was declared a rebel as she had seen Adam Harknes a fugitive, and had failed to report it, in 1684. [RPCS.IX.360]

GILLESPIE, JOHN, in Relicthill, for seeing rebel Robert Cowan in August 1684, was declared a rebel and fugitive in October 1684. [RPCS.IX.372]

GILLILAND, JOHN, was warded in Edinburgh Castle on 10 July 1685, banished to the Plantations on 24 July 1685, and transported via Leith to East New Jersey on 30 July 1685. [ETR] [RPCS.XI.329]

GILLISON, HOMER, from Dumfries was warded in Edinburgh Tolbooth on 20 May 1685, having sworn an Oath of Allegiance was released on 28 May 1685. [ETR]

GILMORE, JAMES, from the Gate of Cumberland, was accused of conversing with rebel John Eastoun, and was imprisoned in October 1684. [RPCS.IX.709]

GILMORE, WILLIAM, a prisoner in Edinburgh Tolbooth, having subscribed to the Test Act, was released on 6 February 1685. [ETR]

GIRVAN, CATHERINE, a prisoner in Leith Tolbooth, was banished to the Plantations on 18 August 1685, then transported via Leith aboard the Henry and Francis bound for East New Jersey on 5 September 1685. [RPCS.XI.154]

GLASGOW, JOHN, from Cavers, Roxburghshire, fought at the Battle of Bothwell Bridge in 1679, was transported via Leith aboard the Crown of London bound for Barbados on 27 November 1679, was shipwrecked off Orkney on 10 December 1679, later transported to Jamaica. [RBM][CEC.212/5][SW.203]

GLASGOW, WILLIAM, from Cavers, Roxburghshire, fought at the Battle of Bothwell Bridge in 1679, was transported via Leith aboard the Crown of London bound for Barbados on 27 November 1679, was shipwrecked off Orkney on 10 December 1679, later transported to Jamaica. [RBM][CEC.212/5][SW.203]

GLASS, WILLIAM, in Cockarne, for attending conventicles, was outlawed on 29 August 1672. [RPCS.III.583]

GLEN, JAMES, a prisoner in Edinburgh Tolbooth in May 1685. [ETR]

GLENCORSE, JOHN, in Mortonmains, for aiding William Milligan a rebel and fugitive, was also declared a rebel and fugitive in 1684. [RPCS.IX.358]

GLENCORSE, THOMAS, for aiding William Milligan a rebel and fugitive, was also declared a rebel and fugitive in 1684. [RPCS.IX.358]

GLENDINNING, JAMES, was educated at the University of St Andrews, minister at Coole or Carnmoney, County Antrim, in

1621, a lecturer at Carrickfergus until the Rebellion of 1641, minister at Kilbarchan, Renfrewshire, from 1647 to 1648, subscribed to the Solemn League and Covenant in 1648, later returned to Ireland. [F.III.149; VII.529]

GLENDINNING, JAMES, of Mochrinie, was accused, in Kirkcudbright on 4 October 1684, of aiding several rebels in 1684. [RPCS.IX.377]

GLOVER, ANDREW, in Hemisfieldtoun, for seeing rebels John Mundall, Peter Coudan and James Glover, who had escaped from Dumfries Tolbooth, and failed to report it, was declared to be a rebel and fugitive in October 1684. [RPCS.IX.370]

GLOVER, JAMES, a rebel in 1684, [RPCS.IX.357]; was imprisoned on 28 November 1684, died in Edinburgh Tolbooth on 13 April 1685. [Nithsdale Martyrs Cross, Dumfries] [ETR]

GLOVER, JANET, a widow, in Hemisfield, Tynwald, for seeing rebel Peter Coudan in July 1684 and not reporting it, was declared to be a rebel and fugitive in October 1684. [RPCS.IX.370]

GLOVER, WILLIAM, former servant to Alexander Williamson in Blackcraig, to be imprisoned in Edinburgh Tolbooth in August 1684. [RPCS.IX.126]

GOLDIE, THOMAS, in Linburn, for aiding rebels, was declared a rebel and fugitive in October 1684. [RPCS.IX.360]

GOODWIN, ROBERT, from Glasgow, was transported via Leith aboard the Henry and Newcastle on 5 September 1685. [RPCS.XI.155]

GORDON, AGNES, in Knoxbrex, was accused, in Kirkcudbright in October 1684, of conversing with rebel Gilbert McGie. [RPCS.IX.374]

GORDON, ALEXANDER, of Knockgray, in the parish of Carsphairn, Kirkcudbrightshire, a suspected Covenanter in 1665. [GC.111]

GORDON, ALEXANDER, born 1650, from Earlston, Berwickshire, fought at the Battle of Bothwell Bridge, Lanarkshire, on 22 June

1679, a prisoner in Edinburgh Tolbooth to be transferred to the Bass Rock in August 1684, escaped from Edinburgh Tolbooth on 4 September 1684, fled to Holland where he died in 1726. [NRS.NRAS.NA.24245][RPCS.IX.99/141][ETR]

GORDON, ALEXANDER of Earlston, Dalry, Ayrshire, was killed at the Battle of Aird's Moss in 1680.

GORDON, ......., of Earlston, a prisoner in Blackness Castle was taken from there to Edinburgh Tolbooth in January 1685. [ETR]

GORDON, ALEXANDER, a Presbyterian minister in northern Ireland in 1679. [RPCS.VI.657]

GORDON, ALEXANDER, of Kinsture, a prisoner in Dumfries for rebellion, to be transferred to Edinburgh Tolbooth, on 2 June 1684. [RPCS.IX.30]

GORDON, ALEXANDER, a merchant in Clauchan, was accused, in Kirkcudbright in 1684, of aiding Robert McClelland of Barscob. [RPCS.IX.376]

GORDON, ALEXANDER, in Airds, was accused, in Kirkcudbright in 1684, of aiding Samuel Arnot a vagrant preacher. [RPCS.IX.376]

GORDON, ANNABELL, then in Edinburgh Tolbooth, was transferred to Dunnottar Castle, Kincardineshire, on 29 July 1685. [ETR]; was banished to the Plantations on 18 August 1685, transported via Leith aboard the <u>Henry and Francis</u> bound for East New Jersey on 5 September 1685. [RPCS.XI.154]

GORDON, BARBARA, in Ballannan, was accused in Kirkcudbright on 7 October 1684, of conversing with rebel John Charters. [RPCS.IX.374]

GORDON, BESSIE, was banished to the Plantations on 18 August 1685, transported via Leith aboard the <u>Henry and Francis</u> bound for East New Jersey on 5 September 1685. [RPCS.XI.164]

GORDON, EDWARD, of Gartcrogo, Dumfries-shire, was indicted for 'hearing and recepting rebellious preachers', in 1684. [RPCS.IX.555]

GORDON, EDWARD, was hanged at Irongray, Kirkcudbrightshire, on 3 March 1685. [Hallhill gravestone, Kirkpatrick-Durham, Kirkcudbrightshire] [Nithsdale Martyrs Cross, Dumfries]

GORDON, JAMES, was captured at the Battle of Dunbar in 1650, transported via London aboard the Unity of Boston bound for New England in November 1650. [SCF.1226]

GORDON, JAMES, was captured at the Siege of Worcester in 1651, and transported via London aboard the John and Sarah bound for Boston, New England, in December 1651. [SD.1.5-6]

GORDON, JAMES, a merchant in Kirkgate, Dumfries, for aiding rebel and conventlicker John Hepburn, was declared a rebel and fugitive in October 1684. [RPCS.IX.372]

GORDON, JAMES, the younger, a merchant in Dumfries, was accused of aiding Andrew Martin of Little Aries a 'declared traitor', was indited in Dumfries in 1684. [RPCS.IX.555]

GORDON, JOHN, was captured at the Siege of Worcester in 1651, transported via London aboard the John and Sarah bound for Boston in December 1651. [SD.1.5-6]

GORDON, JOHN, a burgess of Stranraer, Wigtownshire, a prisoner in Stranraer Tolbooth, accused of treason, was sent to Edinburgh in January 1664. [GC.106]

GORDON, JOHN, of Largmore, died on 6 January 1667 of wounds received at Pentland. [Kells gravestone, Kirkcudbrightshire]

GORDON, JOHN, in Middleton of Dalry, Kirkcudbrightshire, was sought by the Justice Court in August 1667 for his part in the late rebellion. [GC.123] [RPCS.II.345]

GRAHAM, WILLIAM, was killed on 15 March 1684. [Crossmichael gravestone, Kirkcudbrightshire]

GRAHAM, WILLIAM, from Linlithgow, West Lothian, imprisoned in Linlithgow Tolbooth, transported via Glasgow aboard the Pelican of Glasgow bound for Carolina in 1684. [RPCS.VIII.

GRAHAM, WILLIAM, was transported via Leith aboard the John and Nicholas bound for Barbados in December 1685. [ETR]

GRANT, ALASTAIR, was captured at the Siege of Worcester in 1651, and transported via London aboard the John and Sarah bound for New England in November 1651, landed in Boston in February 1652. [SD.1.5-6]

GRANT, DANIEL, was captured at the Siege of Worcester in 1651, and transported via London aboard the John and Sarah bound for New England in November 1651, landed in Boston in February 1652. [SD.1.5-6]

GRANT, JAMES, [1], was captured at the Siege of Worcester in 1651, and transported via London aboard the John and Sarah bound for New England in November 1651, landed in Boston in February 1652. [SD.1.5-6]

GRANT, JAMES, [2], captured at the Siege of Worcester in 1651, and transported via London aboard the John and Sarah bound for New England in November 1651, landed in Boston in February 1652. [SD.1.5-6]

GRANT, JAMES, [3], was captured at the Siege of Worcester in 1651, and transported via London aboard the John and Sarah bound for New England in November 1651, landed in Boston in February 1652. [SD.1.5-6]

GRANT, JOHN, [1], was captured at the Siege of Worcester in 1651, and transported via London aboard the John and Sarah bound for New England in November 1651, landed in Boston in February 1652. [SD.1.5-6]

GRANT, JOHN, [2], was captured at the Siege of Worcester in 1651, and transported via London aboard the John and Sarah bound for New England in November 1651, landed in Boston in February 1652. [SD.1.5-6]

GRANT, JOHN, [3], was captured at the Siege of Worcester in 1651, and transported via London aboard the John and Sarah bound for New England in November 1651, landed in Boston in February 1652. [SD.1.5-6]

GRANT, PATRICK, was captured at the Siege of Worcester in 1651, and transported via London aboard the John and Sarah bound for New England in November 1651, landed in Boston in February 1652. [SD.1.5-6]

GRANT, PETER, was captured at the Battle of Dunbar in 1650, and transported via London aboard the Unity bound for New England in November 1650. [SD.1226]

GRANT, THOMAS, was captured at the Siege of Worcester in 1651, and transported via London aboard the John and Sarah bound for New England in November 1651, landed in Boston in February 1652. [SD.1.5-6]

GRAY, ANDREW, a merchant from Edinburgh, captured the Royalist General Sir James Turner, in Dumfries on 15 November 1666. [Z.192]

GRAY, ARCHIBALD, a skipper in Donaghadee, was accused of transporting a rebel, Gilbert McKie from Scotland to Ireland and back in 1684. [RPCS.II.381]

GRAY, CHARLES, then in Edinburgh Tolbooth, was transferred to Dunnottar Castle, Kincardineshire, on 29 July 1685. [ETR]; was banished to the Plantations on 11 August 1685. [RPCS.XI.126/143/145]

GRAY, GEORGE, was captured at the Battle of Dunbar in 165, then transported via London aboard the Unity bound for New England in November 1650. [CEB]

GRAY, JAMES, from Fenwick, Ayrshire, fought at the Battle of Bothwell Bridge in 1679, GOVAN, JOHN, from Neilston, Renfrewshire, fought at the Battle of Bothwell Bridge in 1679, was transported via Leith aboard the Crown of London bound for Barbados on 27 November 1679, was shipwrecked and drowned off Orkney on 10 December 1679. [RBM]

GRAY, JAMES, was killed at the Battle of Aird's Moss on 22 July 1680. [Muirkirk Monument, Ayrshire]

GRAY, JAMES, the elder, portioner of Chryston, parish of Calder, Mid Lothian, was imprisoned in Edinburgh in 1683. [RPCS.VIII.643]; a prisoner in Edinburgh or Canongait Tolbooth, a rebel, was banished to the Plantations in Carolina on 8 August 1684. [RPCS.IX.95]

GRAY, JAMES, a prisoner in Edinburgh Tolbooth, was banished to the Plantations on 11 August 1685, transported via Leith to Jamaica in August 1685, landed in Port Royal in November 1685 [ETR] [RPCS.XI.330]

GRAY, JOHN, was educated at Edinburgh University, minister at Orwell from 1650 until deprived for keeping conventicles in 1671. [F.V.79]

GRAY, MARGARET, in Hemisfieldtoun, for seeing rebel Peter Coudan and his wife there, and failed to report it, was declared to be a rebel and fugitive in October 1684. [RPCS.IX.370]

GRAZE, JAMES, from Calder, Midlothian, fought at the Battle of Bothwell Bridge in 1679, was transported via Leith aboard the Crown of London bound for Barbados on 27 November 1679, was shipwrecked and drowned off Orkney on 10 December 1679. [RBM]

GREENSHIELDS, JOHN, from Cavers, Roxburghshire, fought at the Battle of Bothwell Bridge in 1679, was transported via Leith aboard the Crown of London bound for Barbados on 27 November 1679, was shipwrecked and drowned off Orkney on 10 December 1679. [RBM]

GREIG, JOHN, son of Reverend James Greig of Loudoun [1597-1635], was educated at Glasgow University, a minister at Carrickfergus and at Newtonards, Ireland, from 1646 until 1650, was imprisoned in Carlingford Castle, Ireland, from 1663 until 1654, he died on 20 July 1670. [FI.37]

GREIG, JOHN, minister in Carstairs, Lanarkshire, was warded in Edinburgh Tolbooth on 15 October 1685. [ETR]

GREIG, WALTER, minister at Balmerino, Fife, from 1621 until 1671, chaplain to Lord Balcarres's Regiment of Horse in the Army of the Solemn League and Covenant in 1644, died on 24 September 1671. [F.V.128][RHCA]

GREIR, ADAM, in West Calder, Mid Lothian, a rebel and rioter, was banished and transported to Virginia, on 30 July 1668. [RPCS.II.503]

GREIR, ANNA, relict of …… in Peeltoun, for aiding rebels, William Herreis, James MacMichael, and two others, was declared to be a rebel and fugitive in October 1684. [RPCS.IX.368]

GRIER, FERGUS, imprisoned in Leith Tolbooth, was transported via Leith aboard the Henry and Francis bound for East New Jersey on 5 September 1685, landed there on 7 December 1685. [RPCS.XI.154] [NWI.I.422]

GREIR, HELEN, spouse of Archibald Broun in Auchinchain, for aiding rebels John and James Carmichael, Robert Grier a chapman, and William Herries, was declared to be a rebel and fugitive in October 1684. [RPCS.IX.367/700]

GRIER, HENRY, in Balmaclellan, Kirkcudbrightshire, was sought by the Justice Court in August 1667 for his part in the late rebellion. [GC.123]

GRIER, JAMES, imprisoned in Leith Tolbooth, was transported via Leith aboard the Henry and Francis bound for East New Jersey on 5 September 1685, landed there on 7 December 1685. [RPCS.XI.154] [NWI.I.422]

GRIER, JOHN, of Dalton, in the parish of Kells, Kirkcudbrightshire, a suspected Covenanter in 1665. [GC.111]

GRIER, JOHN, from Brigmark, Kirkcudbrightshire, a prisoner in Kirkcudbright Tolbooth, was banished to the Plantations on 13 October 1684. [RPCS.X.258]

GRIER, MARIE, in Castle Fairn, for aiding her son William Herries and other rebels and fugitives, was declared to be a rebel and fugitive, in September 1684. [RPCS.IX.373]

GRIER, ROBERT, of Millmark, in the parish of Dalry, Kirkcudbrightshire, a suspected Covenanter in 1665. [GC.111]

GRIER, ROBERT, from Lochenkitt, a rebel in 1666, imprisoned in Edinburgh Tolbooth, was banished to Virginia on 4 August 1668. [RPCS.II.507]; he was granted to Captain Lightfoot, master of the Convertin at Leith bound for Virginia in September 1668. [RPCS.II.534]

GRIER, ROBERT, a chapman, was alleged to be one of the rebels involved in the ambush at Enterkin, Dumfries-shire in 1684. [RPCS.IX.259]

GRIER, THOMAS, in Cormilligan, Glencairn, Dumfries-shire, was banished to the Plantations on 24 October1684, was committed in irons in October 1684 while his wife Catherine Hunter was also committed. [RPCS.IX.587/692]

GRIERSON, ALEXANDER, brother of William Grierson sometime of Lochwhir, and James Grierson the younger of Craignestoun, for going to Thirstoun on the last day of July 1684 and bring back brother William Grierson of Lochwhir, a rebel and fugitive, to Auchinshenemoor, was declared to be rebels and fugitives in October 1684. [RPCS.IX.367]

GRIERSON, ISABEL, at Crossmichael Mill, was accused in Kirkcudbright of conversing with fugitive Andrew Crock, in 1684. [RPCS.IX.374]

GRIERSON, JAMES, of Dargoner, Kirkcudbrightshire, was sought by the Justice Court in August 1667 for his part in the late rebellion. [GC.123]; was released on caution from Ayr Tolbooth on 18 July 1667. [RPCS.II.309]

GRIERSON, JOHN, in Tounfoot, Dunscore, refused to depone and was imprisoned, on 7 August 1684. [RPCS.IX.264]

GRIERSON, JOHN, was killed on 18 December 1684. [St John of Dalry gravestone, Kirkcudbrightshire][GC.317]

GRIERSON, JOHN, was killed on Auchencloy Moor in 1685. [Auchencloy Martyrs Monument, Kirkcudbrightshire]

GRIERSON, ROBERT, tenant of Lochenkit farm, was captured, tried, and banished abroad, but returned to Scotland in 1688. [Larghill Monument, Kirkcudbrightshire]

GRIERSON, ROBERT, was killed at Ingliston Mains on 28 April 1685. [Balmaclellan gravestone, Kirkcudbrightshire] [Nithsdale Martyrs Cross, Dumfries]

GRIERSON, WILLIAM, of Lochtour/Lochwhirr, was wounded at the ambush at Enterkin on 9 October 1684, was declared a rebel and fugitive, a prisoner in Dumfries for rebellion, to be caught and transferred to Edinburgh Tolbooth; to be released on 11 February 1669. [RPCS.IX.30/358; II.598]

GRIEVE, ROBERT, in Maw, for attending conventicles, was outlawed on 29 August 1672. [RPCS.III.583]

GRIEVE, ROBERT, a servant of the widow Annand, was accused of rioting in Edinburgh in 1686. [NRS.JC39.91]

GRIEVE, WILLIAM, from Linlithgow, West Lothian, a prisoner in Canongait Tolbooth, was banished to the Plantations on 27 May 1684, and was transported to Carolina in June 1684. [RPCS.VIII.526/630]

GRIEVE, WILLIAM, a Captain of Lord Angus's Regiment, [the Cameronians], who fought at the Battle of Killiecrankie in 1689. [BK]

GRINDLAY, WILLIAM, from Cavers, Roxburghshire, fought at the Battle of Bothwell Bridge in 1679, was transported via Leith aboard the Crown of London bound for Barbados on 27

November 1679 was shipwrecked and drowned off Orkney on 10 December 1679. [RBM]

GRYCIE, AGNES, wife of John Black, for aiding John MacCall and John Smith rebels, at Thomas Hunter's house in Auchenbreck, was declared a rebel and fugitive in October 1684. [RPCS.IX.365]

GRYCIE, JOHN, in Cleughfoot, for seeing rebel John MacCall weeding the corn of John Laurie in Eshtrees, and later seeing him in Jean Laurie's house at Mollloford, and not reporting same, and failing to report it was declared to be a rebel and fugitive in October 1684. [RPCS.IX.365]

GRYCIE, JOHN, in Tippett, for seeing rebels John Mathieson and another in the Aird Milne, and failing to report it was declared to be a rebel and fugitive in October 1684. [RPCS.IX.365]

GRIME, ALLISTER, was captured at the Battle of Dunbar in 1650 and transported via London aboard the <u>Unity</u> bound for Boston in November 1650. [SCF.1226]

GRINDLAY, WILLIAM, a prisoner in Edinburgh Tolbooth, was transported via Leith to the Plantations in November 1679. [ETR]

GRINLAW, JOHN, in Garloff, was accused, in Kirkcudbright on 4 October 1684, of aiding rebels John Clerk and Gilbert Welsh. [RPCS.IX.378]

GUIDEN, ROBERT, then in Edinburgh Tolbooth, was transferred to Dunnottar Castle, Kincardineshire, on 29 July 1685. [ETR]

GUNN, DANIEL, was captured at the Siege of Worcester in 1651, transported via Gravesend, London, aboard the <u>John and Sarah</u> bound for New England in December 1651. [SD.1.5-6]

GURNER, JAMES, captured at the Siege of Worcester in 1651, transported via London aboard the <u>John and Sarah</u> bound for Boston, New England in December 1651, lander there in February 1652. [SD.1.6-6]

GUTHRIE, FRANCIS, of Gagie, Angus, a possible Covenanter in Ireland in 1640. [NRS.GD188.25.1.4.16]

GUTHRIE, JAMES, minister at Stirling, was accused of holding conventicles was imprisoned in Edinburgh Castle on 23 August 1660, was executed at the Mercat Cross in Edinburgh in 1661. [RPCS.VIII.465]

GUTHRIE, JOHN, born 1632, youngest son of James Guthrie of Pitforthie in Angus, was educated at Glasgow University, minister at Tarbolton, Ayrshire, from 1658 until deprived in 1662, was sought by the Justice Court in August 1667 for his part in the late rebellion. [GC.123] [RPCS.II.345]; was condemned to death but was pardoned, he died in 1669.

GUTHRIES, ROBERT, probably captured at the Battle of Dunbar in 1650 and transported via London to New England in 1650. [NWI.I.159]

GUTHRIE, Reverend WILLIAM, born 1620, son of James Guthrie of Pitforthy in Angus, minister of Fenwick, Ayrshire from 1644 until he was deposed in 1664 for refusing to submit to Episcopacy, probably chaplain of the Earl of Cassillis's Regiment of Foot at the Battle of Dunbar in September 1650, died in Brechin, Angus, on 10 October 1665, buried in Brechin Cathedral. [RHCA] [F.III.93]

HACKSTON, DAVID, of Rathillet, Fife, who assassinated Archbishop Sharp in 1679, fought at the Battle of Bothwell Bridge on 2 June 1679, was captured after the Battle of Aird's Moss in Ayrshire, and executed in 1680, trial papers. [NRS.JC39.115]

HACKSTON, WILLIAM, a tailor from Edinburgh, imprisoned in Edinburgh Tolbooth, was transported via Leith aboard the St Michael of Scarborough bound for the West Indies on 12 December 1678. [RPCS.VI.76]

HACKSTON, WILLIAM, a rebel imprisoned in Edinburgh Tolbooth, was released on 25 September 1684. [RPCS.IX.180][ETR]

HADDOWAY, ARCHIBALD, from Glasgow, a prisoner in Edinburgh Tolbooth, was transported via Leith aboard the St Michael of Scarborough bound for the West Indies on 12 December 1678. [RPCS.VI.76]

HADDOWAY, WILLIAM, a tenant of Torpichen, East Lothian, a rebel and rioter, was banished and transported to Virginia, on 30 July 1668. [RPCS.II.503]

HADDOWAY, Mrs, wife of William Haddoway a rioter in Calder, Mid Lothian, and now a fugitive, to be imprisoned in Edinburgh Tolbooth in June 1668. [RPCS.II.470]

HAFFIE, ANDREW, in Careltoun, was accused, in Kirkcudbright, of aiding rebels and in particular the ministers banished to the Bass Rock in the Firth of Forth, in October 1684. [RPCS.IX.374]

HAGOMAN, JOHN, was captured at the Siege of Worcester in 1651, then transported via London aboard the John and Sarah bound for New England in December 1651, landed in Boston in February 1652. [SD.1.5-6]

HAIR, JOHN, was killed in New Cumnock, Ayrshire, in 1685. [Nithsdale Martyrs Cross, Dumfries]

HAIR, WILLIAM, in Morton Castle, for aiding William Milligan a rebel and fugitive, was also declared a rebel and fugitive in 1684. [RPCS.IX.358]

HAIRSTANES, AGNES, spouse of Fair Thomas Harknes in Lought, Durisdeer, for aiding rebels, was declared a rebel and fugitive in September 1684, [RPCS.IX.373]; refused to take the oath and was imprisoned in Dumfries Tolbooth in October 1684. [RPCS.IX.690]

HAIRSTANES, WILLIAM, in Penphillan, was imprisoned in irons in October 1684. [RPCS.IX.696]

HAISTIE, JOHN, and JANET GIBSON his wife, for aiding William Milligan in Mortonmains a rebel and fugitive, was also declared rebels and fugitives in 1684. [RPCS.IX.359/373]

HAISTIE, WILLIAM, then in Edinburgh Tolbooth, put in irons and imprisoned in Canongait Tolbooth on 29 July 1685. [ETR]

HALDANE, JOHN, a Captain of Lord Angus's Regiment, [the Cameronians], who fought at the Battle of Killiecrankie in 1689.

HALL, DAVID, from Mayfield, was killed on Kirkconnell Moor, Kirkcudbrightshire, in 1685. [Kirkconnell Moor Monument]

HALL, GILBERT, a minister, was accused of holding conventicles and imprisoned in Edinburgh Castle in August 1660, [RPCS.VIII.465];

HALL, HENRY, of Heughheid, with his troop of horse, fought at the Battle of Bothwell Bridge on 2 June 1679, later was captured in Queensferry on 3 June 1680.

HALL, JAMES, a tenant farmer in Argyll, took part in Argyll's Rebellion in 1685, a prisoner in Edinburgh Tolbooth, was banished to the Plantations on 31 July 1685, transported via Leith to Jamaica in August 1685. [RPCS.XI.136]

HALLIDAY, DAVID, portioner of Mayfield, was killed on Kirkconnell Moor on 21 February 1685. [Balmaghie gravestone, Kirkcudbrightshire] [GC.304]

HALLIDAY, DAVID, from Glengape, was killed on 11 July 1685. [Balmaghie gravestone, Kirkcudbrightshire] [GC.304]

HALLIDAY, JOHN, a burgess of Kirkcudbright, was imprisoned in Edinburgh Tolbooth, for his wife's part in the tumult in Kirkcudbright, was released after guaranteeing his wife's future attitude toward bishops, the Church and the State in 1663. [RPCS.I.377]

HALLIDAY, MARION, spouse of William Richardson, was accused of rioting in Kirkcudbright in the parish of Irongray, in 1663. [RPCS.I.373]

HALLIDAY, THOMAS, in Netherthird, was accused, at Kirkcudbright in October 1684, of aiding rebel John Coutart. [RPCS.IX.377]

HALTRIDGE, JOHN, chaplain to Sir William Cunningham of Cunninghamhead, was forbidden to preach in 1664, moved to Ireland, minister at Island Magee in 1672, died in 1697. [F.VII.530]

HALLUME, JOHN, born 1667, tried in Kirkcudbright, he refused to take the Oath of Abduration, and was hanged there in 1685. [St Cuthbert's gravestone, Kirkcudbright]

HAMILTON, ANDREW, a tenant of the laird of Lee, subscribed to a bond on 8 July 1684. [RPCS.IX.211]

HAMILTON, ARCHIBALD, minister at Wigtown, moved to Bangor, Ireland, in 1672, returned to Wigtown in 1689, died on 29 June 1695. [F.VII.530]

HAMILTON, DAVID, was captured at the Siege of Worcester in 1651, then transported via London aboard the John and Sarah bound for New England in December 1651, landed in Boston in February 1652. [SD.1.5-6]

HAMILTON, Sir FREDERICK, of Castle Hamilton, County Leitrim, Ireland, was admitted as a burgess and guilds-brother of Edinburgh on 23 June 1633, he subscribed to the Covenant in Londonderry in 1636, joined the Covenanter Army in Scotland but was killed in 1647. [EBR]

HAMILTON, GEORGE, from Brouncastle, was imprisoned in Edinburgh Tolbooth on 13 November 1684, was banished to the Plantations on 24 December 1684. [RPCS.X.777/269/304][ETR]

HAMILTON, ISABEL, a prisoner in Edinburgh Tolbooth, was transported via Leith to Barbados in December 1665. [ETR]

HAMILTON, JAMES, born 1596, minister at Ballywalter from 1626, was involved in the attempted emigration of 140 settlers via Groomsport aboard the Eagle Wing bound for New England on 9 September 1636, venture failed and returned on 3 November 1636. He publicly prayed at the execution of the Marquis of Argyll at the Mercat Cross of Edinburgh on 27 May 1661.

HAMILTON, JAMES, of Kirktonholm, subscribed to the National Covenant in 1644 and 1649.

HAMILTON, JAMES, was captured at the Siege of Worcester in 1651, then transported via London aboard the John and Sarah bound for New England in December 1651, landed in Boston in February 1652. [SD.1.5-6]

HAMILTON, JAMES, a minister in Edinburgh, was deposed and ordered to leave the town before 1 October 1662. [RPCS.I.264]

HAMILTON, JAMES, of Kittiemuir, Stonehouse, Lanarkshire, was captured at the Battle of Pentland and executed in Edinburgh on 7 December 1666.

HAMILTON, JAMES, a prisoner in Canongait Tolbooth, a rebel, was banished to the Plantations in Carolina on 8 August 1684. [RPCS.IX.95]; originally, he should have gone in Robert Malloch's ship but was changed to the ship of Walter Gibson, a merchant in Glasgow, on 19 August 1684. [RPCS.IX.111][ETR]

HAMILTON, JAMES, a prisoner in Edinburgh Tolbooth, formerly sentenced to transportation, subscribed to a bond undertaking to leave the kingdom within a month, on 29 August 1684. [RPCS.IX.320]

HAMILTON, JOHN, late of Rodgerstoun, a prisoner in Edinburgh Tolbooth, an accessory to the Battle of Bothwell Bridge, Lanarkshire, in 1679, a petition to the Privy Council in 1684; was released. [RPCS.IX.90/97]; a bond, dated 2 August 1684. [RPCS.IX.216]

HAMILTON, JOHN, was killed at the Battle of Aird's Moss on 22 July 1680. [Muirkirk Monument, Ayrshire]

HAMILTON, JOHN, of Hallcraig, was warded in Edinburgh Tolbooth on 13 November 1684. [ETR]

HAMILTON, JOHN, of Craigmuir, was warded in Edinburgh Tolbooth on 13 November 1684. [ETR]

HAMILTON, JOHN, born in Scotland, was educated at Edinburgh University, minister at Donaghadee, died at the Siege of Londonderry in 1689. [FI.39]

HAMILTON, JOHN, born at Sorbie, Wigtownshire, in 1651, was educated at Edinburgh University, minister at Ballee, Ireland, from 1673 until 1685, then at Comber from 1683 to 1689, died on 17 October 1702. [FI.65]

HAMILTON, MATTHEW, servant to a husbandman in Kintyre, Argyll, who had participated in Argyll's Rebellion in 1685, a prisoner in Edinburgh Tolbooth, was stigmatised and banished to the Plantations in July 1685, was transported via Leith to Jamaica on 11 August 1685. [ETR][RPCS.XI.329]

HAMILTON, PATRICK, from Livingstone, West Lothian, fought at the Battle of Bothwell Bridge in 1679, was transported via Leith aboard the Crown of London bound for Barbados on 27 November 1679, was shipwrecked and drowned off Orkney on 10 December 1679. [RBM]

HAMILTON, ROBERT, in Hill, a rebel, subscribed to a bond of the peace in October 1668. [RPCS.II.548]

HAMILTON, ROBERT, son of Claud Hamilton of Kennedy's Ernock, minister of Killieleagh, County Down, amongst those on the attempted emigration to New England in 1636, returned to Carrickfergus, minister of Ballantrae, Ayrshire, from 1642 until 1650, when he is thought to have crossed to Ireland. [F.II.331]

HAMILTON, ROBERT, of Preston, Mid Lothian, led the Covenanters at the Battle of Bothwell Bridge, Lanarkshire, on 22 June 1679.

HAMILTON, ROBERT, of Monkland, Lanarkshire, was found guilty of conversing with the assassins of Archbishop Sharp in July 1684, was sentenced to death but was reprieved. [ETR]

HAMILTON, RORY, was captured at the Siege of Worcester in 1651, then transported via London aboard the John and Sarah bound for New England in December 1651, landed in Boston in February 1652. [SD.1.5-6]

HAMILTON, WILLIAM, of Overton, was warded in Edinburgh Tolbooth on 13 November 1684. [ETR]

HANNA, WILLIAM, in Foulraw, a rebel in 1684, [RPCS.IX.356]; a Covenanter from the Borders, was banished to the American

Plantations on 18 August 1685, was taken from Leith Tolbooth, put in irons and imprisoned in Edinburgh Tolbooth, [ETR], then was transported from Leith aboard the Henry and Francis bound for East New Jersey in September 1685, landed there on 7 December 1685. [RPCS.XI.94/154]

HANNAY, SAMUEL, from Kirkmabreck, Kirkcudbrightshire, fought at the Battle of Bothwell Bridge in 1679, was transported via Leith aboard the Crown of London bound for Barbados on 27 November 1679, was shipwrecked and drowned off Orkney on 10 December 1679. [RBM]

HARDIE, JOHN, born around 1632, from Gordon, Berwickshire, a minister in Leiden and Rotterdam in the Netherlands from 1683 until 1687. [SEC]

HARDIE, WILLIAM, from Kelso, Roxburghshire, fought at the Battle of Bothwell Bridge in 1679, was transported via Leith aboard the Crown of London bound for Barbados on 27 November 1679, was shipwrecked and drowned off Orkney on 10 December 1679. [RBM]

HARKNESS, ADAM, son of Thomas Harkness in Lockerbie, Dumfries-shire, was alleged to be one of the rebels involved in the ambush at Enterkin, Dumfries-shire in 1684. [RPCS.IX.259/260]

HARKNESS, JAMES, in Lockerbie, Dumfries-shire, a Covenanter in 1679, was tried in 1684. [NRS.JC39.53]; was alleged to be one of the rebels involved in the ambush at Enterkin, Dumfries-shire in 1684. [RPCS.IX.259]; born 1651, died 6 December 1723. [Dalgarno gravestone]

HARKNESS, JOHN, a servant of Margaret Frisell in Mitchellslacks, Dumfries-shire, for conversing with William and Thomas Harkness rebels and fugitives, was declared a rebel and fugitive, [RPCS.IX.359]; and was banished to the American colonies on 24 October 1684. [RPCS.X.587]

HARKNESS, THOMAS, in Lockerbie, Dumfries-shire, a Covenanter in 1679, was tried in 1684. [NRS.JC39.53]; was hanged in the

Greenmarket, Edinburgh, in 1684. [Nithsdale Martyrs Cross, Dumfries]

HARKNESS, WILLIAM, a rebel in Closeburn, Dumfries-shire, in August 1684. [RPCS.IX.260/359]

HARPER, JOHN, from Fenwick, Ayrshire, was transported to the colonies, probably New York in 1684. [RPCS.VIII.526]

HARPER, ROBERT, a Covenanter, who was transported to Virginia in June 1669. [RPCS.III.22]

HARROWAY, JOHN, was transported via Leith aboard the St Michael of Scarborough bound for the West Indies on 12 December 1678. [RPCS.VI.76]

HART, ARCHIBALD, in Wicketshaw, a rebel, subscribed to a bond of the peace in October 1668. [RPCS.II.548]

HART, JOHN, for his part in the Pentland Rising of 1666, was beheaded in Glasgow on 19 December 1666. [Glasgow Cathedral]

HART, JOHN, fought at the Battle of Bothwell Bridge, Lanarkshire, on 22 June 1679. [Glasgow Cathedral plaque]

HART, JOHN, was born 1617 in Scotland, was educated at the University of St Andrews, minister at Taughboyne, Monreagh, Ireland, from 1656 until his death there on 8 January 1687, he was imprisoned as a non-conformist in Lifford, Ireland, in 1669. [Cal.SP.Ire.]

HART, MARGARET, a prisoner in Glasgow Tolbooth, took an oath and was released in October 1684. [RPCS.IX.710]

HARVIE, JOHN, from Dalserf, Lanarkshire, was transported via Leith aboard the Henry and Francis bound for East New Jersey on 5 September 1685. [RPCS.XI.329] [NWI.I.423]

HASTIE, WILLIAM, from Carluke, Lanarkshire, was transported via Leith bound for Jamaica in July 1685. [RPCS.XI.136]

HAY, ANDREW, of Craignathan, was warded in Edinburgh Tolbooth on 13 November 1684. [ETR]

HAY, GILBERT, was warded in Edinburgh Tolbooth on 11 February 1686. [ETR]

HAY, JOHN, born 1625, Earl of Tweeddale, died 1697, a Presbyterian who initially supported King Charles I, then fought against him at the Battle of Marston Moor in 1644, and later at Preston, he was imprisoned at the Restoration for defending the Covenanter minister James Guthrie. [Z.198]

HAY, JOHN, a minister in Renfrew until deposed in 1649, settled in Donegal, Ireland, returned to Scotland in 1663. [RPCS.I.342]

HAY, JOHN, of Park, was transferred from Edinburgh Tolbooth to Blackness Castle on 16 September 1684, a prisoner in Edinburgh Tolbooth, was released on 2 August 1685. [ETR]

HAY, JOHN, was transported to the colonies in August 1685. [RPCS.XI.130][NRS.CH2.83.8]

HAY, WILLIAM, a minister in Galloway, was accused of holding conventicles within the Presbytery in 1666. [GC.107]

HAY, WILLIAM, was transported via Leith aboard the St Michael of Scarborough bound for the West Indies on 12 December 1678. [RPCS.VI.76]

HAY, WILLIAM, a Captain of Lord Angus's Regiment, [the Cameronians], who fought at the Battle of Killiecrankie in 1689. [BK]

HAYNING, GRIZEL, sister of John Hayning, for aiding rebel Thomas Hunter in Floors, Thomas Hunter in Dinduff, Walter Smith, and other rebels in her house in Tynron, was declared to be a rebel and fugitive in October 1684. [RPCS.IX.368/369]

HAYNING, JEAN, for aiding rebel ......Harper the younger, in Dunscore in summer 1684, was declared to be a rebel and fugitive in October 1684. [RPCS.IX.370]

HAYNING, JOHN, in Laight and his spouse Janet Houatson, for aiding rebels Gilbert Gilchrist, Alexander Gibson, and Walter Smith, the last two were seen peeling bark in Craigney Wood and not reporting it were declared to be rebels and fugitives in October 1684. [RPCS.IX.368]

HAYNING, JOHN, in Glengaber, Holywood, for seeing rebel William Weir and not reporting it, was declared to be a rebel and fugitive in October 1684. [RPCS.IX.370]

HAYNING, JOHN, in Blackmyre, was accused in Kirkcudbright in October 1684, of conversing with rebel John Corsan in May 1684. [RPCS.IX.376]

HAYNING, JOHN, in Overlagga, was accused, in Kirkcudbright on 4 October 1684, of aiding several rebels in 1684. [RPCS.IX.377]

HAYNING, ROBERT, from Dungegan, Ireland, a rebel in 1666, imprisoned in Edinburgh Tolbooth or Canongait Tolbooth, having taken the Oath of Allegiance, was released on 11 July 1667. [RPCS.II.308]

HAYNING, WILLIAM, in Arnabrie, was accused in Kirkcudbright of conversing with a rebel and fugitive, William Russell, in 1684. [RPCS.IX.374]

HECTOR, ARCHIBALD, who was in Argyll's Rebellion, a prisoner in Edinburgh Tolbooth, was liberated on 12 January 1686. [ETR]

HEDDERICK, JAMES, was captured at the Siege of Worcester, was transported via London aboard the John and Sarah bound for New England in 1651, landed at Boston in February 1653. [SD.1.5-6]

HEDDERICK, WILLIAM, was captured at the Siege of Worcester, was transported via London aboard the John and Sarah bound for New England in 1651, landed at Boston in February 1653. [SD.1.5-6]

HENDERSON, Reverend Alexander, born in Fife, minister of Leuchars. In 1638 he was Moderator of the Glasgow Assembly which deposed bishops and removed the king as head of the Church of Scotland, he jointly drafted the National Covenant of 1638, he died in 1646. [Greyfriars Monument]

HENDERSON, ALEXANDER, an alleged assassin of Archbishop Sharp, fled to Ireland on 7 October 1680. [RPCS.VI.560]

HENDERSON, ANDREW, in Tamenen, for attending conventicles, was outlawed on 29 August 1672. [RPCS.III.583]

HENDERSON, ANDREW, an alleged assassin of Archbishop Sharp, fled to Ireland on 7 October 1680. [RPCS.VI.560]

HENDERSON, CATHERINE, then in Edinburgh Tolbooth, was transferred to Dunnottar Castle, Kincardineshire, on 29 July 1685. [ETR]

HENDERSON, GEORGE, and his son John Henderson, in Kinnaird, for attending conventicles, were outlawed on 29 August 1672. [RPCS.III.584]

HENDERSON, JAMES, Major of Lord Angus's Regiment, [the Cameronians], who fought and was killed at the Battle of Killiecrankie in 1689. [BK]

HENDERSON, JOHN, portioner of Nethertoun, for attending conventicles, was outlawed on 29 August 1672. [RPCS.III.583]

HENDERSON, JOHN, from Ruchoard, was warded in Edinburgh Tolbooth on 28 November 1684, transferred to Dunnottar Castle, Kincardineshire, on 29 July 1685. [ETR]; was banished to the Plantations on 18 August 1685, transported via Leith aboard th Henry and Francis bound for East New Jersey on 5 September 1685, landed there on 7 December 1685. [RPCS.XI.154/289] [NWI.I.423]

HENDERSON, PATRICK, in Blair of Forth, for attending conventicles, was outlawed on 29 August 1672. [RPCS.III.583]

HENDERSON, ROBERT, of East Martin, for attending conventicles, was outlawed on 29 August 1672. [RPCS.III.583]

HENDERSON, ROBERT, in Nethertoun, for attending conventicles, was outlawed on 29 August 1672. [RPCS.III.583]

HENDERSON, THOMAS, in Gateside, Dunscore, 'was committed to the castle' in 1684. [RPCS.IX.702]

HENDERSON, WILLIAM, a shoemaker in East Martin, for attending conventicles, was outlawed on 29 August 1672. [RPCS.III.583]

HENDERSON, WILLIAM, from Livingstone, West Lothian, fought at the Battle of Bothwell Bridge in 1679, was transported November 1679, was shipwrecked and drowned off Orkney on 10 December 1679. via Leith aboard the Crown of London bound for Barbados on 27 [RBM]

HENDRY, ALEXANDER, a prisoner in Edinburgh Tolbooth, willing to go to America [sic] was released to go there on 17 December 1685, was transported via Leith aboard the John and Nicholas bound for Barbados on 17 December 1685. [ETR]

HENDRIE, ROBERT, from Airth, Stirlingshire, fought at the Battle of Bothwell Bridge in 1679, was transported November 1679, was shipwrecked and drowned off Orkney on 10 December 1679. via Leith aboard the Crown of London bound for Barbados on 27 [RBM]

HENSHAW, WILLLAM, a merchant in Glasgow, was transported to the [West] Indies on 13 June 1678. [RPCS.V.474]

HERD, WILLIAM, from Ashkirk, Roxburghshire, fought at the Battle of Bothwell Bridge in 1679, was transported November 1679, was shipwrecked and drowned off Orkney on 10 December 1679. via Leith aboard the Crown of London bound for Barbados on 27 [RBM]

HERIOT, ALEXANDER, a prisoner in Edinburgh Tolbooth, a rebel, was banished to the Plantations in Carolina on 8 August 1684. [RPCS.IX.95/126/130/319]; was released on parole on 20 August 1684 until he could be shipped to Carolina, subject to a penalty of 1000 merks. [RPCS.IX.319]; then in Edinburgh Tolbooth, was transferred to Dunnottar Castle, Kincardineshire, on 29 July 1685. [ETR]

HERRON, ANDREW, in Larg, was accused of conversing with rebel William Kennedy in May 1684. [RPCS.IX.375]

HERRON, PATRICK, was captured at the Siege of Worcester in 1651, was transported via London aboard the John and Sarah bound for New England in December 1651, landed in Boston in February 1652. [SD.1.5-6]

HERON, WILLIAM, was killed at Lochenkit in 1685. [Nithsdale Martyrs Cross, Dumfries]

HERON, WILLIAM, from Glencairn parish, Dumfries-shire, was executed at Kirkpatrick, Irongray, Kirkcudbrightshire, on 2 March 1683. [Largshill Monument, Kirkcudbrightshire]

HERRIES, BESSIE, spouse of Adam Genochen, was accused of rioting in Kirkcudbright in the parish of Irongray, in 1663. [RPCS.I.373]

HERRIES, ROBERT, a surgeon from Dunbarton, was banished to the [West] Indies on 7 November 1678. [RPCS.VI.53]

HERRIES, WILLIAM, a Captain of Lord Angus's Regiment, [the Cameronians], who fought at the Battle of Killiecrankie in 1689. [BK]

HESLOP, AGNES, a servant of James Hunter in Auchenbenyee, for seeing rebels James Hunter the younger in Dinduff, and Gilbert Gilchrist, and failing to report it was declared to be a rebel and fugitive in October 1684. [RPCS.IX.365]

HESLOP, JOHN, from Cavers, Roxburghshire, a prisoner in Edinburgh Tolbooth, having subscribed to the Test Act was released on 21 July 1685. [ETR]

HESLOP, WILLIAM, a cottar in Townhead, for having seen James Douglas and other rebels and not reporting it, was declared to be a rebel and fugitive in October 1684. [RPCS.IX.363]

HEUCHAN, ALEXANDER, in Bardrokott, was accused, in October 1684 in Kirkcudbright, of being at the Battle of Bothwell Bridge in 1679. [RPCS.IX.375]

HIDELSTOUN, ROBERT, at Carse Mill, Dunscore, for aiding rebels, John Pagan, and Peter Stranger, also for seeing five rebels at Jean

MacKenzie's house at Carse Mill and nor reporting it, was declared a rebel and a fugitive in October 1684. [RPCS.IX.369]

HIDELSTOUN, THOMAS, in Gateside, Dunscore, for aiding rebel John Weir, , was declared to be a rebel and fugitive in October 1684. [RPCS.IX.370]

HIDELSTOUN, WILLIAM, at Carse Mill, for seeing five rebels at Jean MacKenzie's house at Carse Mill but nor reporting it, was declared a rebel and a fugitive in October 1684. [RPCS.IX.369]; later 'was committed to the castle'. [RPCS.IX.701]

HIGHBEN, ROBERT, was captured at the Siege of Worcester in 1651, then transported via London aboard the John and Sarah bound for Boston in December 1651. [SD.1.5-6]

HIGGINS, GEORGE, a currier from Linlithgow, West Lothian, was banished to the Plantations on 27 May 1684, then transported via Leith to Carolina in June 1684. [RPCS.VIII.524/526/629]

HODGE, JOHN, an armorer from Glasgow, was banished to the Plantations on 9 October 1684, transported via Leith aboard the Henry and Francis bound for East New Jersey on 5 September 1685, died on voyage. [RPCS.XI.155/289/292] [NWI.I.423]

HODGEON, ADAM, in Douglas, a rebel in Glasgow Tolbooth, was banished to the Plantations in June 1684, and transported via Glasgow aboard the Pelican bound for Carolina, bond by Walter Gibson, a merchant in Glasgow, dated 20 June 1684. [RPCS.IX.208]

HOGG, DANIEL, was captured at the Siege of Worcester in 1651, then transported via London aboard the John and Sarah bound for New England in December 1651, landed in Boston in February 1652. [SD.1.5-6]

HOGG, JOHN, [1], was captured at the Siege of Worcester in 1651, then transported via London aboard the John and Sarah bound for New England in December 1651, landed in Boston in February 1652. [SD.1.5-6]

HOGG, JOHN, [2], was captured at the Siege of Worcester in 1651, then transported via London aboard the John and Sarah bound for New England in December 1651, landed in Boston in February 1652. [SD.1.5-6]

HOGG, JOHN, [3], was captured at the Siege of Worcester in 1651, then transported via London aboard the John and Sarah bound for New England in December 1651, landed in Boston in February 1652. [SD.1.5-6]

HOGG, JOHN, was transported via Leith aboard the John and Nicholas bound for Barbados in December 1685. [RPCS.XI.255][ETR]

HOG, JOHN, born in the 1610s, from Restalrig, Mid Lothian, a minister in exile in Rotterdam, Holland, from 1663 until 1692. [SEC]; probably chaplain to Brymer's Regiment of Foot in the Army of the Covenant in 1648, at the Battle of Dunbar in September 1650. [RHCA]

HOGG, NEIL, was captured at the Siege of Worcester in 1651, then transported via London aboard the John and Sarah bound for New England in December 1651, landed in Boston in February 1652. [SD.1.5-6]

HOG, PATRICK, was warded in Edinburgh Tolbooth on 7 July 1685. [ETR]

HOG, Reverend THOMAS, born 1625 in Tain, minister of Kiltearn, Ross and Cromarty, was outed in 1661, then became a conventricler near Auldearn, to be arrested in 1668, imprisoned in Forres, Edinburgh, and the Bass Rock, was liberated on condition that he abandoned the kingdom on 28 March 1684, later exiled to the Netherlands, returned to Kiltearn at the Restoration, died on 4 January 1692. [RPCS.II.504][ETR] [Kilteard gravestone]

HOGE, JOHN, a prisoner in Canongait Tolbooth, who refused to take an Oath of Allegiance, was banished to the American Plantations on 17 December 1685. [ETR]

HOLME, JOHN, reader in Hutton, accused of conversing with rebel James Reston, to appear before the Lords of Judiciary on 1 November 1684. [RPCS.IX.513]

HOLM, Lady, a prisoner in Kirkcudbright Tolbooth, was banished to the Plantations on 13 October 1684. [RPCS.X.258]

HOLMES, ALEXANDER, son of James Holmes a tenant in Greenock, a prisoner in Canongait Tolbooth, having subscribed to a bond, was released on 23 August 1684. [RPCS.IX.314]

HOLMES, ANGUS, was warded in Edinburgh Tolbooth on 10 July 1685. [ETR]

HOLMES, JAMES, a tenant in Greenock, who attended a conventicle near Greenock, was to be captured and imprisoned in Edinburgh Tolbooth in August 1684. [RPCS.IX.131]

HOLMES, MARGARET, a prisoner in Edinburgh Tolbooth, to be transported to the Plantations on 11 August 1685, was stimatised, and transported via Leith to Jamaica in August 1685. [RPCS.XI.330][ETR]

HOME, DAVID, former minister at Coldingham, was accused of attending a conventicle in Edinburgh in February 1669. [RPCS.II.615]

HOME, GEORGE, was captured at the Siege of Worcester in 1651, then transported via London aboard the John and Sarah bound for New England in December 1651, landed in Boston in February 1652. [SD.1.5-6]

HOME, THOMAS, was captured at the Battle of Dunbar, transported via London aboard the Unity bound for Boston, New England, in November 1650. [CEB]

HOOD, ADAM, then in Edinburgh Tolbooth, was transferred to Dunnottar Castle, Kincardineshire, on 29 July 1685. [ETR]; was banished to the Plantations on 18 August 1685, then transported via Leith aboard the Henry and Francis bound for East New Jersey on 5 September 1685, landed there on 7 December 1685. [RPCS.XI.154/289/292][NWI.I.423]

HOOP, MARY, servant to Janet Wilson, a tenant in Crawfordtoun, for rebels, William Herries, William Corsan, James MacMichael, Robert Greir a chapman, and others, was declared a rebel and a fugitive in October 1684. [RPCS.IX.369]

HOPKIRK, JAMES, from Cavers, Roxburghshire, fought at the Battle of Bothwell Bridge in 1679, was transported November 1679, was shipwrecked and drowned off Orkney on 10 December 1679. via Leith aboard the Crown of London bound for Barbados on 27 [RBM]

HORNE, ANDREW, in Dewgley, and his son John Horne, for attending conventicles, were outlawed on 29 August 1672. [RPCS.III.583]

HORNE, HENRY, in Kinross, for attending conventicles, was outlawed on 29 August 1672. [RPCS.III.583]

HORNE, JOHN, in Tamenen, for attending conventicles, was outlawed on 29 August 1672. [RPCS.III.583]

HORN, THOMAS, from Maybole, Ayrshire, fought at the Battle of Bothwell Bridge in 1679, was transported November 1679, was shipwrecked and drowned off Orkney on 10 December 1679. via Leith aboard the Crown of London bound for Barbados on 27 [RBM]

HORNE, WILLIAM, imprisoned in Edinburgh Tolbooth, was transported via Leith aboard the John and Nicholas bound for the West Indies on 17 December 1685. [ETR]

HORNER, BARBARA, from Dinduff, was banished to the Plantations in October 1684. [RPCS.X.587]

HOUSTOUN, DAVID, was born 1633 in Renfrewshire, was educated in Glasgow University, minister at Glenarm and Ballymoney from 1661 until 1672, died 8 December 1696, buried at Connor, Ireland. [FI.67]

HOUSTON, JAMES, from Balmaghie, Kirkcudbrightshire, fought at the Battle of Bothwell Bridge in 1679, was transported via Leith aboard the Crown of London bound for Barbados on 27

November 1679, was shipwrecked and drowned off Orkney on 10 December 1679. [RBM]

HOW, DANIEL, was captured at the Siege of Worcester in 1651, then transported via London aboard the John and Sarah bound for New England in December 1651, landed in Boston in February 1652. [SD.1.5-6]

HOWATSON, JAMES, in Craigbuy, Penpont, and his wife, for aiding rebels Daniel MacMichael, John Clerk, and other rebels, were declared rebels and fugitives in October 1684. [RPCS.IX.363]; was banished to the Plantations on 24 October 1684, [RPCS.X.587]; refused to take the Test Oath and was imprisoned in October 1684. [RPCS.IX.691];

HOWATSON, JOHN, son of John Howatson in Nether Dalvein, having carrying the wounded William Grierson from Enterkin to Thirstoun, was declared a rebel and fugitive in 1684. [RPCS.IX.358]

HOWATSON, JOHN, in Nether Dalvein, and his wife ..... Menzies, having harboured rebels and fugitives, were also declared rebels and fugitives in 1684. [RPCS.IX.358]

HOWATSON, JOHN, and his wife .....Goldie, in Laight, for aiding rebels and fugitives, were declared to be rebels and fugitives, in September 1684. [RPCS.IX.373]

HOWIE, JOHN, a prisoner in Edinburgh Tolbooth, to be transported to the Plantations, was transported via Leith to Barbados on 22 December 1665. [ETR]

HOWIE, JOHN, a prisoner in Edinburgh Tolbooth, was transported via Leith to Jamaica in August 1685. [ETR]

HOWIE, SAMUEL, a prisoner in Edinburgh Tolbooth, to be transported to the Plantations on 11 August 1685. [ETR][RPCS.XI.329]

HOWNAME, WALTER, from Teviotdale, was transported via Leith bound for Jamaica in August 1685, landed in Port Royal. [RPCS.XI.330]

HUDSON, DANIEL, was captured at the Siege of Worcester in 1651, then transported via London aboard the John and Sarah bound for New England in December 1651, landed in Boston in February 1652. [SD.1.5-6]

HUDSON, JOHN, was captured at the Siege of Worcester in 1651, then transported via London aboard the John and Sarah bound for New England in December 1651, landed in Boston in February 1652. [SD.1.5-6]

HUME, ALESTER, was captured at the Siege of Worcester in 1651, then transported via London aboard the John and Sarah bound for New England in December 1651, landed in Boston in February 1652. [SD.1.5-6]

HUME, DAVID, [1], was captured at the Siege of Worcester in 1651, then transported via London aboard the John and Sarah bound for New England in December 1651, landed in Boston in February 1652. [SD.1.5-6]

HUME, DAVID, [2], was captured at the Siege of Worcester in 1651, then transported via London aboard the John and Sarah bound for New England in December 1651, landed in Boston in February 1652. [SD.1.5-6]

HUME, DAVID, born 1625, was educated at Edinburgh University, minister at Coldingham, Berwickshire, from 1658 until deprived in 1662, held conventicles in 1679, took refuge in Holland, a minister in exile in the Netherlands from 1681 until 1687, was declared a fugitive in 1684, returned to Scotland and died in Edinburgh on 15 December 1687, buried in Greyfriars. [F.II.37] [SEC]

HUME, JOHN, was captured at the Siege of Worcester in 1651, then transported via London aboard the John and Sarah bound for New England in December 1651, landed in Boston in February 1652. [SD.1.5-6]

HUME, THOMAS, was captured at the Siege of Worcester in 1651, then transported via London aboard the John and Sarah bound for New England in December 1651, landed in Boston in February 1652. [SD.1.5-6]

HUMPER, WALTER, from Dalmellington, Ayrshire, fought at the Battle of Bothwell Bridge in 1679, was transported via Leith aboard the Crown of London bound for Barbados on 27 November 1679 was shipwrecked and drowned off Orkney on 10 December 1679. [RBM]

HUNTER, ANN, died in Dumfries Tolbooth in 16... [Nithsdale Martyrs Cross, Dumfries]

HUNTER, ARCHIBALD, a rebel and fugitive in 1684. [RPCS.IX.360]

HUNTER, ELIZABETH, 168-. [Nithsdale Martyrs Cross, Dumfries]

HUNTER, GEORGE, in Holme, for aiding rebels John MacCall and Thomas Hunter, was declared to be a rebel and fugitive in October 1684. [RPCS.IX.365]

HUNTER, JAMES, servant to Robert Scott in Coshogle, having aided the wounded rebel William Grierson of Lochwhir after the Enterkin ambsh, was declared a rebel and fugitive in 1684. [RPCS.IX.358]

HUNTER, JAMES, in Holme, for aiding rebels Gilbert Gilchrist, James Douglas, and Thomas Hunter in Breckindide, was declared to be a rebel and fugitive in October 1684. [RPCS.IX.365]

HUNTER, JOHN, a rebel imprisoned in Dumfries Tolbooth, having subscribed to the bond of peace, was released on 23 February 1669. [RPCS.II.608]

HUNTER, JOHN, a cottar in Townhead, for having seen James Douglas and other rebels and not reporting it was declared to be a rebel and fugitive in October 1684. [RPCS.IX.363]

HUNTER, JOHN, in Fleuchlarg, Tynron, for aiding rebels William Coran from Jedburgh, Thomas Hunter in Woodend, and John Gibson in Englstoun, and for others, was declared to be a rebel and fugitive in October 1684. [RPCS.IX.368]

HUNTER, JOHN, a prisoner in Canongait Tolbooth, who refused to take an Oath of Allegiance, was banished to th American Plantations on 17 December 1685, then transported via Leith aboard the John and Nicholas bound for Barbados in December 1685. [ETR] [RPCS.XI.166]

HUNTER, JOHN, was killed at Corehead in 1685. [Tweedsmuir gravestone, Peebles-shire]

HUNTER, ROBERT, in Hattock, for aiding rebels – the two Thomas Hunters, Gilbert Gilchrist, Walter Smith, and James Douglas in March 1684, was declared to be a rebel and fugitive in October 1684. [RPCS.IX.365]

HUNTER, THOMAS, the elder, and his wife Barbara Horner in Dunduff, Penpont, for aiding rebels including their son Thomas Hunter, were declared to be rebels and fugitives, in September 1684. [RPCS.IX.360/373]; was imprisoned in October 1684 and transported to the Plantations in October 1684. [RPCS.IX.691;X.587]

HUNTER, THOMAS, and Katherine Hunter in Cormilligan, for aiding Archibald Hunter in Terraran, and Robert Ferguson, rebels and fugitives, were declared to be rebels and fugitives, in September 1684. [RPCS.IX.373]

HUNTER, WILLIAM, in Ladywell for aiding the two rebels Thomas Hunter in March 1684, was declared to be a rebel and fugitive in 1684. [RPCS.IX.365]; he was captured at Auchenday then taken to Kirkcudbright Tolbooth, where he was executed in 1684. [St Cuthbert's gravestone, Kirkcudbright] [Nithsdale Martyrs Cross, Dumfries]

HUTCHISON, ANDREW, was educated at Edinburgh University, minister at Stewarton, Ayrshire from 1647 until 1662 when he refused to conform to Episcopacy. [F.III.125]

HUTCHISON, GEORGE, a minister in Edinburgh, was deposed and ordered to leave the town before 1 October 1662. [RPCS.I.264]

HUTCHESON, GEORGE, from Straiton, Ayrshire, fought at the Battle of Bothwell Bridge in 1679, was transported via Leith aboard the Crown of London bound for Barbados on 27 November 1679, was shipwrecked and drowned off Orkney on 10 December 1679. [RBM]

HUTCHISON, ISABEL, was transferred from Leith Tolbooth to Edinburgh Tolbooth on 21 August 1685. [ETR]

HUTCHISON, JAMES, former minister in Killelan, was warded in Edinburgh Tolbooth on 15 October 1684, and was released on 7 May 1685. [ETR]

HUTCHISON, JOHN, in Newbottle, was sought by the Justice Court in August 1667 for his part in the late rebellion. [GC.123] [RPCS.II.345]

HUTCHISON, JOHN, of Hairlaw, Dumfries-shire, a farmer, was imprisoned in Edinburgh Tolbooth, then transported via Leith aboard the John and Francis bound for East New Jersey on 5 September 1685, died on voyage. [RPCS.XI.155/475/477/501/559] [NWI.I.423]

HUTCHESON, ROBERT, was transported via Leith to Jamaica in August 1685. [RPCS.XI.136]

HYND, SAMUEL, was warded in Edinburgh Tolbooth on 10 July 1685. [ETR]

HYSLOP, JOHN, was warded in Edinburgh Tolbooth on 28 May 1685. [ETR]

INGLIS, ARCHIBALD, minister at Moffat, Dumfries-shire, from 1660 until 1662 when he refused to submit to Episcopacy. [F.II.216]

INGLIS, HELEN, a widow in Cupar, Fife, for attending conventicles, was outlawed on 29 August 1672. [RPCS.III.583]

INGLIS, JAMES, was captured at the Siege of Worcester in 1651, then transported via London aboard the John and Sarah bound for New England in December 1651, landed in Boston in February 1652. [SD.1.5-6]

INGLIS, JOHN, in Borg, for collecting funds for the rebels, was accused, in Kirkcudbright in October 1684, of conversing with rebel Gilbert McGie. [RPCS.IX.374]

INGLIS, PATRICK, was captured at the Siege of Worcester in 1651, then transported via London aboard the John and Sarah bound for New England in December 1651, landed in Boston in February 1652. [SD.1.5-6]

INGLIS, RICHARD, was captured at the Siege of Worcester in 1651, then transported via London aboard the John and Sarah bound for New England in December 1651, landed in Boston in February 1652. [SD.1.5-6]

INGLIS, THOMAS, from Livingston, West Lothian, fought at the Battle of Bothwell Bridge in 1679, was transported via Leith aboard the Crown of London bound for Barbados on 27 November 1679 was shipwrecked and drowned off Orkney on 10 December 1679. [RBM]

INGLIS, WILLIAM, a mason in Glasgow, a rebel in Glasgow Tolbooth, was banished to the Plantations in June 1684, and transported via Glasgow aboard the Pelican bound for Carolina, bond by Walter Gibson, a merchant in Glasgow, dated 20 June 1684. [RPCS.IX.208]

INNES, ALEXANDER, was captured at the Battle of Dunbar in 1650, then transported via London aboard the Unity bound for New England in November 1650 [SD.1.5-6]

IRELAND, JOHN, in Auchincairn, Dumfries-shire, for conversing with rebel Robert Lauchlison, was declared a rebel and fugitive in October 1684. [RPCS.IX.372]; was warded in Edinburgh Tolbooth on 10 July 1685, to be transported via Leith bound for Jamaica on 11 August 1685. [ETR]

IRVING, FRANCIS, born around 1610, from Kirkmahoe, Dumfriesshire, a minister in exile in the Netherlands from 1679 until 1685. [SEC]

IRVING, JANET, in Nether Almerness, Buittle, Kirkcudbrightshire, fugitives and fanatics in 1684. [RPCS.IX.571]

IRVING, JEAN, spouse of John Kirko a wright in Tynwald, for aiding rebel ....Harper the younger, in Dunscore in summer 1684, was declared to be a rebel and fugitive in October 1684. [RPCS.IX.370]

IRVING, JOHN, the elder, a merchant in Dumfries, for conversing with fugitive, James Garmorie in Hienanatie, was declared a rebel and fugitive in October 1684. [RPCS.IX.372];'was committed to prison' in 1684. [RPCS.IX.703]

IVAR, JOHN, was transported via Leith to Jamaica in August 1685. [RPCS.XI.136]

IVAR, MALCOLM, for taking part in Argyll's Rebellion was banished to the Plantations on 30 July 1685. [RPCS.XI.126]

JACKSON, ANNABELL, then in Edinburgh Tolbooth, was transferred to Dunnottar Castle, Kincardineshire, on 29 July 1685. [ETR]; was banished to the Plantations on 18 August 1685, was transported via Leith aboard the Henry and Francis bound for East New Jersey on 5 September 1685. [RPCS.XI.154/291]

JACKSON, GEORGE, who had been banished to Flanders, was tried in 1684 for having attended conventicles. [NRS.JC39.93]

JACKSON, JAMES, was captured at the Siege of Worcester in 1651, then transported via London aboard the John and Sarah bound for New England in December 1651, landed in Boston in February 1652. [SD.1.5-6]

JACKSON, JOHN, a servant from Glasgow, then in Edinburgh Tolbooth, put in irons and imprisoned in Canongait Tolbooth on 29 July 1685, [ETR]; was banished to the Plantations on 30 July 1685, then transported via Leith bound for Jamaica in August 1685, landed at Port Royal in November 1685. [RPCS.XI.329]

JACKSON, PATRICK, was captured at the Siege of Worcester in 1651, then transported via London aboard the <u>John and Sarah</u> bound for New England in December 1651, landed in Boston in February 1652. [SD.1.5-6]

JACKSON, PATRICK, was warded in Edinburgh Tolbooth on 28 May 1685, having taken the Oath of Abjuration was released on 21 July 1685. [ETR]

JACKSON, THOMAS, was banished to the Plantations on 24 August 1685, then transported via Leith aboard the <u>Henry and Francis</u> bound for East New Jersey on 5 September 1685, he died on the voyage. [RPCS.XI.114/145/159] [NWI.I.423]

JACKSON, WALTER, was captured at the Siege of Worcester in 1651, then transported via London aboard the <u>John and Sarah</u> bound for New England in December 1651, landed in Boston in February 1652. [SD.1.5-6]

JACKSON, WILLIAM, was sought by the Justice Court in August 1667 for his part in the late rebellion. [GC.123]; was sentenced to transportation to the American Plantations in 1685. [NRS.JC39.77]; was taken from Edinburgh Tolbooth to be put aboard the <u>Henry and Francis</u> bound for East New Jersey ion 5 September 1685, landed there on 7 December 1685. [ETR] [RPCS.XI.125/127/159] [NWI.I.423]

JAMIESON, ALEXANDER, from Mauchline, Ayrshire, took part in Argyll's Rebellion in 1685, was warded in Edinburgh Tolbooth on 10 July 1685, then banished to the Plantations on 29 July 1685, stigmatised and transported via Leith to Jamaica on 11 August 1685. [ETR] [RPCS.XI.136]

JAMIESON, ARCHIBALD, imprisoned in Edinburgh Tolbooth, was transported via Leith to East New Jersey on 31 July 1685. [RPCS.XI.131]

JAMIESON, DAVID, was captured at the Siege of Worcester in 1651, then transported via London aboard the <u>John and Sarah</u>

bound for New England in December 1651, landed in Boston in February 1652. [SD.1.5-6]

JAMIESON, DAVID, a 'sweet singer', was banished to the Plantations on 5 May 1684, was transported via Leith to New York on 19 May 1684. [RPCS.VIII.516]

JAMIESON, DAVID, from Linlithgow, West Lothian, was banished to the Plantations on 27 May 1684, transported via Leith to Carolina on 29 May 1684. [RPCS.VIIII.526]

JAMIESON, GEORGE, in Openshaw, a prisoner in Edinburgh Tolbooth, having subscribed to the Test Act, was released on 6 February 1685. [ETR]

JAMIESON, NEIL, was captured at the Siege of Worcester in 1651, then transported via London aboard the John and Sarah bound for New England in December 1651, landed in Boston in February 1652. [SD.1.5-6]

JACKSON, PATRICK, was captured at the Siege of Worcester in 1651, then transported via London aboard the John and Sarah bound for New England in December 1651, landed in Boston in February 1652. [SD.1.5-6]

JAMESON, EDWARD, minister at Swinton and Simprin, Berwickshire, from 1647 until deprived in 1661, in 1676 he was outlawed for preaching at conventicles. [F.II.59]

JANSEN, NICOLAS, a Dutchman involved in Argyll's Rebellion, died a prisoner in Edinburgh Tolbooth, 30 September 1685. [ETR]

JARDINE, ANDREW, for his part in Argyll's Rebellion, was stigmatised then banished to the Plantations on 28 July 1685, transported on 4 August 1685. [RPCS.XI.329]

JARDINE, KATHERINE, in Fardine, Dunscore, for aiding rebels John Weir and Robert Lauchlison, and for seeing rebel John Greir the elder, but not reporting it, was declared to be a rebel and fugitive, in October 1684. [RPCS.IX.370]

JARDINE, WILLIAM, was captured at the Battle of Dunbar, then transported via London aboard the Unity bound for New England in November 1650. [SD.1.5-6]

JASON, JAN, a Dutchman, was warded in Edinburgh Tolbooth on 11 August 1685 for his part in Argyll's Rebellion, was liberated on 30 March 1686. [ETR]

JOHNSTONE, ALEXANDER, son of the late Archibald Johnstone of Warriston, having taken the Oath of Allegiance, was released from Edinburgh Tolbooth on 9 July 1685. [ETR]

JOHNSTONE, ARCHIBALD, of Warriston, jointly drafted the National Covenant of 1638, sent from England to be imprisoned in Scotland in May 1663, to be brought from Leith and imprisoned in Edinburgh Tolbooth in May 1663. [RPCS.I.369/370/371]

JOHNSTONE, DONALD, took part in Argyll's Rebellion in 1685, was banished to the Plantations on 30 July 1685, then transported via Leith to Jamaica in August 1685. [RPCS.XI.136]

JOHNSTONE, ELIZABETH, spouse of John Muirhead in the Mains of Crawfordton, for aiding rebels Alexander Muirhead sometime of Glen Crosh and John Smith a tailor, was declared a rebel and a fugitive in October 1684. [RPCS.IX.369]

JOHNSTONE, GABRIEL, a Presbyterian minister who fled from Scotland to Ireland in 1669. [Cal.SP.Ire.1669]

JOHNSTONE, GEORGE, minister in Edinburgh Tolbooth on 17 June 1685. [ETR]

JOHNSTON, GEORGE, from Midcalder, Midlothian, was taken from Edinburgh Tolbooth to be put aboard the Henry and Francis bound for East New Jersey ion 5 September 1685, landed there on 7 December 1685. [RPCS.XI.125/127/159] [NWI.I.423]

JOHNSTON, JAMES, for his part in the Pentland Rising of 1666, was hanged in Glasgow on 19 December 1666. [Glasgow Cathedral]

JOHNSTONE, JAMES, fought at Bothwell Bridge on 22 June 1679. [Glasgow Cathedral plaque]

JOHNSTONE, JAMES, in Hayhill, a rebel in 1684. [RPCS.IX.356]

JOHNSTONE, JOHN, a merchant burgess of Edinburgh, a rebel imprisoned in Edinburgh Tolbooth, was released on 25 September 1684. [RPCS.IX.180][ETR]

JOHNSTON, NEIL, was captured at the Siege of Worcester in 1651, then transported via London aboard the John and Sarah bound for New England in December 1651, landed in Boston in February 1652. [SD.1.5-6]

JOHNSTONE, ROBERT, of Craigielands, Dumfries-shire, was indicted for 'hearing and recepting rebellious preachers', in 1684. [RPCS.IX.555]

JOHNSTONE, WILLIAM, of Laverocklaw, was educated at the University of St Andrews, minister at Coldstream, Berwickshire, from 1659 until deprived in 1662. [F.II.41]

JOHNSTONE, WILLIAM, in Burnside, Kirkmaho, for seeing rebel Robert Cowan raking in Andrew Fraser's meadow in Glenmade in July 1684, was declared to be a rebel and fugitive in October 1684. [RPCS.IX.370]

JOHNSTONE, WILLIAM, a gardener on the Fyntulloch Estate, Wigtownshire, was executed in 1685. [Wigtown gravestone]

JONES, PATRICK, was captured at the Siege of Worcester in 1651, then transported via London aboard the John and Sarah bound for New England in December 1651, landed in Boston in February 1652. [SD.1.5-6]

KEIR, PATRICK, from Kincardine on Forth, fought at the Battle of Bothwell Bridge in 1679, was transported via Leith aboard the Crown of London bound for Barbados on 27 November 1679, was shipwrecked and drowned off Orkney on 10 December 1679. [RBM][ETR]

KEITH, ALEXANDER, minister of Strathbrock in West Lothian, husband of Margaret Hamilton, later in Ireland by 5 March 1657. [NRS.GD30.1339/1349]

KEITH, ALEXANDER, a fencing master, was accused of rioting in Edinburgh in January 1686. [NRS.JC39.91]

KEITH, GEORGE, of Aden, Aberdeenshire, Captain of the Earl Marischal's Regiment of the Army of the Solemn League and Covenant, fought at the Sieges of Newcastle, Hereford and Newark in 1644. [RHCA]

KEITH, WILLIAM, the Earl Marischal, with 1500 Covenanters, fought the Royalists under Viscount Aboyne at Megray Hill near Stonehaven, Kincardineshire on 15 June 1639.

KELL, NEIL, was transported via Leith to Jamaica on 7 August 1685. [RPCS.XI.130]

KELLO, JOHN, was banished to the Plantations on 6 August 1684, transported via Leith to Carolina in August 1684. [RPCS.IX.95]

KELLIE, CHRISTIAN, then in Edinburgh Tolbooth, was transferred to Dunnottar Castle, Kincardineshire, on 29 July 1685. [ETR]

KELLIE, KATHERINE, was banished to the Plantations on 18 August 1685, was transported via Leith aboard the Henry and Francis bound for East New Jersey on 5 September 1685, died on the voyage. [RPCS.XI.154/292] [NEWI.I.423]

KELLY, JOHN, a baker in Dunbar, East Lothian, a prisoner in Edinburgh or Canongait Tolbooth, later in Dunnottar Castle, a rebel, was banished to the Plantations on 5 February 1685, then transported via Leith aboard the Henry and Francis bound for East New Jersey on 5 September 1685, landed there on 7 December 1685. [RPCS.X.129/335] [NWI.1.423]

KELSO, WILLIAM, a surgeon apothecary in Ayr, fought at the Battle of Bothwell Bridge, Lanarkshire, on 22 June 1679, escaped via Ireland, aboard the Anne and Hester bound for Boston, New England, in April 1680. [SPC.1682.441] [UJA.2.1.274]

KELTON, THOMAS, was captured at the Battle of Dunbar, then transported via London aboard the Unity bound for New England in November 1650. [SD.1.5-6]

KELVIN, THOMAS, was imprisoned in Edinburgh Tolbooth on 14 April 1685. [ETR]

KEMPER, DANIEL, was captured at the Siege of Worcester in 1651, then transported via London aboard the John and Sarah bound for New England in December 1651, landed in Boston in February 1652. [SD.1.5-6]

KENNAN, ANDREW, in Kirkcudbright, was accused, in Kirkcudbright in October 1684, of conversing with rebels, John Coultart and William Campbell. [RPCS.IX.374]

KENNEDY, ANDREW, of Clowburn, was imprisoned in Edinburgh Tolbooth on 13 November 1684, was transferred to Canongait Tolbooth on 12 September 1685. [ETR]

KENNEDY, BESSIE, from Cockethill, was transported to the Plantations in October 1684. [RPCS.X.587]

KENNEDY, GILBERT, born 1627, second son of Colonel Gilbert Kennedy of Ardmillan in Ayrshire, was educated at Glasgow University, minister at Girvan from 1651 until deprived in 1662, was accused of keeping conventicles in 1679, moved to Ireland, minister at Dundonald and Holywood from 1673 until his death on 6 February 1688, buried in Dundonald. [F.III.41; VII.531] [FI.70]

KENNEDY, JOHN, from Closeburn, Dumfriesshire, fought at the Battle of Bothwell Bridge in 1679, was transported via Leith aboard the Crown of London bound for Barbados on 27 November 1679, was shipwrecked and drowned off Orkney on 10 December 1679. [RBM]

KENNEDY, JOHN, was stigmatised, banished to the Plantations on 28 July 1685, and transported via Leith to Jamaica in August 1685. [RPCS.XI.329]

KENNEDY, JOHN, of Glenure, a Covenanter in 1679, was tried in 1685. [NRS.JC39.70]

KENNEDY, THOMAS, of Grange, was found guilty of attending conventicles and was fined 314 pounds Scots and imprisoned in Edinburgh Tolbooth, in August 1684. [RPCS.IX.130]

KENNEDY, THOMAS, born 1625, eldest son of Colonel Gilbert Kennedy of Ardmillan in Ayrshire, was educated at Glasgow University, minister at Donaghmore, County Tyrone, from 1646, died on 9 February 1716. [FI.44]

KENNEDY, THOMAS, formerly a minister in Leswalt, Wigtownshire, in 1654, was deprived in 1662, minister in Carland, County Tyrone in 1662, in Newtonards by 1672 returned to Scotland in 1689, then back to Carland in 1693, died 9 February 1716, [F.VII.531]; deeds 1677 & 1687. [NRS.RD2.44.470; RD2.68]

KENNEDY, THOMAS, of Grange, a Covenanter in 1679, was tried in 1685. [NRS.JC39.70]

KENNIE, JOHN, was transported via Leith aboard the Henry and Francis bound for East New Jersey on 5 September 1685, landed there on 7 December 1685. [NWI.I.423]

KEOCHTAN, ALEXANDER, a burgess of Kirkcudbright, was imprisoned in Edinburgh Tolbooth, for his wife's part in the tumult in Kirkcudbright, was released after guaranteeing his wife's future attitude toward bishops, the Church and the State in 1663. [RPCS.I.377]

KER, ANDREW, in Auchingassell, for aiding rebel Gilbert Gilchrist in July 1684, was declared to be a rebel and fugitive in October 1684. [RPCS.IX.366]

KER, ANNA, relict of John Duncan, to be tortured unless she identified the rebels who attempted to kill the Archbishop of St Andrews and the Bishop of Orkney, in 1668, was banished to the Plantations on 29 July 1668. [RPCS.II.495]

KERR, ANNA, [probably the relict of John Duncan above], spouse of John Binning of Dalvennan, was warded in Edinburgh Tolbooth, on 3 December 1684. [ETR]

KER, CUTHBERT, and his wife Marian Grierson, in Craig, for aiding rebels John MacMillan and two others, were declared to be rebels and fugitives in October 1684. [RPCS.IX.365]

KERR, DANIEL, from Ottar's Land in Argyll, for joining Argyll's Rebellion, was banished to the Plantations pn 9 July 1685, and transported via Leith to New England on 9 July 1685. [RPCS.XI.94/313]

KER, DANIEL, of Kersland, a Captain of Lord Angus's Regiment, [the Cameronians], in 1689. [BK]

KER, GILBERT, a plotter and rebel in Ireland in 1663. [RPCS.I.371]

KER, JAMES, of Grange, born 1601, was educated at Edinburgh University, minister at Abbotrule, Roxburghshire, from 1624 until deprived in 1662, in 1680 he was imprisoned for holding conventicles, he died in 1694. [F.III.121]

KER, JOHN, in Dalyean, for aiding rebels at Dalyean in 1684, was declared a rebel and fugitive in October 1684. [RPCS.IX.364]

KER, ROBERT, of Kersland, was sought by the Justice Court in August 1667 for his part in the late rebellion. [GC.123]

KERR, WALTER, from Lanarkshire, was transported via Leith aboard the Henry and Francis bound for East New Jersey on 5 September 1685, landed on 7 December 1685. [RPCS.XI.173][NWI.I.423]

KERR, WILLIAM, a Covenanter who escaped from Wigtown Tolbooth and attempted to flee to Ireland via Port Patrick in 1684. [RPCE.IX.381]

KER, ......, of Kersland, a Captain of Lord Angus's Regiment, [The Cameronians], who fought at the Battle of Dunkeld in August 1689. [BK]

KEVAN, Mrs, mother of le late William Russell, was accused in Kirkcudbright of conversing with a rebel and fugitive, William Russell, in 1684. [RPCS.IX.374]

KEY, JOHN, was captured at the Battle of Dunbar in 1650, transported via London aboard the Unity bound for Boston, New England, in November 1650. [CEB]

KIDD, DAVID, a weaver from Logie, was transported via Leith aboard the St Michael of Scarborough bound for the West Indies on 12 December 1678. [RPCS.VI.76]

KID, JAMES, born around 1666, a minister in exile in the Netherlands around 1685. [SEC]

KIDD, JOHN, from Livingstone, West Lothian, was transported via Glasgow aboard the Pelican bound for Carolina in June 1684. [RPCS.IX.208]

KIDD, PETER, minister at Carluke, Lanarkshire, was warded in Edinburgh Tolbooth on 15 October 1684. [ETR]

KILGOUR, Major, fought at the Battle of Rullion Green in 1666. [Z.193]

KILLEN, JOHN, from Shotts, Lanarkshire, fought at the Battle of Bothwell Bridge in 1679, was transported via Leith aboard the Crown of London bound for Barbados on 27 November 1679, was shipwrecked and drowned off Orkney on 10 December 1679. [RBM]

KILPATRICK, HUGH, minister at Lurgan in 1686, returned to Scotland in 1690, minister at Old Cumnock, Ayrshire, then at Ballymoney, Ireland, in 1695, died in 1712. [F.VII.531]

KILPATRICK, JOHN, in Whitfall, Dumfries-shire, for seeing rebel William Milligan since he broke prison in Dumfries, and not reported it, was declared to be a rebel and fugitive in October 1684. [RPCS.IX.373]

KINCAID, JOHN, from Chalcarrock, was warded in Edinburgh Tolbooth on 28 November 1684, was transferred to Dunnottar

Castle, Kincardineshire, on 29 July 1685, was transported via Leith aboard the Henry and Francis bound for East New Jersey on 5 September 1685, landed there on 7 December 1685. [RPCS.XI.154] [ETR] [NWI.I.423]

KING, JOHN, father and son, in Little Govan, Glasgow, were tried in 1679. [NRS.JC39.102]

KINGHOLME, JOHN, in Cubbocks, was accused, in Kirkcudbright on 4 October 1684 of aiding Mr Renwick and other rebels in 1684. [RPCS.IX.377]

KIRK, ANDREW, servant to the miller at Glenesland, for conversing with rebels John Smith and Robert Cunningham at Janet MacEwan's barn at Merkland, was declared to be a rebel and fugitive in October 1684. [RPCS.IX.370]

KIRK, JAMES, of Sundaywell, was sought by the Justice Court in August 1667 for his part in the late rebellion. [GC.123]

KIRK, JAMES, from Largo, Fife, fought at the Battle of Bothwell Bridge in 1679, was transported via Leith aboard the Crown of London bound for Barbados on 27 November 1679, was shipwrecked and drowned off Orkney on 10 December 1679. [RBM] [ETR]

KIRK, JOHN, from Ceres, Fife, was transported via Leith aboard the Crown of London bound for Barbados on 27 November 1679, was shipwrecked and drowned off Orkney on 10 December 1679. [RBM][ETR]

KIRK, ROBERT, from Orwell, Kinross, fought at the Battle of Bothwell Bridge in 1679, was transported via Leith aboard the Crown of London bound for Barbados on 27 November 1679, was shipwrecked off Orkney on 10 December 1679, later transported to Jamaica. [RBM][CEC.212/5][ETR]

KIRKO, AGNES, in Peeltoun, for aiding rebels and fugitives, was declared to be a rebel and fugitive, in September 1684. [RPCS.IX.373]

KIRKO, ELIZABETH, and Katherine Kirko, for aiding rebels and fugitives, were declared to be rebels and fugitives, in September 1684. [RPCS.IX.373]

KIRKO, JOHN, a ruling elder of the kirk, was accused of holding conventicles and imprisoned in Edinburgh Castle in August 1660, [RPCS.VIII.465];

KIRKO, JAMES, in Faldoun, Keir, a fugitive in May 1683. [RPCS.VIII.609]; was killed in Dumfries in 1685. [Nithsdale, Martyrs Monument, Dumfries]

KIRKWALL, ELIZABETH, was stigmatised and banished to the Plantations on 28 July 1685, was transported via Leith to Jamaica on 7 August 1685. [RPCS.XI.329]

KIRKWOOD, JAMES, then in Edinburgh Tolbooth, was banished to the Plantations on 5 February 1685, transferred to Dunnottar Castle, Kincardineshire, on 29 July 1685, transported via Leith aboard th Henry and Francis bound for East New Jersey on 5 September 1685. [ETR] [RPCS.XI.154]

KIRKPATRICK, THOMAS, and his spouse Janet Milligan, for aiding rebels Thomas Hunter and .....MacTurk in May 1684, were declared to be rebels and fugitives in October 1684. [RPCS.IX.365]

KIRKWOOD, JAMES, in Over Blackcraig, to be imprisoned in Edinburgh Tolbooth in August 1684. [RPCS.IX.126]

KITTOCH, JOHN, imprisoned in Edinburgh Tolbooth for being in Argyll's Rebellion, was released on 25 March 1686. [ETR]

KNOX, JOHN, a minister who was warded in Edinburgh Tolbooth on 27 November 1684. [ETR]

LAHLESON, MARION, a widow, in Burnhead, Dunscore, accused of aiding rebels, was a prisoner bound for Dumfries was liberated by Roger Pagan a rebel in August 1684. [RPCS.IX.265/701]

LAING, JAMES, the younger, in Kilpatrick, was warded in Edinburgh Tolbooth on 27 April 1684, believed to have participated in the 'late rebellion', having taken the Test Oath, was liberated on 23 January 1685. [ETR]

LAING, WILLIAM, was captured at the Siege of Worcester in 1651, then transported via London aboard the <u>John and Sarah</u> bound for New England in December 1651, landed in Boston in February 1652. [SD.1.5-6]

LAING, WILLIAM, a farmer from Cavers, Roxburghshire, was transported via Leith aboard the <u>St Michael of Scarborough</u> bound for the West Indies on 12 December 1678. [RPCS.VI.76]

LAING, WILLIAM, from Hawick, Roxburghshire, was banished to the Plantations on 5 May 1684, was transported via Leith to New York on 19 May 1684. [RPCS.VII.216/709]

LAMB, ALEXANDER, from Straiton, Ayrshire, fought at the Battle of Bothwell Bridge in 1679, was transported via Leith aboard the <u>Crown of London</u> bound for Barbados on 27 November 1679, was shipwrecked and drowned off Orkney on 10 December 1679. [RBM]

LAMB, WILLIAM, a journeyman tailor in Edinburgh, was imprisoned in Edinburgh Tolbooth for aiding rebel John Dick, was liberated on 22 April 1684. [ETR]

LAMOND, ARCHIBALD, from Kilbride, Argyll, participated in Argyll's Rebellion, was transported via Leith to Jamaica in August 1685. [RPCS.XI.307] [LC.289]

LAMOND, SORLEY, from Drum, participated in Argyll's Rebellion, was transported via Leith to Jamaica in August 1685. [RPCS.XI.307] [LC.289]

LAMONT, ALEXANDER, of Monidrynan, was accused of participating in the Earl of Argyll's Rebellion in 1685 and was tried in 1687. [NRS.JC39.88]

LAMONT, ARCHIBALD, of Stronalbanach, subscribed in Inveraray, Argyll, to a bond undertaking that he will not assist the Earl of

Argyll or any other rebel under a penalty of 2,000 merks, dated 27 August 1684. [RPCS.IX.318]

LAMONT, WALTER, was educated at St Andrews University, a minister who went to Ireland to become minister at Temple Patrick in 1643. [F.V.117]

LANG, PATRICK, a maltman in Greenock, who attended a conventicle near Greenock, was to be captured and imprisoned in Edinburgh Tolbooth in August 1684. [RPCS.IX.131]

LANGLANDS, JOHN, was educated at Edinburgh University, minister at Wilton, Roxburghshire, from 1641 under 1669, he refused to convert to Episcopacy or subscribe to the Test Oath. [F.II.142]

LATIMER, JOHN, a rebel, in June 1683. [RPCS.IX.356]

LATIMER, MATHEW, a rebel, in June 1683. [RPCS.IX.356]

LATIMER, THOMAS, a rebel, in June 1683. [RPCS.IX.356]

LAUCHLAN, JOHN, in Lanark, a rebel imprisoned in Lanark Tolbooth, to be transferred to Edinburgh Tolbooth, on 30 July 1668. [RPCS.II.503]

LAUCHLAN, MARGARET, born 1622, was accused of conventicle keeping, imprisoned in Wigtown Tolbooth in 1685, and was drowned on 11 May 1685. [GC.413] [Wigtown gravestone]

LAUCHLISON, MARION, in Burnhead, Dunscore, Dumfries-shire, for aiding rebels, James Corsan from Jedburgh, John Pagan and ..... Lauchlison, was declared a rebel and a fugitive in October 1684, and was transported to the colonies in October 1684. [RPCS.IX.369; X.587]

LAUCHLISON, ROBERT, a rebel and fugitive in 1684. [RPCS.IX.361]

LAUDER, JOHN, minister at Dalziel, Lanarkshire, was warded in Edinburgh Tolbooth, on 15 October 1684. [ETR]

LAURIE, GILBERT, of Crossrig, born 1652, was educated at Edinburgh University, fled to Holland, a minister in exile there, was ordained by the Scots Presbytery in London in 1686, went to America, later was minister of Hutton and Fishwick, Berwickshire, from 1693 until his death on 3 September 1727. [F.II.52] [SEC]

LAURIE, JEAN, in Penpont, for aiding rebels William Milligan and John MacCall, was declared to be a rebel and fugitive in October 1684. [RPCA.IX.367]

LAURIE, JOHN, in Eshtrees, Penpont, for meeting rebels John MacCall in Glencairn and William Milligan, and not reporting it was declared to be a rebel and fugitive in October 1684. [RPCS.IX.366]

LAURIE, PETER, in Nether Balgrahill, Penpont, for aiding rebels John MacCall and William Milligan in Floors, also Thomas Hunter in Breckinside, was declared to be a rebel and fugitive in October 1684. [RPCS.IX.366]; was committed to the castle, took the Test, and was liberated. [RPCS.IX.699]

LAURIE, THOMAS, in Balgrahill, Penpont, for aiding rebels Gilbert Gilchrist, the Corsans from Jedburgh, ...Ferguson, and Thomas Hunter in Woodend, was declared to be a rebel and fugitive in October 1684. [RPCS.IX.365]

LAURIE, THOMAS, in Malloford, having seen the rebel William Milligan in his mother's house in Mallowford but failed to report it, also having seen the rebel John MacCall on Tibbers Moor, was declared to be a rebel and fugitive in October 1684. [RPCS.IX.366]

LAUTHER, JOHN, former minister at Dalziel, Lanarkshire, a prisoner in Edinburgh Tolbooth, was released on 27 March 1685. [ETR]

LAW, DAVID, was accused oт participating in the Earl of Argyll's Rebellion in 1685, was tried for treason in 1685. [NRS.JC39.72]; was warded in Edinburgh Tolbooth on 10 July 1685, was banished on 24 July 1685, but later hanged in the Grassmarket in Edinburgh on 12 August 1685. [ETR][RPCS.XI.114]

LAW, JAMES, from Kirkliston, West Lothian, was transported to the West Indies on 1 August 1678. [RPCS

LAW, JAMES, was warded in Edinburgh Tolbooth on 11 February 1686. [ETR]

LAWSON, JAMES, in Auchnotoroch, was tried in 1684 for his part in the 1679 Rebellion, in 1684, [NRS.JC39.51]; was executed in Glasgow on 24 October 1684. [Townhead Martyrs Memorial, Glasgow]

LAWSON, MARION, was banished to the Plantations on 28 July 1685, then transported via Leith to Jamaica in August 1685. [RPCS.XI.329]

LAWSON, WILLIAM, a prisoner in Edinburgh Tolbooth, willing to go to America was released to go to Barbados aboard the John and Nicholas on 17 December 1685. [ETR]

LEARMONT, Major JOSEPH, of Newholm, fought at Rullion Green on 28 November 1666, and was sought by the Justice Court in August 1667 for his part in the late rebellion. [GC.123] [RPCS.II.345][Z.194]

LECKIE, WILLIAM, a merchant from Glasgow, was banished to the West Indies on 13 June 1678. [RPCS.V.474]

LEITCH, DAVID, chaplain of Keith's Regiment of Foot, was captured at the Siege of Worcester in 1651. [RHCA.380]

LENNOX, ROBERT, from Irelandtoun, Girthon, Kirkcudbrightshire, was killed on Kirkconnell Moor, Kirkcudbrightshire, in 1685. [Kirkconnell Moor Monument] [Girthon gravestone, Kirkcudbrightshire] [GC.305]

LENNOX, THOMAS, imprisoned for rebellion, petitioned for liberty in 1668, which was granted. [RPCS.II.424/428]

LERMONT, PETER, from Shotts, Lanarkshire, fought at the Battle of Bothwell Bridge in 1679, was transported via Leith aboard the Crown of London bound for Barbados on 27 November 1679, was shipwrecked and drowned off Orkney on 10 December 1679. [RBM]

LESLIE, ALEXANDER, [1582-1661], previously of the Dutch and Swedish armies, a Field Marshal in Swedish Service, returned to Scotland to command the Scots Army in 1639 during the Bishop's War, fought at Newburn and at the Siege of Newcastle, in Ireland, and at Marston Moor in 1642. King Charles I surrendered to Alexander Leslie, 1st Earl of Leven, in May 1646. Leslie was at the Battle of Dunbar in 1650 where he was captured in August 1651. [RHCA]

LESLIE, DAVID, was appointed as commander of the Scots Army on 2 September 1650, fought and was defeated by Oliver Cromwell at Dunbar on 3 September 1650. [RHCA]

LESLIE, MARGARET, was warded in Edinburgh Tolbooth, on 3 December 1684, was transferred to Dunnottar Castle, Kincardineshire, on 29 July 1685, then banished to the Plantations on 18 August 1685, transported via Leith aboard the Henry and Francis bound for East New Jersey on 5 September 1685, landed there on 7 December 1685. [RPCS.XI.154/292] [ETR] [NWI.I.423]

LETHANGIE, HENRY, in Finlary, Orwell, for attending conventicles, was outlawed on 29 August 1672. [RPCS.III.583]

LETHANGIE, ROBERT, in Parkhead of Burley, for attending conventicles, was outlawed on 29 August 1672. [RPCS.III.583]

LEYDON, JAMES, from Cavers, Roxburghshire, was transported via Leith aboard the Crown of London bound for Barbados on 27 November 1679, was shipwrecked and drowned off Orkney on 10 December 1679. [RBM]

LICKPRIVICK, JAMES, from Cathcart, Glasgow, was transported via Leith aboard the St Michael of Scarborough bound for the West Indies on 12 December 1678. [RPCS.VI.76]

LICKPERICK, JOHN, from Kirkconnell, a prisoner in Canongait Tolbooth, undertook to live orderly and attend his parish church in a bond of 6 September 1684. [RPCS.IX.348]

LIDDELL, DAVID, chaplain to Maule's Foot and Horse Regiments, was captured after the Siege of Worcester in 1651. [RHCA.391]

LIDDLE, JAMES, was captured at the Battle of Dunbar in 1650, transported via London aboard the Unity bound for Boston, New England, in November 1650. [SCF.1226]

LILBOURNE, JAMES, from Shotts, Lanarkshire, fought at the Battle of Bothwell Bridge in 1679, was transported via Leith aboard the Crown of London bound for Barbados on 27 November 1679, was shipwrecked and drowned off Orkney on 10 December 1679. [RBM][ETR]

LINDSAY, JAMES, uncle to Maynes, Dumfries-shire, was indicted for 'hearing and recepting rebellious preachers', in 1684. [RPCS.IX.555]

LINDSAY, JAMES, a Captain of Lord Angus's Regiment, [the Cameronians], who fought at the Battle of Killiecrankie in 1689. [BK]

LINDSAY, JOHN, was accused of keeping conventicles and imprisoned in Edinburgh Tolbooth, released on parole in September 1668. [RPCS.II.536]

LINDSAY, WILLIAM, minister at Dreghorn, Ayrshire, was banished to Ireland in 1638. [RPCS.I.291]

LINN, ALEXANDER, a shepherd, was killed in 1685. [Craigmeddie Fell, Wigtownshire]

LINNING, THOMAS, born around 1657, a minister in exile in Leeuwarden, Friesland, in the Netherlands, from 1685 until 1689, he was ordained in Emden, Groningen, in 1688. [SEC]

LINING, ....., in Polmadie or Little Giveand, who attended a conventicle near Greenock, was to be captured and imprisoned in Edinburgh Tolbooth in August 1684. [RPCS.IX.131]

LINTRON, JANET, was banished to the Plantations on 18 August 1685, then transported via Leith aboard the Henry and Francis bound for East New Jersey on 5 September 1685. [RPCS.XI.164]

LISTON, PATRICK, in Calder, and his son William Liston, were sought by the Justice Court in August 1667 for their part in the late rebellion. [GC.123] [RPCS.II.345]

LITHGOW, JOHN, born 1620, a minister in Ireland, minister of Ewes, Dumfries-shire, from 1646 until 1664 when he refused to conform to Episcopacy, he then preached at conventicles for which he was imprisoned in Edinburgh Tolbooth then confined to the Bass Rock, thereafter he was abroad until 1690. [F.II.233]

LITHGOW, MARGARET, then in Edinburgh Tolbooth, was transferred to Dunnottar Castle, Kincardineshire, on 29 July 1685. [ETR]

LITTLE, MARGARET, in Walltrees, for aiding rebels Ringan Steel, Thomas Hunter, Gilbert Gilchrist, John MacCall, John Clerk, and William Milligan, was declared to be a rebel and fugitive R October 1684, was imprisoned. [RPCS.IX.363/697]

LIVINGSTONE, GRISSELL, spouse to Alexander Keathtoun, was accused of rioting in Kirkcudbright in the parish of Irongray, in 1663. [RPCS.I.373]

LIVINGSTONE, Reverend JOHN, born 21 June 1603 in Monyabroch, Kilsyth, Stirlingshire, was educated at the Universities of Glasgow and St Andrews, minister at Killinchy, County Down, in 1630, participated in the unsuccessful emigrant voyage of the Eagle Wing to New England, in September 1636, he subscribed to the National Covenant in 1638, minister at Stranraer from 1638 until 1648, a military chaplain of the Earl of Cassillis's Regiment during the Bishops War of 1639-1640, was at the Battle of Newburn, minister of Ancrum, Roxburghshire, from 1648 until ousted in 1662, was exiled to Rotterdam in the Netherlands in 1663, where he died on 9 August 1672. [Ancrum gravestone] [F.II.100; III.99; VII.531]

LIVINGSTONE, ROBERT, born 13 December 1654 in Ancrum, Roxburghshire youngest son of Reverend John Livingstone, moved to Rotterdam, Holland, in 1663, emigrated to New England in 1674, a fur trader in Albany, New York, by 1684, a public official in New York, died in 1728. [NRS.GD1.478.880] [NYD.3.401]

LIVINGSTONE, WILLIAM, was banished to the Plantations on 26 August 1685. [ETR]

LOCKHART, GAVIN, was warded in Edinburgh Tolbooth on 10 July 1685, was banished to the Plantations on 25 August 1685, then transported via Leith aboard the <u>Henry and Francis</u> bound for East New Jersey on 5 September 1685, landed there on 7 December 1685. [ETR][RPCS.XI.129/162/330] [NWI.I.423]

LOCKHART, Captain ROBERT, fought at Rullion Green in 1666. [Z.193]

LOCKHART, ROBERT, was killed on 1 May 1685. [Eaglesham gravestone, Renfrewshire]

LOCKHART, WILLIAM, of Wicketshaw, was sought by the Justice Court in August 1667 for his part in the late rebellion. [GC.123] [RPCS.II.345]

LOCKIE, JOHN, in the Lowis in Glaseneuksland, to be imprisoned in Edinburgh Tolbooth in August 1684. [RPCS.IX.126]

LOGAN, CHARLES, at the Castle of Cumlock, subscribed to a bond that he would live orderly and keep his parish church, subject to a penalty of 500 merks, dated in Edinburgh on 28 August 1684. [RPCS.IX.318]

LOGAN, GEORGE, of Logan, was warded in Edinburgh Tolbooth on 28 October 1684, and having subscribed to the Oath of Allegiance and to a bond committing him to a 10,000 merks penalty, was released on 21 July 1685. [ETR]

LOGAN, JAMES, of Bogue, in the parish of Dalry, a suspected Covenanter in 1665. [GC.111]

LOGIE, JOHN, in Bush, was accused, in Kirkcudbright in 1684, of conversing with …..McMillan a rebel. [RPCS.IX.376]

LOGUAIRD, MAXIMUS, a Dutchman, was warded in Edinburgh Tolbooth on 11 August 1685 for his part in Argyll's Rebellion, was liberated on 30 March 1686. [ETR]

LOOKEP, PATRICK, a wright, for employing rebels Walter Smith and Alexander Smith, to peel bark in Craignie Wood, was declared to be a rebel and fugitive in October 1684. [RPCS.IX.367]

LORIMER, JOHN, in Cleughhead, for aiding rebels John MacCall and William Milligan, was declared to be a rebel and fugitive in October 1684. [RPCS.IX.367]

LORIMER, ROBERT, in Tibers, for aiding James Douglas sometime in Auchinskeoch in March 1684, was declared to be a rebel and fugitive in October 1684. [RPCS.IX.367]

LOVE, JOHN, father and son, in Little Govan, Glasgow, were tried in 1679. [NRS.JC39.102]

LOURIE, BESSIE, a widow, was accused of rioting in Kirkcudbright in the parish of Irongray, in 1663. [RPCS.I.373]

LOURIE, GAVIN, in Redmyre, a fugitive, was warded in Edinburgh Tolbooth on 2 July 1684, was liberated on 14 August 1684. [ETR]

LOWE, ALISTAIR, was captured at the Siege of Worcester in 1651, then transported via London aboard the John and Sarah bound for New England in December 1651, landed at Boston in February 1652. [SD.1.5-6]

LOWRIE, JAMES, for attending conventicles, was outlawed on 29 August 1672. [RPCS.III.583]

LUNDIE, JOHN, of Baldasterd, was accused of attending conventicles in Fife in 1668. [RPCS.II.491]

MCADAM, ARCHIBALD, took part in Argyll's Rebellion and was transported via Leith to New England in July 1685. [RPCS.IX.94]

MACADAM, GILBERT, of Waterhead in the parish of Casphairn, a suspected Covenanter in 1665. [GC.111]

MCADAM, GILBERT, from Dalmellington, a rebel in Glasgow Tolbooth, was banished to the Plantations in June 1684, and transported via Glasgow aboard the Pelican bound for Carolina, bond by Walter Gibson, a merchant in Glasgow, dated 20 June 1684. [RPCS.IX.208, X.244]

MCADAM, QUENTIN, from Dalmellington, Ayrshire, fought at the Battle of Bothwell Bridge in 1679, was transported via Leith aboard the Crown of London bound for Barbados on 27 November 1679, was shipwrecked off Orkney on 10 December 1679, later transported to Jamaica. [RBM][SW.199]

MCADAM, QUENTIN, in Craigingillan, was accused, in Kirkcudbright in 1684, of aiding William Gilchrist a vagrant preacher, and for conversing with Gilbert McAdam. [RPCS.IX.376]

MCADAM, WILLIAM, in Arrow, to be tried accused of rebellion, on 3 June 1684. [RPCS.IX.205]

MCADAM, WILLIAM, in Minnivey, to be tried accused of rebellion, on 3 June 1684. [RPCS.IX.205]

MACALASTAIR, DANIEL, was captured at the Siege of Worcester in 1651, then transported via London aboard the John and Sarah bound for New England in December 1651, landed at Boston in February 1652. [SD.1.5-6]

MACALASTAIR, JOHN, was captured at the Siege of Worcester in 1651, then transported via London aboard the John and Sarah bound for New England in December 1651, landed at Boston in February 1652. [SD.1.5-6]

MCALISTER, JOHN, of Kinlochchysport, [sic], subscribed to a bond that he would not aid the Earl of Argyll, subject to a penalty of 2000 merks, at Inveraray on 27 August 1684. [RPCS.IX.320]

MACANDREW, WILLIAM, was captured at the Siege of Worcester in 1651, then transported via London aboard the John and Sarah bound for New England in December 1651, landed at Boston in February 1652. [SD.1.5-6]

MCARTER, ANDREW, was warded in Edinburgh Tolbooth on 28 November 1684, and on 28 May 1685. [ETR]

MCARTHUR, GILBERT, a drover from Islay, Argyll, imprisoned in Paul's Work, Edinburgh, was banished to the Plantations on 24 July 1685, then transported via Leith bound for Jamaica in August 1685. [RPCS.XI.329]

MACARTNEY, GEORGE, of Blacket, a leading Covenanter who was repeatedly fined and imprisoned in the 1660s-1690s. [BMF.95]

MACAULAY, ALEXANDER, Captain of Argyll's Regiment at Ballycastle, Ulster, in 1642. [SCIC]

MACAULAY, ANDREW, was killed at Caldons, Loch Trool, on 23 January 1685. [Newton Stewart gravestone, Kirkcudbrightshire]

MCAULAY, MALCOLM, took part in Argyll's Rebellion, was banished to the Plantations on 31 July 1685, and transported via Leith bound for Jamaica in August 1685. [RPCS.XI.136]

MCBRAIR, DAVID, of Newark, Kirkcudbrightshire, settled in Ireland by 1665. [RPCS.II.58]

MCBRAIR, THOMAS, was tried for participating in the tumult in the parish of Irongray, Kirkcudbrightshire, in 1663. [RPCS.I.376]

MCBRATNEY, JOHN, from Galloway, was transported via Leith aboard the Crown of London bound for Barbados on 27 November 1679, was shipwrecked off Orkney on 10 December 1679, later transported to Jamaica. [RBM] [CEC.212/5]

MCBRIDE, JOHN, took part in Argyll's Rebellion in 1685, and was transported via Leith to New England on 6 July 1685. [RPCS.XI.114/119]

MCBRYD, JOHN, was liberated from Edinburgh Tolbooth on 29 July 1685. [ETR]

MCBURNIE, GEORGE, was accused, in Kirkcudbright in October 1684, of aiding rebel Alexander McBurnie . [RPCS.IX.377]

MACBURNIE, ROBERT, in Tibers, for aiding rebels James MacMillan and Walter Mitchell, was declared to be a rebel and fugitive in October 1684. [RPCS.IX.367]

MCCAIGE, JAMES, of Milnton, and his wife Janet Gibson, fugitives in May 1683. [RPCS.VIII.609]

MCCAIG, JANET, spouse of Thomas Watson, was accused of aiding rebels including Robert Cowan, Archibald Hunter, John Frisell, son of Thomas Frisell in Auchincairn, was declared a rebel and fugitive, in October 1684. [RPCS.IX.360]

MCCAIRTNEY, ANDREW, then in Edinburgh Tolbooth, was transferred to Dunnottar Castle, Kincardineshire, on 29 July 1685. [ETR]

MCCAIRTNEY, ANDREW, a prisoner in Edinburgh Tolbooth, having taken the Oath of Abjuration was released on 21 July 1685. [ETR]

MCCAIRTNEY, GEORGE, in Balmagie, was accused in Kirkcudbright of conversing with Robert McCairtney, a fugitive, in 1684

MCCALINDEN, ALASTER, was captured at the Siege of Worcester in 1651, then transported via London aboard the John and Sarah bound for New England in December 1651, landed at Boston in February 1652. [SD.1.5-6]

MCCALL, JAMES, was captured at the Battle of Dunbar in 1650, and transported via London aboard the Unity bound for New England in December 1650.[SH.15]

MCCALL, JOHN, died at the Battle of Bothwell Bridge, Lanarkshire, on 22 June 1679. [Nithsdale, Martyrs Monument, Dumfries]

MCCALL, JOHN, in Glen Manno, for aiding John Clerk, Daniel Carmichael, and two other rebels in March 1684, was declared to be a rebel and fugitive in 1684, was imprisoned in October 1684. [RPCS.IX.360/363/691]

MCCALL, JOHN, in Laight, Tynron, for aiding rebels Walter Smith, Alexander Gibson, Thomas Hunter in Woodend, John MacCall in Poundland, and William Milligan in Floore, was declared to be a rebel and fugitive in October 1684. [RPCS.IX.368]

MCCALL, MARTIN, was transported to the colonies in July 1685. [RPCS.XI.129]

MCCALL, THOMAS, a cottar in Airkland, for seeing rebels Gilbert Gilchrist and John MacColl but not reporting it, was declared to be a rebel and fugitive in October 1684. [RPCS.IX.363]

MCCALL, THOMAS, in Glen Whargan, for aiding Gilbert Gilchrist and three other rebels in April 1684, was declared a rebel and fugitive in October 1684. [RPCS.IX.363/374]

MCCALL, WILLIAM, took part in Argyll's Rebellion in 1685, was stigmatised and banished to the Plantations on 31 July 1685, and transported via Leith to Jamaica in August 1685. [RPCS.XI.136]

MCCALLUM, ARCHIBALD, took part in Argyll's Rebellion in 1685, was stigmatised and banished to the Plantations on 31 July 1685, and transported via Leith to Jamaica in August 1685. [RPCS.XI.136]

MCCALLUM, DUNCAN, a tenant farmer at Otter in Argyll, took part in Argyll's Rebellion, was banished to the Plantations on 30 July 1685, and transported via Leith to New England in July 1685. [RPCS.IX.94/136]

MCCALLUM, JOHN, took part in Argyll's Rebellion in 1685, then was banished to the Plantations on 30 July 1685, and transported via Leith aboard the Henry and Francis in August 1685. [RPCS.XI.126]

MACCALLUM, MALCOLM, was captured at the Battle of Dunbar in 1650, the transported via London aboard the Unity bound for New England in December 1650. [SCF.1226]

MCCALLUM, NEIL, took part in Argyll's Rebellion in 1685, was banished to the Plantations on 31 July 1685, and transported via Leith to Jamaica in August 1685. [RPCS.XI.330]

MCCALMAN, WILLIAM, from Culbratton, was warded in Edinburgh Tolbooth on 28 November 1684, was transferred to Dunnottar Castle, Kincardineshire, on 29 July 1685, was transported via Leith aboard the Henry and Francis bound for East New Jersey on 5 September 1685. [ETR] [RPCS.X.612]

MCCANN, DANIEL, was captured at the Siege of Worcester in 1651, then transported via London aboard the John and Sarah bound for New England in December 1651, landed at Boston in February 1652. [SD.1.5-6]

MACCARTNEY, JOHN, from Kirkcudbright, fought at the Battle of Bothwell Bridge in 1679, was transported via Leith aboard the Crown of London bound for Barbados on 27 November 1679, was shipwrecked off Orkney on 10 December 1679, later was transported to Jamaica. [RBM][SW.202]

MCCARTNEY, ROBERT, in Orr, a rebel in 1666, imprisoned in Edinburgh Tolbooth or Canongait Tolbooth, having taken the Oath of Allegiance, was released on 11 July 1667. [RPCS.II.308]

MCCAULAY, JAMES, was captured at the Siege of Worcester in 1651, then transported via London aboard the John and Sarah bound for New England in December 1651, landed at Boston in February 1652. [SD.1.5-6]

MCCAULAY, MALCOLM, was transported via Leith to Jamaica in August 1685. [RPCS

MCCAULL, ROBERT, in Glenhead, was accused, in Kirkcudbright in 1684, of conversing with Gilbert McAdam in Craigingillan, William McMillan in Marsalloch, and for hearing Reverend William Gilchrist. [RPCS.IX.376]

MCCAULL, THOMAS, in Merkland of Burnside, was accused, in Kirkcudbright in 1684, of aiding rebels and fugitives. [RPCS.IX.376]

MCCAVERS, CHRISTIAN, was accused of rioting in Kirkcudbright in the parish of Irongray, in 1663. [RPCS.I.373/408]; a rioter, was imprisoned in Kirkcudbright Tolbooth, then to stand at the market cross there on two days in September 1683. [GC.105]

MCCHARLATIE, JOHN, took part in Argyll's Rebellion, was banished to the Plantations on 31 July 1685, then transported via Leith to Jamaica in August 1685. [RPCS.XI.136

MCCHISHOLME, JOHN, from Spittal, a prisoner in Canongait Tolbooth, was banished to the Plantations in Carolina on 19 June 1684, then transported via Leith to Carolina on 19 October 1684. [RPCS.IX.15]

MCCLELLAND, ANDREW, was banished to the Plantations on 18 August 1685, then transported via Leith aboard the <u>Henry and Francis</u> bound for East New Jersey on 5 September 1685. [RPCS.XI.155]

MCCLELLAND, ROBERT, was banished to the Plantations on 18 August 1685, then transported via Leith aboard the <u>Henry and Francis</u> bound for East New Jersey on 5 September 1685. [RPCS.XI.154]

MCCLINTOCK, JAMES, a merchant in Glasgow, was banished to the Plantations in June 1684, then transported via Glasgow aboard the <u>Pelican</u> bound for Carolina in June 1684. [RPCS.IX.208]

MCCORMACK, ANDREW, a minister from Ireland who was killed at the Battle of Rullion Green on 26 November 1666. [Z.194]

MCILVRA, MARTIN, minister on Iona from 1643 until he was deposed in 1648 'for complying with the rebels'. [F.IV.111]

MACINTOSH, DANIEL,

MCKIE, MARION, in Over Senwick, was accused, in Kirkcudbright on 4 October 1684, of aiding rebel John Richardson. [RPCS.IX.375]

MCKINNA, DAVID, in Blackneuk, was accused, in Kirkcudbright in 1684, of aiding rebels and fugitives. [RPCS.IX.376]

MACLAMEROCH, WILLIAM, at Ard Mill, and his spouse Isobel Greir, for aiding rebels John Mathieson and two others, was declared to be a rebel and fugitive in October 1684. [RPCS.IX.367]

MCCLANROES, JOHN, was killed at the Battle of Bothwell Bridge on 22 June 1679. [Nithsdale, Martyrs Monument, Dumfries]

MCCLALLAND, JOHN, born 1609 in Kirkcudbright, was educated at Glasgow University, a schoolmaster in County Down, attempted to emigrate to New England on the Eagle Wing in 1636, returned to Scotland and died in 1650. [PHS]

MCCLARTIE, NEILL, from Argyll to Ireland before 1654. [RSA.2.71]

MACCLEIKERAYE, JOHN, a prisoner in Edinburgh Tolbooth, was transported via Leith to the colonies on 27 November 1679. [ETR]

MCCLELLAND, DAVID, in Kirkcudbright, was accused, in Kirkcudbright in October 1684, of conversing with rebel Alexander McKean. [RPCS.IX.374]

MCCLELLAN, ELIZABETH, spouse to Alexander McLean, was accused of rioting in Kirkcudbright in the parish of Irongray, in 1663. [RPCS.I.373]

MCCLELLAN, JANET, in Logan, Buittle, Kirkcudbrightshire, a fugitive and fanatic in 1684. [RPCS.IX.571]

MCCLELLAN, JOHN, of Barscobe, leader of the Galloway horse, fought at the Battle of Rullion Green on 28 November 1666, was sought by the Justice Court in August 1667 for his part in the late rebellion. [GC.123] [Z.199] [RPCS.II.345][Z192]

MCCLELLAN, ROBERT, of Balmageichan, was sought by the Justice Court in August 1667 for his part in the late rebellion. [GC.123][RPCS.II.345]; was warded in Edinburgh Tolbooth on 28 November 1684. [ETR]

MCCLINTOCK, JAMES, a merchant in Glasgow, a rebel in Glasgow Tolbooth, was banished to the Plantations in June 1684, and transported via Glasgow aboard the Pelican bound for Carolina, bond by Walter Gibson, a merchant in Glasgow, dated 20 June 1684. [RPCS.IX.208]

MCCLIVE, JOHN, was killed at Caldons, Loch Trool, on 23 January 1685. [Newton Stewart gravestone, Kirkcudbrightshire]

MCCLUIR, GILBERT, in Dalmellington, to be tried accused of rebellion, 3 June 1684. [RPCS.IX.205]

MCCLURE, ELISABETH, from Barley, Kirkcudbrightshire, was banished to the Plantations on 23 October 1684. [RPCS.X.257]

MCCLURE, MARY, from Barley, Kirkcudbrightshire, was banished to the Plantations on 23 October 1684. [RPCS.X.257]

MACCOLM, DAVID, was captured at the Siege of Worcester in 1651, and transported via London aboard the John and Sarah bound for Boston in December 1651, landed there in February 1652. [SD.1.5-6]

MACCOLM, JOHN, was captured at the Siege of Worcester in 1651, and transported via London aboard the John and Sarah bound for Boston in December 1651, landed there in February 1652. [SD.1.5-6].

MACCONE, NEIL, was captured at the Siege of Worcester in 1651, and transported via London aboard the John and Sarah bound for Boston on 13 May 1652.

MCCONN, FINLAY, was captured at the Siege of Worcester in 1651, and transported via London aboard the John and Sarah bound for Boston in December 1651, landed there in February 1652. [SD.1.5-6]

MCCONNELL, ALEXANDER, was captured at the Siege of Worcester in 1651, and transported via London aboard the John and Sarah bound for Boston in December 1651. [SD.1.5-6]

MCCONNELL, CANA, was captured at the Siege of Worcester in 1651, and transported via London aboard the John and Sarah bound for Boston in 1651. [SD.1.5-6]

MCCONNELL, DANIEL, was captured at the Siege of Worcester in 1651, and transported via London aboard the John and Sarah bound for Boston in 1651. [SD.1.5-6]

MCCONNELL, JAMES, from Kirkmichael, Ayrshire, fought at the Battle of Bothwell Bridge in 1679, was transported via Leith aboard the Crown of London bound for Barbados on 27 November 1679, was shipwrecked and drowned off Orkney on 10 December 1679. [RBM]

MCCONNELL, WILLIAM, was captured at the Siege of Worcester in 1651, and transported via London aboard the John and Sarah bound for Boston in 1651. [SD.1.5-6]

MCCONOCHIE, DUGAL, a servant of Craiginterve, banished to the Plantations for his part in Argyll's Rebellion on 30 July 1685. [RPCS.XI.126]

MCCONOCHIE, JOHN, banished to the Plantations for his part in Argyll's Rebellion on 30 July 1685, then transported via Leith to Jamaica in August 1685. [RPCS.XI.126]

MCCONOCHIE, NEIL, banished to the Plantations for his part in Argyll's Rebellion on 30 July 1685, then transported via Leith bound for Jamaica in August 1685. [RPCS.XI.126]

MCCORKADALE, ARCHIBALD, was transported via Leith to Jamaica in 1685. [RPCS.XI.136]

MCCORMICK, ANDREW, born 1620s, minister at Magherally, near Banbridge, Ireland, by 1655, was ejected in 1661, crossed over to Scotland, joined the Pentland Rising and fought at Rullion Green where he was killed on 28 November 1666. [Magherally monument] [FI.46]

MCCORNOCK, JOHN, from Colmonell, Ayrshire fought at the Battle of Bothwell Bridge in 1679, was transported via Leith aboard the Crown of London bound for Barbados on 27 November 1679, was shipwrecked and drowned off Orkney on 10 December 1679. [RBM]

MCCOWAN, NEIL, was captured at the Siege of Worcester in 1651, and transported via London aboard the John and Sarah bound for Boston in 1651. [SD.1.5-6]

MCCOY, HUGH, was captured at the Siege of Worcester in 1651, and transported via London aboard the John and Sarah bound for Boston in 1651. [SD.1.5-6]

MCCREATH, JAMES, was captured at the Siege of Worcester in 1651, and transported via London aboard the John and Sarah bound for Boston in 1651. [SD.1.5-6]

MCCREATH, PATRICK was captured at the Siege of Worcester in 1651, and transported via London aboard the John and Sarah bound for Boston in 1651. [SD.1.5-6]

MCCRORY, ALISTER, was captured at the Siege of Worcester in 1651, and transported via London aboard the John and Sarah bound for Boston in 1651. [SD.1.5-6]

MACCUBBIN, ALEXANDER, was hanged on 3 March 1685. [Hallhill gravestone, Kirkpatrick-Durham, Kirkcudbrightshire]

MCCUBBIN, DAVID, from Dalry, Ayrshire, fought at the Battle of Bothwell Bridge in 1679, was transported via Leith aboard the Crown of London bound for Barbados on 27 November 1679, was shipwrecked and drowned off Orkney on 10 December 1679. [RBM]

MACCUBBIN, JAMES, in Marqhirn, Kirkcudbrightshire, for aiding his brother, a rebel, Alexander MacCubbin and his wife, was declared to be a rebel and fugitive in October 1684, was banished to the Plantations on 24 October 1684. [RPCS.IX.367/587]

MACCUBBIN, JOHN, in Penpont, having seen the rebel William Milligan in the house of Jean Douglas in Eshtrees in June 1684, and failed to report it, was declared to be a rebel and fugitive in October 1684. [RPCS.IX.366]

MCCUEAN, WALTER, was banished to the Plantations on 18 August 1685. [RPCS.XI.154]

MCCUIN, WILLIAM, in Crockcatford, was accused, in Kirkcudbright on 4 October 1684, of aiding rebel Gilbert Welch. [RPCS.IX.378]

MCCULLIE, JOHN, was banished to the Plantations on 24 July 1685. [RPCS.XI.114]

MCCULLIE, WILLIAM, in Whytrewe, born 1654, single, admitted that he and his brother had attended field conventicles, in 1684. [RPCS.IX.522]

MCCULLOCH, WILLIAM, from Dalry, Ayrshire, fought at the Battle of Bothwell Bridge in 1679, was transported via Leith aboard the Crown of London bound for Barbados on 27 November 1679, was shipwrecked and drowned off Orkney on 10 December 1679. [RBM]

MCCUTCHONE, JAMES, in Dalmellington, to be tried accused of rebellion, 3 June 1684. [RPCS.IX.205]

MCDICHMAYE, WALTER, a prisoner in Edinburgh Tolbooth, was transported via Leith to the colonies on 27 November 1679. [ETR]

MCDONELL, JOHN, was captured at the Siege of Worcester in 1651, and transported via London aboard the John and Sarah bound for Boston in 1651. [SD.1.5-6]

MCDOUGALL, ALLAN, of Gallonach, subscribed in Inveraray, Argyll, to a bond undertaking that he will not assist the Earl of Argyll or any other rebel under a penalty of 10,000 merks, dated 27 August 1684. [RPCS.IX.318]

MCDOUGALL, DUNCAN, from Argyll, participated in Argyll's Rebellion and was transported via Leith to Jamaica in August 1685. [RPCS.XI.136]

MCDOUNIE, JOHN, participated in Argyll's Rebellion and was transported via Leith to Jamaica in August 1685. [RPCS.XI.136]

MCDOWELL, ALEXANDER, was captured at the Siege of Worcester in 1651, and transported via London aboard the John and Sarah bound for Boston in 1651. [SD.1.5-6]

MCDUGAL, CHARLES, and Janet McDugal, children of Ninian McDugal in Corra, Buittle, Kirkcudbrightshire, fugitives and fanatics in 1684. [RPCS.IX.571]; Charles McDougall from

Kirkcudbrightshire, was transported to the Plantations of colonies in October 1684. [RPCS.X.258]

MCEACHERN, PATRICK, was captured at the Siege of Worcester in 1651, and transported via London aboard the John and Sarah bound for Boston in 1651. [SD.1.5-6]

MACEACHTER, JOHN, in Arminnie, was accused in Kirkcudbright of conversing with a rebel and fugitive, William Russell, in 1684. [RPCS.IX.374]

MCEWAN, ARCHIBALD, from Argyll, participated in Argyll's Rebellion and was transported via Leith to Jamaica in August 1685. [RPCS.XI.136]

MCEWAN, DONALD, a rebel in Argyll's Rebellion, a prisoner in Edinburgh Tolbooth to be returned to the ship at Leith bound for Jamaica on 12 August 1685. [ETR][RPCS.XI.136]

MCEWAN, DUNCAN, was transported via Leith aboard the Henry and Francis bound for East New Jersey in July 1685. [RPCS.XI.131]

MCEWAN, JOHN, was transported via Leith aboard the Henry and Francis bound for East New Jersey in July 1685, landed there on 7 December 1685. [RPCS.XI.131][NWI.I.423]

MCEWAN, ROBERT, was transported via Leith aboard the Henry and Francis bound for East New Jersey in July 1685, landed there on 7 December 1685. [NWI.I.423]

MCEWAN, WALTER, was transported via Leith aboard the Henry and Francis bound for East New Jersey in July 1685, landed there on 7 December 1685. [NWI.I.423]

MCFADZEAN, JANET, from Portrack, Dumfries-shire, spouse of John Harper, was transported to the colonis on October 1684. [RPCS.X.590]

MCGACHIN, JAMES, from Dalry, a prisoner in Canongait Tolbooth, was banished to the Plantations in Carolina in 1684. [RPCS.XI.15]

MCGARRON, ROBERT, from Maybole, Ayrshire, fought at the

Battle of Bothwell Bridge in 1679, was transported via Leith aboard the Crown of London bound for Barbados on 27 November 1679, was shipwrecked and drowned off Orkney on 10 December 1679. [RBM]

MCGAVIN, HUGH, was liberated from Edinburgh Tolbooth on 30 July 1685 having taken an Oath of Allegiance. [ETR]

MCGAVIN, WILLIAM, from Tarbolton, a prisoner in Glasgow Tolbooth, accused of participating in the Battle of Bothwell Bridge on 22 June 1679, to be taken to Edinburgh Tolbooth, in June 1684. [RPCS.IX.1]

MCGEE, JOHN, from Kirkcudbright, fought at the Battle of Bothwell Bridge in 1679, was transported via Leith aboard the Crown of London bound for Barbados on 27 November 1679, was shipwrecked off Orkney on 10 December 1679, later was transported to Jamaica. [CEC.212/5][SW.202] [RBM]

MACGHIE, ANDREW, chaplain of Cranston's Horse Regiment, a prisoner after the Siege of Worcester in 1651. [RHCA.366]

MCGIBBON, ARCHIBALD, took part in Argyll's Rebellion in 1685, was warded in Edinburgh Tolbooth on 10 July 1685, [ETR], then transported via Leith bound for Jamaica in August 1685. [RPCS.XI.329]

MCGIBBON, DUGALL, who was in Argyll's Rebellion in 1685, a prisoner in Edinburgh Tolbooth, was liberated on 12 January 1686. [ETR]

MCGIBBON, HECTOR, who was in Argyll's Rebellion in 1685, was transported via Leith to Jamaica in August 1685. [RPCS.XI.329]

MCGIBBON, JOHN, from Glenowkeill, who was in Argyll's Rebellion in 1685, was transported via Leith to Jamaica in August 1685. [RPCS.XI.329]

MCGIBBON, Dr, was warded in Edinburgh Tolbooth on 10 July 1685. [ETR]

MCGIE, JEAN, was taken from Leith Tolbooth, put in irons and imprisoned in Edinburgh Tolbooth, in 1685, [ETR], then banished to the Plantations on 15 August 1685, transported via Leith aboard the <u>Henry and Francis</u> bound for East New Jersey on 5 September 1685, landed there on 7 December 1685. [RPCS.XI.154/166/292] [NWI.I.423]

MCGIE, JEAN, was banished to the Plantations on 18 August 1685, then transported via Leith aboard the <u>Henry and Francis</u> bound for East New Jersey on 5 September 1685, landed there on 7 December 1685. [RPCS.XI.154/166/292] [NWI.I.423]

MCGIE, WILLIAM, in Borland, was accused, in Kirkcudbright in October 1684, of conversing with rebel Gilbert McGie. [RPCS.IX.374]

MCGILCHRIST, JAMES, was warded in Edinburgh Tolbooth on 1 November 1684, was released on 27 March 1685. [ETR]

MACGILL, DAVID, in Earlston near Dalry, Ayrshire, a rebel and fugitive, whose wife was tortured and died in 1660s? [Z.196]

MACGILL, JAMES, was captured at the Siege of Worcester in 1651, and transported via London aboard the <u>John and Sarah</u> bound for Boston in 1651, landed there in February 1652. [SD.1.5-6]

MCGILL, ROBERT, from Galashiels, Selkirkshire, fought at the Battle of Bothwell Bridge in 1679, was transported via Leith aboard the <u>Crown of London</u> bound for Barbados on 27 November 1679, was shipwrecked off Orkney on 10 December 1679, later transported to Jamaica. [RBM][CEC212/5][ETR]

MCGILL, WILLIAM, a writer in Minnigaff, was accused, in Kirkcudbright on 4 October 1684, of conversing with rebel, William Kennedy sometime in Barnkirk in June 1684. [RPCS.IX.375]

MCGILLICH, JOHN, from Argyll, for participating in Argyll's Rebellion, was transported via Leith to Jamaica in August 1685. [RPCS.XI.329]

MCGIRR, THOMAS, was killed at the Battle of Bothwell Bridge, Lanarkshire, on 22 June 1679. [Nithsdale, Martyrs Monument, Dumfries]

MACGOWN, ALEXANDER, born 1605, son of William MacGown in Dumfries, was educated at the University of St Andrews, minister at Mouswald, Dumfries-shire from 1637 until 1664 when he was suspended for refusing to conform to Episcopacy, he died in Dumfries on 28 April 1664. [F.II.219]

MCGOWAN, ANDREW, in Quarters, was accused, in Kirkcudbright in October 1684, of taking part of the Rebellion of 1679 and aiding rebels. [RPCS.IX.377]

MCGOWAN, HUGH, was warded in Edinburgh Tolbooth on 22 July 1685. [RPCS.IX.163]

MCGOWAN, JOHN, for participating in Argyll's Rebellion, was transported via Leith to Jamaica in August 1685. [RPCS.XI.329]

MCHARG, ARCHIBALD, in Minnievick, was accused, in Kirkcudbright in October 1684, of conversing with Archibald Stewart in January 1684. [RPCS.IX.375]

MCHARIE, JOHN, from Maybole, Ayrshire, fought at the Battle of Bothwell Bridge in 1679, was transported via Leith aboard the Crown of London bound for Barbados on 27 November 1679, was shipwrecked and drowned off Orkney on 10 December 1679. [RBM]

MCKECHNIE, WALTER, from Glasgow, fought at the Battle of Bothwell Bridge in 1679, was transported via Leith aboard the Crown of London bound for Barbados on 27 November 1679, was shipwrecked and drowned off Orkney on 10 December 1679. [RBM]

MCKENZIE, THOMAS, from Liberton, Midlothian, fought at the

Battle of Bothwell Bridge in 1679, was transported via Leith aboard the Crown of London bound for Barbados on 27 November 1679, was shipwrecked off Orkney on 10 December 1679, later transported to Jamaica. [RBM][CEC.212/5][SW.202]

MACKERVAIL, DAVID, from Glencairn, Dumfriesshire, fought at the Battle of Bothwell Bridge in 1679, was transported via Leith aboard the Crown of London bound for Barbados on 27 November 1679, was shipwrecked and drowned off Orkney on 10 December 1679. [RBM]

MACKHELLIN, DANIEL, was captured at the Siege of Worcester in 1651, was transported via London aboard the John and Sarah bound for Boston in December 1651, landed there in February 1652, [SD.1.5-6]

MCHUTCHEON, HUGH, a merchant from Blackrewe, a rebel, newly returned from Holland, was captured taken to Ardmillan, then imprisoned in Ayr in 1684. [RPCS.IX.513]

MCILLIGAN, JOHN, was accused of holding conventicles in Moray in 1668, to be arrested. [RPCS.II.504]

MCILMUN, ALEXANDER, of Kinlochlean, was accused of participating in the Earl of Argyll's Rebellion of 1685 and tried in 1687. [NRS.JC39.88]

MCILROY, GILBERT, a prisoner in Edinburgh Tolbooth, to be transported to the Plantations on 11 August 1685. [ETR]

MCILROY, WILLIAM, a prisoner in Edinburgh Tolbooth, to be transported to the Plantations on 11 August 1685. [ETR]

MCILVAY, DUNCAN, a prisoner in Edinburgh or Canongait Tolbooth, a rebel, was banished to the Plantations in Carolina on 8 August 1684. [RPCS.IX.95]

MCILVIE, JOHN, a shoemaker from Kilmarnock, Ayrshire, a rebel imprisoned in Canongait Tolbooth, was released in September 1684. [RPCS.IX.170]

MCILVORY, JOHN, from Craigintyrie, took part in Argyll's Rebellion in 1685, was transported via Leith bound for Jamaica in August 1685. [RPCS.XI.136]

MCILVRA, MARTIN, minister on Iona from 1643 until he was deposed in 1648 'for complying with the rebels'. [F.IV.111]

MCILWRAITH, JOHN, in Balloch, who was in the Rebellion of 1679, later took the Bond, by October 1684. [RPCS.IX.515]

MCILWRAITH, MATTHEW, was shot dead in 168-. [Colmonell gravestone]

MACINTAGGART, JOHN, a servant from Argyll, took part in Argyll's Rebellion in 1685, then transported via Leith bound for Jamaica in August 1685. [RPCS.XI.136]

MACINTOSH, DANIEL, was captured at the Siege of Worcester in 1651, then transported via London aboard the John and Sarah bound for New England in December 1651, landed at Boston in February 1652. [SD.1.5-6]

MACINTOSH, WILLIAM, was captured at the Siege of Worcester in 1651, then transported via London aboard the John and Sarah bound for New England in December 1651, landed at Boston in February 1652. [SD.1.5-6]

MCINTYRE, ARCHIBALD, from Glendaruel, took part in Argyll's Rebellion in 1685, was transported via Leith bound for Jamaica in August 1685. [RPCS.XI.329]

MCINTYRE, MALCOLM, was captured at the Battle of Dunbar in 1650, the transported via London aboard the Unity bound for Boston in 1650, [SD.1.5-6]

MCINTYRE, MALCOLM, was captured at the Siege of Worcester in 1651, then transported via London aboard the John and Sarah bound for Boston in December 1651, landed there in February 1652. [SD.1.5-6]

MCINTYRE, ROBERT, was captured at the Battle of Dunbar in 1650, the transported via London aboard the Unity bound for Boston in 1650, [SCF.1226]]

MCISAAC, MURDOCH, from Machrimore, Kintyre, Argyll, took part in Argyll's Rebellion, was transported via Leith to New England in July 1685. [RPCS.XI.94/310]

MCIVAR, ANGUS, from Glassary, Argyll, took part in Argyll's Rebellion, was transported via Leith to New England in July 1685. [RPCS.XI.94/310]

MCIVAR, DONALD, from Argyll, took part in Argyll's Rebellion, was transported via Leith to Jamaica in August 1685. [RPCS.XI.136]

MCIVAR, DUNCAN, from Argyll, took part in Argyll's Rebellion, was transported via Leith to Jamaica in August 1685. [RPCS.XI.136]

MCIVAR, JOHN, from Tulloch in Argyll, took part in Argyll's Rebellion, was transported via Leith to Jamaica in August 1685. [RPCS.XI.136]

MCJARROW, JAMES, in Shang, a rebel, was captured and imprisoned in Ayr Tolbooth in 1684. [RPCS.IX.513]

MCKAIL, HUGH, born 1640, son of Matthew McKail, was licenced by the Presbytery of Edinburgh, a covenanting preacher who was tortured and later executed at the Market Cross of Edinburgh on 22 December 1666. [F.III.230][Z.195]

MCKAIL, JAMES, was captured at the Siege of Worcester in 1651, was transported via London aboard the John and Sarah bound for Boston in December 1651, landed there in February 1652, [SD.1.5-6]

MCKAIRNE, NEIL, from Argyll, took part in Argyll's Rebellion, was transported via Leith to Jamaica in August 1685. [RPCS.XI.136]

MCKAY, ALEXANDER, was captured at the Siege of Worcester in 1651, was transported via London aboard the John and Sarah bound for Boston in December 1651, landed there in February 1652, [SD.1.5-6]

MCKAY, DUNCAN, from Skipnish, Kintyre, Argyll, took part in Argyll's Rebellion, was transported via Leith to Jamaica in August 1685. [RPCS.XI.136]

MCKAY, HUGH, was captured at the Siege of Worcester in 1651, was transported via London aboard the John and Sarah bound for Boston in December 1651, landed there in February 1652, [SD.1.5-6]

MCKAY, JOHN, was captured at the Siege of Worcester in 1651, was transported via London aboard the John and Sarah bound for Boston in December 1651, landed there in February 1652, [SD.1.5-6]

MCKAY, MARTIN, was transported via London bound for Jamaica in August 1685. [RPCS.XI.136]

MCKAY, NEIL, as captured at the Siege of Worcester in 1651, was transported via London aboard the John and Sarah bound for Boston in December 1651, landed there in February 1652, [SD.1.5-6]

MCKEAN, ALESTAR, was captured at the Siege of Worcester in 1651, was transported via London aboard the John and Sarah bound for Boston in December 1651, landed there in February 1652, [SD.1.5-6]

MCKAY, DANIEL, was captured at the Siege of Worcester in 1651, was transported via London aboard the John and Sarah bound for Boston in December 1651, landed there in February 1652, [SD.1.5-6]

MCKEAN, EDWARD, was shot dead in 1685. [Barr gravestone] [F.3.17]

MCKEAN, JOHN, was captured at the Siege of Worcester in 1651, was transported via London aboard the John and Sarah bound for Boston in December 1651, landed there in February 1652, [SD.1.5-6]

MCKEAN, NEIL, was captured at the Siege of Worcester in 1651, was transported via London aboard the John and Sarah bound for Boston in December 1651, landed there in February 1652, [SD.1.5-6]

MCKEAN, PATRICK, was captured at the Siege of Worcester in 1651, was transported via London aboard the John and Sarah bound for Boston in December 1651, landed there in February 1652, [SD.1.5-6]

MCKEAN, ROBERT, was captured at the Siege of Worcester in 1651, was transported via London aboard the John and Sarah bound for Boston in December 1651, landed there in February 1652, [SD.1.5-6]

MCKEAN, SAMUEL, was captured at the Siege of Worcester in 1651, was transported via London aboard the John and Sarah bound for Boston in December 1651, landed there in February 1652, [SD.1.5-6]

MCKEAN, WILLIAM, was captured at the Siege of Worcester in 1651, was transported via London aboard the John and Sarah bound for Boston in December 1651, landed there in February 1652, [SD.1.5-6]

MCKECHAN, WALTER, from Shirgarton, was transported via Leith aboard the St Michael of Scarborough bound for the West Indies on 12 December 1678. [RPCS.VI.76]

MCKECHNIE, JOHN, from Galloway, was nearly liberated from a military escort at Enterkin Pass in Dumfries-shire, later was imprisoned in Edinburgh where he died in 1684. [GC.314]

MACKEICHAN, NEIL, from Baranazarw, Lorne, Argyll, took part in Argyll's Rebellion, was transported via Leith to Jamaica in August 1685. [RPCS.XI.136]

MACKEITH, DAVID, was captured at the Siege of Worcester in 1651, was transported via London aboard the John and Sarah bound for Boston in December 1651, landed there in February 1652, [SD.1.5-6]

MCKELLAR, ANGUS, from Argyll, in Argyll's Rebellion, was transported via Leith to New England in July 1685. [RPCS.XI.94]

MCKELLO, DONALD, from Argyll, in Argyll's Rebellion, was transported via Leith to New England in July 1685. [RPCS.XI.136]

MCKELLO, DUGALD, from Argyll, in Argyll's Rebellion, was transported via Leith to Jamaica in August 1685. [RPCS.XI.136]

MCKELLO, JOHN, from Argyll, in Argyll's Rebellion, was transported via Leith to Jamaica in August 1685. [RPCS.XI.136]

MCKELLO, MARTIN, from Argyll, in Argyll's Rebellion, was transported via Leith to Jamaica in August 1685. [RPCS.XI.136]

MACKEN, WILLIAM, was captured at the Siege of Worcester in 1651, was transported via London aboard the John and Sarah bound for Boston in December 1651, landed there in February 1652, [SD.1.5-6]

MACKENTHOW, JOHN, was captured at the Siege of Worcester in 1651, was transported via London aboard the John and Sarah bound for Boston in December 1651, landed there in February 1652, [SD.1.5-6]

MACKEOUN, CUTHBERT, and William MacMartin in Bankhead, Tynron, for aiding rebels James and John Gibson, and five others, was declared to be a rebel and fugitive in October 1684. [RPCS.IX.368]

MCKEON, JOHN, in Kirkcudbright, was accused, in Kirkcudbright in October 1684, of conversing with rebel Alexander McKean. [RPCS.IX.374]

MACKETH, NEIL, was captured at the Siege of Worcester in 1651, was transported via London aboard the John and Sarah bound for Boston in December 1651, landed there in February 1652, [SD.1.5-6]

MACKIE, HILL, was captured at the Siege of Worcester in 1651, was transported via London aboard the John and Sarah bound for Boston in December 1651, landed there in February 1652, [SD.1.5-6]

MACKIE, JAMES, from Denny, Stirlingshire, fought at the Battle of Bothwell Bridge in 1679, was transported via Leith aboard the Crown of London bound for Barbados on 27 November 1679, was shipwrecked and drowned off Orkney on 10 December 1679. [RBM]

MCKIE, MARION, in Over Senwick, was accused, in Kirkcudbright on 4 October 1684, of aiding rebel John Richardson. [RPCS.IX.375]

MCKIE, PATRICK, in Gleckmallock, was accused, in Kirkcudbright in October 1684, of conversing with rebel William Stewart in 1682. [RPCS.IX.375]

MACKIE, RORY, was captured at the Siege of Worcester in 1651, was transported via London aboard the John and Sarah bound for Boston in December 1651, landed there in February 1652, [SD.1.5-6]

MCKIE, WILLIAM, was transported from Leith to New Jersey in July 1685. [RPCS.XI.95]

MCKILLON, DONALD, from Glendaurel, was in Argyll's Rebellion, transported via Leith to Jamaica in August 1685. [RPCS.XI.136]

MCKINLAY, NEIL, took part in Argyll's Rebellion in 1685, then transported via Leith bound for Jamaica in August 1685. [RPCS.XI.136]

MCKINNA, DAVID, in Blackneuk, was accused, in Kirkcudbright in 1684, of aiding rebels and fugitives. [RPCS.IX.376]

MACKINNA, JOHN, in Craignee, Tynron, and his wife Margaret Laurie, for aiding rebels Walter Smith, Alexander Gibson, and Thomas Hunter in Breckinside, were declared to be rebels and fugitives in October 1684. [RPCS.IX.368]

MCKINNELL, ARCHIBALD, in Algirth, saw rebels Robert Lauchlison and John Weir and failed to report them, was declared as a rebel and fugitive in October 1684. [RPCS.IX.361]

MCKINNON, JOHN, was captured at the Siege of Worcester in 1651, was transported via London aboard the <u>John and Sarah</u> bound for Boston in December 1651, landed there in February 1652, [SD.1.5-6]

MCKINNON, JOHN, from Duppen of Kintyre, was in Argyll's Rebellion, transported via Leith to Jamaica in August 1685. [RPCS.XI.236]

MCKINNEY, JEAN, in Grangeburn, Dunscore, Dumfries-shire, accused of aiding rebels, a prisoner bound for Dumfries, was liberated by Roger Pagan a rebel in August 1684. [RPCS.IX.265]

MCKNACHT, JOHN, son of Patrick McKacht in Cumnock, a rebel was sought in 1667. [RPCS.II.345]

MCKNACHT, PATRICK, in Cumnock, a rebel was sought in 1667. [RPCS.II.345]

MCKNAIGHT, DAVID, in Beckbie, was accused, in Kirkcudbright in 1684, of conversing with rebel John Corsan, in midsummer 1684. [RPCS.IX.376]

MCKNAUGHT, JOHN, in Middletoun of Dalry, a rebel sought in 1667. [RPCS.II.345]

MCKNAIGHT, JOHN, in Larg, was accused, in Kirkcudbright, in October 1684, of conversing with John Corsan a rebel in June 1684. [RPCS.IX.376]

MCKNAIGHT, JOHN, in Overtoun of Dalry, was accused in Kirkcudbright on 4 October 1684, of conversing with George Douglas of Old Clauchan and harbouring other fugitives in 1684. [RPCS.IX.377]

MCKNAIGHT, WILLIAM, in Meikle Careltoune, was accused, in October 1684 in Kirkcudbright, of conversing with rebel John Clinton. [RPCS.IX.374]

MCKNISH, JOHN, the younger, in Littleton, was accused, in Kirkcudbright in October 1684, of conversing with rebel Gilbert McGie. [RPCS.IX.374]

MCKROYK, ANDREW, in Kirkcudbright, was accused, in Kirkcudbright in October 1684, of conversing with rebel Alexander McKean. [RPCS.IX.374]

MCLACHLAN, WILLIAM, was educated at Glasgow University, minister at Kilmartin, Argyll, from 1669 until 1689, he settled in Ireland after August 1690 and died there. [F.IV.13

MCLAUCHLAN, ARCHIBALD, of Kylinuchanich, subscribed in Inveraray, Argyll, to a bond undertaking that he will not assist the Earl of Argyll or any other rebel under a penalty of 1,000 pounds Scots, dated 28 August 1684. [RPCS.IX.318]

MCLAUCHLAN, JOHN, formerly servant to Craigintyrie, in Argyll's Rebellion, imprisoned in Edinburgh Tolbooth, was released on 12 January 1686. [ETR]

MCLAUCHLAN, MARGARET, born 1621, tenant in Drumjargon, relict of John Mulligan a carpenter, was accused of attending a conventicle, and was drowned at Bladnoch in the Solway at Wigtown on 11 May 1685. [Wigtown Monument]

MCLEAN, ALEXANDER, a burgess of Kirkcudbright, was imprisoned in Edinburgh Tolbooth, for his wife's part in the tumult in Kirkcudbright, was released after guaranteeing his wife's future attitude toward bishops, the Church and the State in 1663. [RPCS.I.377]

MCLEAN, ANDREW, from Argyll, was in Argyll's Rebellion, a prisoner in Edinburgh Tolbooth, to be transported to Jamaica on 11 August 1685. [ETR][RPCS.XI.330]

MCKINNON, JOHN, from Duppen of Kintyre, Argyll, was in Argyll's Rebellion, transported via Leith to Jamaica in August 1685. [RPCS.XI.236]

MCLEAN, DUNCAN, from Argyll, was in Argyll's Rebellion, transported via Leith to Jamaica in August 1685. [RPCS.XI.236]

MCLEAN, HUGH, from Argyll, was in Argyll's Rebellion, transported via Leith to Jamaica in August 1685. [RPCS.XI.330]

MCLEAN, JAMES, a tailor in Barnrosh, was accused in Kirkcudbright on 7 October 1684, of conversing with rebels John Charters and William Halliday. [RPCS.IX.374]

MCLEAN, JOHN, was liberated from Edinburgh Tolbooth on 29 July 1685. [ETR]

MCLEAN, JOHN, from Portindryan, Argyll, was in Argyll's Rebellion, transported via Leith to Jamaica in August 1685. [RPCS.XI.330]

MCLEAN, THOMAS, in Blackmyre, was accused in Kirkcudbright in October 1684, of conversing with rebel John Corsan in May 1684. [RPCS.IX.376]

MCLEAN, WILLIAM, was in Argyll's Rebellion, transported via Leith to Jamaica in July 1685. [RPCS.XI.114]

MCLEAN, WILLIAM, was liberated from Edinburgh Tolbooth on 29 July 1685. [ETR]

MCLEAN, ......, was captured at the Siege of Worcester in 1651, was transported via London aboard the John and Sarah bound for Boston in December 1651, landed there in February 1652, [SD.1.5-6]

MCLELLAN, ANDREW, died aboard the Henry and Francis when bound for East New Jersey in 1685. [Nithsdale, Martyrs Monument, Dumfries]

MCLELLAN, JOHN, fought at the Battle of Bothwell Bridge in 1679, was transported via Leith aboard the Crown of London bound for

Barbados on 27 November 1679, was shipwrecked and drowned off Orkney on 10 December 1679. [RBM]

MCLELLAN, MARGARET, was banished to the Plantations in 1685, then transported via Leith aboard the Henry and Francis bound for East New Jersey ON 5 September 1685, died on the voyage. [RPCS.XI.154/291/292][NWI.I.423]

MCLELLAN, ROBERT, then in Edinburgh Tolbooth, was transferred to Dunnottar Castle, Kincardineshire, on 29 July 1685. [ETR]; was banished to the Plantations on 18 August 1685, then transported via Leith aboard the Henry and Francis bound for East New Jersey on 5 August 1685. [RPCS.XI.155]

MACLEOD, JOHN, was captured at the Siege of Worcester in 1651, was transported via London aboard the John and Sarah bound for Boston in December 1651, landed there in February 1652, [SD.1.5-6]

MACLEOD, MURTLE, was captured at the Siege of Worcester in 1651, was transported via London aboard the John and Sarah bound for Boston in December 1651, landed there in February 1652, [SD.1.5-6]

MCLINE, ALEXANDER, from Argyll, was in Argyll's Rebellion, transported via Leith to Jamaica in August 1685. [RPCS.XI.136]

MACLOUN, JOHN, in Auchinnaight, for aiding rebels John MacColl, Gilbert Gilchrist, and the Corsans from Glencairn, in April 1684, was declared to be a rebel and fugitive in October 1684. [RPCS.IX.366]

MCLURG, ...., of Minigaff, a Covenanter that Graham of Claverhouse, was determined to hang in 1682. [BK.15]

MCLURG, MARGARET, wife of Alexander Milligan, was banished to the Plantations on 17 October 1684. [RPCS.X.612]

MCLURG, THOMAS, from Colmonell, Ayrshire, fought at the Battle of Bothwell Bridge in 1679, was transported via Leith aboard the Crown of London bound for Barbados on 27

November 1679, was shipwrecked and drowned off Orkney on 10 December 1679. [RBM]

MCMEEKEN, GILBERT, of Killingtringen, 'parish of Canmonell' a Covenanter in 1679, was tried in 1685. [NRS.JC39.70]; admitted that he attended conventicles, and fined on 17 July 1684. [RPCS.IX.53/58]

MCMICHAEL, DANIEL, was killed at Dalveen in 1683. [Durisdeer gravestone, Nether Dalveen, Thornhill, Dumfries-shire] [Nithsdale, Martyrs Monument, Dumfries]

MCMICHAEL, DUNCAN, from Islay, Argyll, was in Argyll's Rebellion, transported via Leith to Jamaica in August 1685. [RPCS.XI.136]

MACMICHAEL, JAMES, was alleged to be one of the rebels involved in the ambush at Enterkin, Dumfries-shire in 1684. [RPCS.IX.259]; he was killed on Auchencloy Moor on 18 December 1684. [Auchencloy Martyrs Monument, Kirkcudbrightshire] [Nithsdale, Martyrs Monument, Dumfries] [GC.315]

MCMICHAEL, ROBERT, from Dalry, a prisoner in Canongait Toolbooth, subscribed to a bond undertaking to live orderly, attend his parish church, and compear when requested. [RPCS.IX.343]

MCMICHAEL, ROGER, from Dalry, Galloway, a rebel who was transported via Leith to Jamaica in August 1685. [RPCS.XI.316]

MCMICHAN, JOHN, minister at Dalry, was accused, in Kirkcudbright on 4 October 1684 of aiding Robert McClelland of Barscob, Thomas Vernor, William Edgar of Gordonstoun, and James McAdam in Clauchan, rebels in 1684. [RPCS.IX.377]

MCMICHAN, WILLIAM, was warded in Edinburgh Tolbooth on 22 July 1685, was liberated on 30 July 1685 having taken an Oath of Allegiance. [RPCS.IX.163/168]

MCMILLAN, ALEXANDER, in Marnhold, was accused, in Kirkcudbright on 4 October 1684, of aiding several rebels in 1684.

[RPCS.IX.377]; was transported via Leith to Barbados in December 1685. [RPCS.XI.386][ETR]

MCMILLAN, ALEXANDER, from Dumfries, was warded in Edinburgh Tolbooth on 28 November 1684, having subscribed to the Test Act, was released on 5 February 1685. [ETR]

MCMILLAN, ALEXANDER, from Galloway, a prisoner in Canongait Tolbooth, who refused to take an Oath of Allegiance, was banished to the American Plantations on 17 December 1685, was transported via Leith aboard the John and Nicholas bound for Barbados in December 1685. [ETR][RPCS.XI.386]

MCMILLAN, ANTHONY, in Kirrochie, was accused, in Kirkcudbright in October 1684, of conversing with rebel Anthony Stewart in February 1684. [RPCS.IX.375]

MCMILLAN, DUNCAN, from Carradale, Kintyre, Argyll, was in Argyll's Rebellion, transported via Leith to Jamaica in August 1685. [RPCS.XI.329]

MCMILLAN, JAMES, in Briddinoch, was accused, in Kirkcudbright in 1684, of aiding rebels William McMillan in Marbreck, James Clark there, and for hearing William Gilchrist a vagrant preacher. [RPCS.IX.376]

MACMILLAN, JOHN, was captured at the Battle of Dunbar in 1650, was transported via London aboard the Unity bound for Boston in November 1650. [SCF.1226]

MACMILLAN, JOHN, was fined in Kirkcudbright for non-conformity in 1662. [Carsphairn gravestone, Kirkcudbrightshire]

MCMILLAN, JOHN, in Burnhead, was accused, in Kirkcudbright in 1684, of aiding rebels and fugitives. [RPCS.IX.376]

MCMILLAN, JOHN, from Argyll, was in Argyll's Rebellion in 1685, transported via Leith to Jamaica in August 1685. [RPCS.XI.94]

MCMILLAN, ROBERT, in Cairniehill, was accused, in Kirkcudbright in 1684, of aiding rebels and fugitives, James McMichan and

William Herries, also hearing rebellious preachers, and being in the rebellion of 1679. [RPCS.IX.376]

MCMILLAN, WILLIAM, servant of a tenant of Maxwelltoun, imprisoned in Canongait Tolbooth suspected of being a rebel, having taken the Oath of Allegiance, was released on 18 July 1667. [RPCS.II.399]

MCMILLAN, WILLIAM, of Caldow in Balmaclellan, fled to Ireland to avoid persecution, returned to hold conventicles around 1673, was imprisoned in Kirkcudbright Tolbooth in November 1676, was taken via Edinburgh to Dunnottar Castle, Kincardineshire. [GC.350]

MCMILLAN, WILLIAM, in Midcarminoch, was accused, in Kirkcudbright in 1684, for corresponding with David McGill in Dalshangin, William McMillan in Marscalloch, and for hearing Reverend William Gilchrist a vagrant preacher. [RPCS.IX.376]

MCMILLAN, WILLIAM, was transported via Leith aboard the Henry and Francis bound for East New Jersey on 5 September 1685, died on the voyage. [NWI.I.423]

MCMIN, WALTER, and his brother James McMin, sons of John McMin in Buittle Mill, Kirkcudbrightshire, fugitives and fanatics in 1684. [RPCS.IX.571]

MCMURRIE, JAMES, from Straiton, Ayrshire, fought at the Battle of Bothwell Bridge in 1679, was transported via Leith aboard the Crown of London bound for Barbados on 27 November 1679, was shipwrecked and drowned off Orkney on 10 December 1679. [RBM]

MCNAB, JAMES, was captured at the Siege of Worcester in 1651 and transported via Gravesend, London, aboard the John and Sarah bound for Boston, New England, in December 1651, landed in February 1652. [SD.1/5-6]

MCNAUGHT, JOHN, in Middleton of Dalry, was sought by the Justice Court in August 1667 for his part in the late rebellion. [GC.123]

MCNEIL, ALASTAIR, was captured at the Siege of Worcester, transported via London aboard the John and Sarah bound for Boston in December 1651, landed there in February 1652. [SD.1.5-6]

MCNEIL, ARCHIBALD, from Argyll, for taking part in Argyll's Rebellion was transported via Leith to Jamaica in August 1685. [RPCS.XI.136]

MCNEIL, DONALD, was captured at the Siege of Worcester, transported via London aboard the John and Sarah bound for Boston in December 1651, landed there in February 1652. [SD.1.5-6]

MCNEIL, HECTOR, from Argyll, for being in Argylls Rebellio, was transported via Leith to Jamaica in August 1685. [RPCS.XI.136]

MCNEIL, JAMES, was captured at the Siege of Worcester, transported via London aboard the John and Sarah bound for Boston in December 1651, landed there in February 1652. [SD.1.5-6]

MCNEIL, JOHN, from Argyll, took part in Argyll's Rebellion in 1685, was transported via Leith to Jamaica in August 1685. [RPCS.XI.136]

MCNEILL, MALCOLM, formerly servant to Craigintyrie, in Argyll's Rebellion, imprisoned in Edinburgh Tolbooth, was released on 12 January 1686. [ETR]

MCNEIL, PATRICK, was captured at the Siege of Worcester, transported via London aboard the John and Sarah bound for Boston in December 1651, landed there in February 1652. [SD.1.5-6]

MCNEISH, DONALD, was captured at the Siege of Worcester, transported via London aboard the John and Sarah bound for

Boston in December 1651, landed there in February 1652. [SD.1.5-6]

MCNEISH, PATRICK, was captured at the Siege of Worcester, transported via London aboard the John and Sarah bound for Boston in December 1651, landed there in February 1652. [SD.1.5-6]

MCNESTER, ALESTER, was captured at the Siege of Worcester, transported via London aboard the John and Sarah bound for Boston in December 1651, landed there in February 1652. [SD.1.5-6]

MCNURE, JOHN, from St Ninian's, Stirlingshire, fought at the Battle of Bothwell Bridge in 1679, was transported via Leith aboard the Crown of London bound for Barbados on 27 November 1679, was shipwrecked and drowned off Orkney on 10 December 1679. [RBM]

MCPHUN, ARCHIBALD, of Drip, was accused of participating in the Earl of Argyll's Rebellion and tried in 1687. [NRS.JC39.88]

MCPHUN, JOHN, of Invernydan, was accused of participating in the Earl of Argyll's Rebellion of 1685 and tried in 1687. [NRS.JC39.88]

MCQHAE, JAMES, in Pluntoun, was accused, in Kirkcudbright on 4 October 1684, of aiding fugitive William Campbell. [RPCS.IX.375]

MCQUEEN, AMOS, was captured at the Siege of Worcester, transported via London aboard the John and Sarah bound for Boston in December 1651, landed there in February 1652. [SD.1.5-6]

MCQUEEN, DUNCAN, from Argyll, took part in Argyll's Rebellion and was transported via Leith to Jamaica in August 1685. [RPCS.XI.136]

MCQUEEN, GEORGE, was captured at the Siege of Worcester, transported via London aboard the John and Sarah bound for Boston in December 1651, landed there in February 1652. [SD.1.5-6]

MCQUEEN, HUGH, from Argyll, for being in Argyll's Rebellion, was transported via Leith to Jamaica in August 1685. [RPCS.XI.136]

MCQUEEN, HUGH, from Argyll, for being in Argyll's Rebellion, was transported via Leith to Jamaica in August 1685. [RPCS.XI.136]

MCQUEEN, ROBERT, from Nithsdale, was banished to the Plantations on 25 August 1685, then transported via Leith aboard the <u>Henry and Francis</u> bound for East New Jersey on 5 September 1685, landed there on 7 December 1685. [RPCS.XI.154]

MCQUEEN, WALTER, was banished to the Plantations on 25 August 1685, then transported via Leith aboard the <u>Henry and Francis</u> bound for East New Jersey on 5 September 1685, landed there on 7 December 1685. [RPCS.XI.154]

MACQUHAN, ANDREW, from Kirkcudbright, fought at the Battle of Bothwell Bridge in 1679, was transported via Leith aboard the <u>Crown of London</u> bound for Barbados on 27 November 1679, was shipwrecked off Orkney on 10 December 1679 later transported to Jamaica. [RBM] [SW.202]

MACQUHAN, THOMAS, from Kirkcudbright, fought at the Battle of Bothwell Bridge in 1679, was transported via Leith aboard the <u>Crown of London</u> bound for Barbados on 27 November 1679, was shipwrecked off Orkney on 10 December 1679 later transported to Jamaica. [RBM] [SW.202]

MCQUILLAN, DANIEL, was captured at the Siege of Worcester in 1651, transported via London aboard the <u>John and Sarah</u> bound for Boston in December 1651, landed there in February 1652. [SD.1.5-6]

MCQUILLAN, JOHN, was captured at the Siege of Worcester in 1651, transported via London aboard the <u>John and Sarah</u> bound for Boston in December 1651, landed there in February 1652. [SD.1.5-6]

MCREADY, JOHN, from Ratho, was transported via Leith t the West Indies in August 1678. [RPCS.V.488]

MCROBERT, ANDREW, was killed on Kirkconnell Moor, Kirkcudbrightshire, on 21 February 1685. [Kirkconnell Moor Monument] [Twynholm gravestone, Kirkcudbrightshire] [GC.305]

MACROSKIE, THOMAS, in Barholm, was accused, in Kirkcudbright in October 1684, of conversing with rebel Hendry McCulloch, sometime in Barholm, in June 1683. [RPCS.IX.376]

MCSHANE, JOHN, was captured at the Battle of Dunbar in 1650, then transported via London aboard the <u>Unity</u> bound for Boston in November 1650. [SCF.1226]

MACSHELLIE, JOHN, in Whiteside, was accused, in Kirkcudbright in 1684, of conversing with rebel John Bell from Whiteside, in September 1683. [RPCS.IX.376]

MCTAGGART, ALEXANDER, in Dalnae, was accused, in Kirkcudbright in October 1684, of conversing with Anthony Stewart in September 1683. [RPCS.IX.375]

MCTAGGART, JOHN, from Penninghame, Wigtownshire, MACQUHAN, ANDREW, from Kirkcudbright, fought at the Battle of Bothwell Bridge in 1679, was transported via Leith aboard the <u>Crown of London</u> bound for Barbados on 27 November 1679, was shipwrecked off Orkney on 10 December 1679. [RBM]

MCTAGGART, JOHN, in Craigmark, to be tried accused of rebellion, 3 June 1684. [RPCS.IX.205]

MCTAILLOUR, DONALD, from Fordie in Perthahire, was in Argyll's Rebellion in 1685, transported via Leith to Jamaica in August 1685. [RPCS.XI.329]

MCTHOMAS, ALISTER, was captured at the Siege of Worcester in 1651, transported via London aboard the <u>John and Sarah</u> bound for Boston in December 1651, landed there in February 1652. SD.1.5-6]

MCTIRE, JOHN, from Kirkmichael, Ayrshire, MACQUHAN, ANDREW, from Kirkcudbright, fought at the Battle of Bothwell Bridge in 1679, was transported via Leith aboard the <u>Crown of London</u> bound for Barbados on 27 November 1679, was shipwrecked off Orkney on 10 December 1679 later transported to Jamaica. [RBM] [SW.202]

MCTOUCHER, WILLIAM, in Dalmellington, to be tried accused of rebellion, 3 June 1684. [RPCS.IX.205]

MCTURK, JAMES, the younger, in Holme of Dalqhairn, was accused, in Kirkcudbright in 1684, of conversing with rebels John Fraser and John Clerk in Marbrack, and for hearing William Gilchrist. [RPCS.IX.376]

MCURICH, ARCHIBALD, a herd from Argyll, was in Argyll's Rebellion, transported via Leith to New England in July 1685. [RPCS.XI.312/330]

MCVERRAN, DONALD, was in Argyll's Rebellion, then transported via Leith to Jamaica in August 1685. [RPCS.XI.136]

MCVEY, DONALD, was in Argyll's Rebellion, then transported via Leith to Jamaica in August 1685. [RPCS.XI.136]

MCVICAR, DONALD, from Inveraray, Argyll, was in Argyll's Rebellion, then transported via Leith to Jamaica in August 1685. [RPCS.XI.94/312]

MCVICAR, DUNCAN, born 1668, son of baillie McVicar in Campbeltown, Argyll, was in Argyll's Rebellion, then transported via Leith to Jamaica in August 1685. [RPCS.XI.94/317]

MCVIG, DUNCAN, from Argyll, was in Argyll's Rebellion, then transported via Leith to Jamaica in August 1685. [RPCS.XI.329]

MCWALTER, JOHN, was warded in Edinburgh Tolbooth on 22 July 1685, was liberated on 29 July 1685. [RPCS.IX.163/165]

MCWALTER, THOMAS, was captured at the Battle of Dunbar in 1650, transported via London aboard the Unity bound for Boston in November 1650. [SCF.1226]

MCWALTER, WALTER, was captured at the Battle of Dunbar in 1650, transported via London aboard the Unity bound for Boston in November 1650. [SCF.1226]

MCWHAE, ROBERT, in Borgue, Kirkcudbrightshire, was killed in 1685. [Kirkandrews gravestone, Gatehouse of Fleet, Kirkcudbrightshire]

MCWHANNELL, JOHN, in Gleckmallock, was accused, in Kirkcudbright in October 1684, of conversing with rebel William Stewart in 1682. [RPCS.IX.375]

MCWHIDDIE, ALLAN, from Argyll, in Argyll's Rebellion, was transported via Leith to Jamaica in August 1685. [RPCS.XI.136]

MCWHIRTER, JOHN, from Maybole, Ayrshire,

fought at the Battle of Bothwell Bridge in 1679, was transported via Leith aboard the Crown of London bound for Barbados on 27 November 1679, was shipwrecked and drowned off Orkney on 10 December 1679. [RBM]

MCWILLIAM, DANIEL, was captured at the Siege of Worcester in 1651, transported via London aboard the John and Sarah bound for Boston in December 1651, landed there in February 1652. [SD.1.5-6]

MCWILLIAM, DAVID, was captured at the Siege of Worcester in 1651, transported via London aboard the John and Sarah bound for Boston in December 1651, landed there in February 1652. [SD.1.5-6]

MCWILLIAM, GELLUST, was captured at the Siege of Worcester in 1651, transported via London aboard the John and Sarah bound for Boston in December 1651, landed there in February 1652. [SD.1.5-6]

MCWILLIE, JOHN, from Argyll, in Argyll's Rebellion in 1685, a prisoner in Edinburgh Tolbooth, to be transported to the Plantations on 11 August 1685 via Leith to Jamaica. [ETR] [RPCS.329]

MACHANE, MATTHEW, in Eaglesham, a rebel in Glasgow Tolbooth, was banished to the Plantations in June 1684, and transported via Glasgow aboard the Pelican bound for Carolina, bond by Walter Gibson, a merchant in Glasgow, dated 20 June 1684. [RPCS.IX.208]

MACK, GEORGE, in Caldergreen, a rebel, subscribed to a bond of the peace in October 1668. [RPCS.II.548]

MACK, JAMES, a prisoner in Canongait Tolbooth, who refused to take an Oath of Allegiance, was banished to the American Plantations on 17 December 1685, then transported via Leith aboard the John and Nicholas bound for Barbados in December 1685. [ETR][RPCS.XI.386]

MACKIE, JAMES, in Cubbocks, was accused, in Kirkcudbright on 4 October 1684 of aiding Mr Renwick and other rebels in 1684. [RPCS.IX.377]

MAINE, HENRY, born 1625 in Linlithgow, West Lothian, was educated at Edinburgh University, minister at Islandmagee, Ulster, from 1649, he was subject to persecution there and imprisoned in Carrickfergus in 1650, later minister at Houston, Renfrewshire, from 1650 until his death in October 1651. [CEG][FI.45][F.III.139; VII.532]

MAIN, JOHN, for his part in the Pentland Rising of 1666, was beheaded in Glasgow on 19 December 1666. [Glasgow Cathedral]

MAIN, JOHN, from Old Monkland, Lanarkshire, fought at Bothwell Bridge, Lanarkshire, on 22 June 1679. [Glasgow Cathedral plaque]

MAIR, WILLIAM, from Stirling, was transported via Leith aboard the Henry and Francis bound for East New Jersey on 5 September 1685, landed there on 7 December 1685. [RPCS.XI][NWI.I.423]

MAITLAND, ELIZABETH, was taken from Leith Tolbooth, put in irons and imprisoned in Edinburgh Tolbooth, in 1685. [ETR]

MAITLAND, JOHN, 1616-1682, 2$^{ND}$ Earl of Lauderdale, initially a Covenanter but later a Royalist. [NRS.GD1.1428]

MAITLAND, JOHN, was banished to the Plantations on 16 May 1684, transported via Glasgow aboard the Pelican bound for Carolina in 1684. [RPCS.VIII.720]

MAITLAND, MARGARET, was taken from Leith Tolbooth, put in irons and imprisoned in Edinburgh Tolbooth, in 1685. [ETR]

MAKIN, JANET, spouse of Alexander Moffat in Gilchristland, for seeing the rebel John Frisell and failing to report it, was declared to be a rebel and fugitive in October 1684. [RPCS.IX.361]

MALCOLM, JOHN, from Dalry, Galloway, fought at the Battle of Bothwell Bridge in 1679, was transported via Leith aboard the Crown of London bound for Barbados on 27 November 1679, was shipwrecked off Orkney on 10 December 1679 later transported to Jamaica. [RBM] [SW.202]

MALCOLM, JOHN, in Sundaywall, for aiding rebels, Robert Cunningham, Gilbert Gilchrist, and John MacCall, in June 1684, was declared to be a rebel and fugitive in October 1684. [RPCS.IX.370]

MALCOLM, JOHN, from Dalry, was captured at the Battle of Ayrsmoss on 22 July 1680, and was hanged in the Grassmarket, Edinburgh, in August 1680. [GC.185]

MANN, DANIEL, was captured at the Siege of Worcester in 1651, transported via London aboard the John and Sarah bound for Boston in December 1651, landed there in February 1652. [SD.1.5-6]

MANN, JOHN, was captured at the Siege of Worcester in 1651, transported via London aboard the John and Sarah bound for Boston in December 1651, landed there in February 1652. [SD.1.5-6]

MANN, PATRICK, was captured at the Siege of Worcester in 1651, transported via London aboard the John and Sarah bound for Boston in December 1651, landed there in February 1652. [SD.1.5-6]

MANUEL, JAMES, a maltman from Glasgow, was transported via Glasgow to the West Indies in June 1678. [RPCS.V.474]

MANSON, ALEXANDER, was transported via Leith to Jamaica in August 1685. [ETR][RPCS.XI.329]

MARNOCH, GILBERT, a chapman, was transported via Leith aboard the St Michael of Scarbourough bound for the West Indies in August 1678. [RPCS.VI.76]

MARSHALL, ALEXANDER, was banished to the Plantations on 24 July 1685. [RPCS.XI.114]

MARSHALL, JOHN, a smith from Glasgow, was transported to the West Indies in June 1678. [RPCS.V.474]

MARSHALL, JOHN, in Shotts, Lanarkshire, a rebel in Glasgow Tolbooth, was banished to the Plantations in June 1684, and transported via Glasgow aboard the Pelican bound for Carolina, bond by Walter Gibson, a merchant in Glasgow, dated 20 June 1684. [RPCS.IX.208][NRS.S/H]

MARSHALL, JOHN, then in Edinburgh Tolbooth, was transferred to Dunnottar Castle, Kincardineshire, on 29 July 1685. [ETR]; was transported via Leith aboard the Henry and Francis bound for East New Jersey on 5 September 1685, landed there on 7 December 1685. [RPCS.XI.167/289/292] [NWI.I.423]

MARSHALL, MICHAEL, from Strathaven, was transported via Leith aboard the Henry and Francis bound for East New Jersey on 5 September 1685, landed there on 7 December 1685. [RPCS.XI.159] [NJSA.EJ Deeds.Liber A, Fo.225]

MARSHALL, THOMAS, from Shotts, Lanarkshire, a rebel in Glasgow Tolbooth, was banished to the Plantations in June 1684, and transported via Glasgow aboard the Pelican bound for Carolina, bond by Walter Gibson, a merchant in Glasgow, dated 20 June 1684. [RPCS.IX.208]

MARSHALL, WILLIAM, was transported via Leith to Jamaica in August 1685, landed at Port Royal in November 1685. [RPCS.XI.329] [LJ.157

MARTIN, DANIEL, was captured at the Siege of Worcester in 1651, transported via London aboard the <u>John and Sarah</u> bound for Boston in December 1651, landed there in February 1652. [SD.1.5-6]

MARTIN, GEORGE, a notary, was executed in the Grassmarket of Edinburgh, 'for denying authority', on 22 February 1684. [ETR]

MARTIN, JAMES, a maltman in Greenock, who attended a conventicle near Greenock, was to be captured and imprisoned in Edinburgh Tolbooth in August 1684. [RPCS.IX.131]

MARTIN, JAMES, a tenant in Hemisfield for seeing rebel and not reporting it, was declared to be a rebel and fugitive in October 1684. [RPCS.IX.370]

MARTIN, JOHN, possibly from Stonehouse, Lanarkshire, was killed at the Battle of Drumclog on 1 June 1679

MARTIN, JOHN, from Borgue, Kirkcudbrightshire, MACQUHAN, ANDREW, from Kirkcudbright, fought at the Battle of Bothwell Bridge in 1679, was transported via Leith aboard the <u>Crown of London</u> bound for Barbados on 27 November 1679, was shipwrecked off Orkney on 10 December 1679 later transported to Jamaica. [RBM] [SW.202]

MARTIN, JOHN, in Ayr, a rebel in 1679, was tried in 1685. [NRS.JC39.75]; then in Edinburgh Tolbooth, was transferred to Dunnottar Castle, Kincardineshire, on 29 July 1685. [ETR]

MARTIN, JOHN, from Kirkmichael, Argyll, in Argyll's Rebellion, was transported via Leith aboard the <u>Henry and Francis</u> bound for East New Jersey on 5 September 1685, landed there on 7 December 1685] [ETR] [RPCS.XI.114/129/136/154/330] [NWI.I.423]

MARTIN, ROBERT, born 1592, was educated at the University of St Andrews, minister at Eckford, Roxburghshire, from 1641 until his death on 12 August 1665, he refused to conform to Episcopacy. [F.II.110]

MARTIN, ROBERT, clerk to the Justice Court, was tried for treason as an accessory to the Rebellion of 1679. [NRS.JC39.66]

MARTIN, ROBERT, in Nether Barndennoch and his wife Margaret Hidelstone and their son Robert Martin, for aiding rebels John MacMillan a chapman, Thomas Hunter in Dinduff, and seven others, were declared to be rebels and fugitives in October 1684. [RPCS.IX.361]

MASON, ALEXANDER, a prisoner in Edinburgh Tolbooth, to be transported to the Plantations on 11 August 1685. [ETR]

MASON, JOHN, was captured at the Battle of Dunbar in 1650, transported via London aboard the Unity bound for Boston in November 1650. [SCF.1226]

MATHER, AGNES, in the mills of Forth, for attending conventicles, was outlawed on 29 August 1672. [RPCS.III.583]

MATHER, DAVID, from Bridgeness, West Lothian, was transported in August 1670. [RPCS.III.206]

MATHER, JOHN, from Jedburgh, Roxburghshire, MACQUHAN, ANDREW, from Kirkcudbright, fought at the Battle of Bothwell Bridge in 1679, was transported via Leith aboard the Crown of London bound for Barbados on 27 November 1679, was shipwrecked and drowned off Orkney on 10 December 1679. [RBM]

MATHER, WILLIAM, in Mitchellslacks, for seeing William Harkness a rebel in July 1684, and not reporting it, was declared a rebel and fugitive in 1684. [RPCS.IX.359]

MATHIE, THOMAS, from Monklands, Lanarkshire, fought at the Battle of Bothwell Bridge in 1679, was transported via Leith aboard the Crown of London bound for Barbados on 27 November 1679, was shipwrecked and drowned off Orkney on 10 December 1679. [RBM] [SW.202]

MATHIESON, JOHN, tenant of Rosehill, Closeburn, Dumfries-shire, imprisoned in Canongait Tolbooth, was banished to the colonies on 19 June 1684, was transported via Leith to Carolina in June 1684, returned via New York in 1687, died on 1 October 1709. [ETR] [Closeburn gravestone, Thornhill, Dumfries-shire] [RPCS.XI.15]

MATHIESON, JOHN, a Captain of Lord Angus's Regiment, [the Cameronians], who fought at the Battle of Killiecrankie in 1689. [BK]

MAVOR, ALEXANDER, and his son Mark Mavor, from Glen Urquhart, was transported in 1685. [RPCS.X.165]

MAXTON, NEIL, was captured at the Siege of Worcester in 1651, transported via London aboard the John and Sarah bound for Boston in December 1651, landed there in February 1652. [SD.1.5-6]

MAXWELL, AGNES, was accused of rioting in Kirkcudbright in the parish of Irongray, in 1663, she subscribed to a bond on 17 August 1663, undertaking to stand at the market cross of Kirkcudbright bearing a notice accepting fault for causing a tumult. [RPCS.I.373/408]; a rioter, was imprisoned in Kirkcudbright Tolbooth, then to stand at the market cross there on two days in September 1683. [GC.105]

MAXWELL, ALEXANDER, was captured at the Battle of Dunbar in 1650, transported via London aboard the Unity bound for Boston in November 1650. [SCF.1226]

MAXWELL, CHARLES, from Nether Keir in Nithsdale, Dumfries-shire, was transported to the colonies in October 1684. [RPCS.X.587]

MAXWELL, DANIEL, was captured at the Siege of Worcester in 1651, transported via London aboard the John and Sarah bound for Boston in December 1651, landed there in February 1652. [SD.1.5-6]

MAXWELL, EDWARD, of Millingtoun, Holywood, for having his child baptised irregularly, was declared to be a rebel and fugitive in October 1684. [RPCS.IX.370]

MAXWELL, EDWARD, of Hills, was accused, in Kirkcudbright in October 1684, of aiding Gilbert Welch who fought in the Rebellion of 1679. [RPCS.IX.378]

MAXWELL, GABRIEL, son of John Maxwell of Stanelie, was educated at Glasgow University, minister of Dundonald, Ayrshire, from 1642, was chaplain to Lieutenant General Leslie's regiment in 1647, was at the Battle of Mauchline Moor in 1648 and in the Pentland Rising of 1666, was sought by the Justice Court in August 1667 for his part in the late rebellion. [GC.123] [RPCS.II.345];fled to Ireland in 1669. [F.3.35] [Cal.SP.Ire.1669]

MAXWELL, HUGH, of Dalswinton, Dumfries-shire, for aiding rebels, John Johnstone, also Robert Neilson and family, and Robert Morrein, was declared a rebel and fugitive in October 1684. [RPCS.IX.372/555]; was warded in Edinburgh Tolbooth on 28 November 1684. [ETR]

MAXWELL, JAMES, from Cathcart, Glasgow, was transported via Leith aboard the St Michael of Scarborough bound for the West Indies on 12 December 1678.
[RPCS.VI.76]

MAXWELL, JAMES, the younger, from Cathcart, Glasgow, was transported via Leith aboard the St Michael of Scarborough bound for the West Indies on 12 December 1678. [RPCS.VI.76]

MAXWELL, JOHN, in Gribtoun, was indited in Dumfries for harbouring James McGill in Gribtoun, a declared traitor, in 1684. [RPCS.IX.555]

MAXWELL, ROBERT, from Cathcart, Glasgow, was transported via Leith aboard the St Michael of Scarborough bound for the West Indies on 12 December 1678. [RPCS.VI.76]

MAXWELL, WILLIAM, of Monreif, the younger, was sought by the Justice Court in August 1667 for his part in the late rebellion. [GC.123] [RPCS.II.1667]

MAXWELL, ROBERT, born 1611 in Glasgow, was educated at Glasgow University, minister at Monkton and Prestwick, Ayrshire, from 1640 until 1665, having refused to conform to Episcopacy he was deposed, in 1677 he was imprisoned for holding conventicles, he died in Bogton House, Cathcart, Glasgow, on 26 March 1686. [F.III.56] [Glasgow Cathedral gravestone]

MAXWELL, ZACHARIE, was warded in Edinburgh Tolbooth, on 8 October 1684. [ETR]

MECHLANE, ELIZABETH, was transported to the colonies in October 1684. [RPCS.X.251]

MEIKLE, ROBERT, a minister, was transported via Leith aboard the St Michael of Scarborough bound for the West Indies on 12 December 1678. RPCS.VI.76]

MELDRUM, GEORGE, a minister from Crombie, Aberchirder a prisoner in Edinburgh Tolbooth on 17 June 1685, was transported to the colonies in February 1685. [ETR][RPCS.X.165]

MEIN, ALEXANDER, from Kirkcudbright, was transported to the colonies in October 1684. [RPCS.X.257]

MELVILL, ROBERT, minister at Simprin, Berwickshire, from 1641, was chaplain to the Army to the Solemn League and Covenant in Newcastle in 1644, died around 1653. [F.II.62] [RHCA]

MENZIES, ANDREW, in Beckbie, was accused, in Kirkcudbright in October 1684, of conversing with rebel John Corsan, in Summer 1683. [RPCS.IX.376]

MENZIES, EDWARD, servant to Margaret Frisell, for conversing with rebels William and Thomas Harkness at Mitchellslacks in August 1684, was declared a rebel and fugitive in 1684. [RPCS.IX.359]

MENZIES, GEORGE, in Gaitslack, Dumfries-shire, for aiding rebels Thomas and William Harkness at his shieling at Kirkop, was declared a rebel and fugitive in October 1684. [RPCS.IX.372]

MERCER, ROBERT, chaplain to Aldie's Horse Regiment, in the Army of the Kingdom, was captured at the Siege of Worcester in 1651. [RHCA.360]

MERCHISTON, ROBERT, born 1637, son of Reverend David Merchiston in Ormiston, was educated at Edinburgh University minister at Kirkpatrick-Juxta -Dungree from 1664 until 1681 when he was deprived for refusing to take the Test Act, he died on 5 November 1697. [F.II.211]

MERK, JAMES, chaplain of Rothiemay's Regiment of Foot, was captured at the Siege of Worcester in 1651. [RHCA.396]

MIDDLETON, JOHN, Colonel of Middleton's Regiment of Horse in the Army of the Solemn League and Covenant until 1647. Later became Earl of Middleton by Charles II, and in 1666 the Governor of Tangier where he died. [RHCA.170][Z.181]

MILLER, ALEXANDER, in Colliston, for attending conventicles, was outlawed on 29 August 1672. [RPCS.III.583]

MILLER, ALEXANDER, was captured at the Siege of Worcester in 1651, transported via London aboard the John and Sarah bound for Boston in December 1651, landed there in February 1652. [SD.1.5-6]

MILLER, ANDREW, born 1630, was educated at Glasgow University, minister at Dailly, Ayrshire, from 1660 until deprived in 1662, minister in Neilston, Renfrewshire, from 1672 until 15 October 1684 when he was imprisoned in Edinburgh Tolbooth and in Blackness Castle until 12 March 1685 when he was released, he died in January 1686. [F.III.158] [ETR]

MILLER, JAMES, in Colliston, for attending conventicles, was outlawed on 29 August 1672. [RPCS.III.583]

MILLER, JAMES, from Kirkcaldy, Fife, was transported via Leith aboard the <u>St Michael of Scarborough</u> bound for the West Indies on 12 December 1678. [RPCS.VI.76]

MILLER, JOHN, from Glasford, Lanarkshire, fought at the Battle of Bothwell Bridge in 1679, was transported via Leith aboard the <u>Crown of London</u> bound for Barbados on 27 November 1679, was shipwrecked and drowned off Orkney on 10 December 1679. [RBM] [SW.202]

MILLER, JOHN, in Greenhead, a prisoner in Glasgow Tolbooth, accused of participating in the recent rebellion, to be taken to Edinburgh Tolbooth, in June 1684. [RPCS.IX.1]

MILLER, THOMAS, from Ceres, Fife, fought at the Battle of Bothwell Bridge in 1679, was transported via Leith aboard the <u>Crown of London</u> bound for Barbados on 27 November 1679, was shipwrecked off Orkney on 10 December 1679, later transported to Jamaica. [RBM] [SW.200] [CEC.212/5] [ETR]

MILLER THOMAS, fought at the Battle of Bothwell Bridge in 1679, was transported via Leith aboard the <u>Crown of London</u> bound for Barbados on 27 November 1679, was shipwrecked and drowned off Orkney on 10 December 1679. [RBM]

MILLER, WILLIAM, from Glasgow, fought at the Battle of Bothwell Bridge in 1679, was transported via Leith aboard the <u>Crown of London</u> bound for Barbados on 27 November 1679, was shipwrecked and drowned off Orkney on 10 December 1679. [RBM] [SW.202]

MILLER, WILLIAM, from Monklands, Lanarkshire, fought at the Battle of Bothwell Bridge in 1679, was transported via Leith aboard the <u>Crown of London</u> bound for Barbados on 27 November 1679, was shipwrecked and drowned off Orkney on 10 December 1679. [RBM] [SW.202]

MILLER, WILLIAM, from Glencairn, Nithsdale, , fought at the Battle of Bothwell Bridge in 1679, was transported via Leith aboard the <u>Crown of London</u> bound for Barbados on 27

November 1679, was shipwrecked off Orkney on 10 December 1679, later transported to Jamaica. [RBM] [SW.202] [CEC.212/5]

MILLIGAN, JOHN, from Glencairn, Nithsdale, , fought at the Battle of Bothwell Bridge in 1679, was transported via Leith aboard the Crown of London bound for Barbados on 27 November 1679, was shipwrecked and drowned off Orkney on 10 December 1679. [RBM] [SW.202] [CEC.212/5]

MILLIGAN, THOMAS, from Glencairn, Nithsdale, , fought at the Battle of Bothwell Bridge in 1679, was transported via Leith aboard the Crown of London bound for Barbados on 27 November 1679, was shipwrecked off Orkney on 10 December 1679, later transported to Jamaica. [RBM] [SW.202] [CEC.212/5]

MILLER, PATRICK, in Orphat, for attending conventicles, was outlawed on 29 August 1672. [RPCS.III.583]

MILLER, ROBERT, a mason in the parish of Rutherglen, Lanarkshire, a Covenanter in 1679, imprisoned in Edinburgh Tolbooth, was tried in 1685, then hanged at the Gallowlee on 28 January 1685. [NRS.JC39.67] [ETR]

MILLER, ROBERT, was educated at the University of Glasgow, minister at Ochiltree, Ayrshire, from 1661 until deprived in 1662, a minister in exile in Leiden in the Netherlands from 1662 until 1669, he also went to France and returned to Scotland in 1669. [SEC]

MILLER, ROBERT, a shoemaker in Kinswaid, for attending conventicles, was outlawed on 29 August 1672. [RPCS.III.583]

MILLER, THOMAS, and his spouse Elspeth Ferguson in Glan Gar, for aiding rebels Thomas Hunter in Breckinside, Thomas Hunter in Woodend, and …..MacTurk, were declared to be rebels and fugitives in October 1684. [RPCS.IX.365]

MILLER, WILLIAM, a prisoner in Dumfries Tolbooth, was transferred to Edinburgh Tolbooth in September 1668. [RPCS.II.536]

MILLER, ......, of Waxford, was fined 300 merks for attending a conventicle in Ayrshire in 1668. [RPCS.II.444]

MILLIGAN, GEORGE, in Buss, having conversed with William Milligan a rebel and fugitive, was also declared to be a rebel, and fugitive in 1684. [RPCS.IX.359]

MILLIGAN, JAMES, in Knocknou, was accused, in Kirkcudbright on 4 October 1684 of aiding Mr Renwick and other rebels in 1684. [RPCS.IX.377]

MILLIGAN, JANET, a servant in Airkland, for seeing rebels Gilbert Gilchrist and John MacColl but not reporting it, was declared to be a rebel and fugitive in October 1684. [RPCS.IX.363]

MILLIGAN, JOHN, from Glencairn, Nithsdale, fought at the Battle of Bothwell Bridge in 1679, was transported via Leith aboard the Crown of London bound for Barbados on 27 November 1679, was shipwrecked and drowned off Orkney on 10 December 1679. [RBM] [SW.202] [CEC.212/5]

MILLIGAN, JOHN, in Floors, for aiding his brother and rebel, William Milligan, was declared to be a rebel and fugitive, in September 1684. [RPCS.IX.373]

MILLIGAN, JOHN, in Burn, for conversing with his son John Milligan, a fugitive who had escaped from Dumfries Tolbooth, for aiding a rebel and fugitive, was declared to be a rebel and fugitive, in September 1684. [RPCS.IX.373]

MILLIGAN, ROBERT, was killed at Scarvating in 1679. [Nithsdale Martyrs Monument, Dumfries-shire]

MILLIGAN, ROBERT, in Breckinside, for aiding rebels, William Corsan from Jedburgh and John Gibson in Englistoun, was declared to be a rebel and fugitive in October 1684. [RPCS.IX.368]

MILLIGAN, THOMAS, from Glencairn, Nithsdale, fought at the Battle of Bothwell Bridge in 1679, was transported via Leith aboard the Crown of London bound for Barbados on 27 November 1679, was shipwrecked off Orkney on 10 December 1679, later transported to Jamaica. [RBM] [SW.202] [CEC.212/5]

MILLIGAN, WILLIAM, a rebel imprisoned in Dumfries Tolbooth, escaped in 1684; his wife Margaret Milligan, having harbouring and aiding him, was declared to be a rebel, she was transported to the colonies in October 1684. [RPCS.IX.359; X.587]

MILNE, WILLIAM, a tenant farmer in Kincorth, Aberdeenshire, was killed on 10 July 1645. [St Fittock's church, Nigg, Aberdeenshire]

MILROY, JOHN, a chapman on the Fyntulloch Estate, Wigtownshire, was executed in 1685. [Wigtown gravestone]

MILWARD, DAVID, was captured at the Siege of Worcester in 1651, transported via London aboard the John and Sarah bound for Boston in December 1651, landed there in February 1652. [SD.1.5-6]

MILWARD, JAMES, was captured at the Siege of Worcester in 1651, transported via London aboard the John and Sarah bound for Boston in December 1651, landed there in February 1652. [SD.1.5-6]

MIRRIE, JAMES, from Cumnock, Ayrshire, fought at the Battle of Bothwell Bridge in 1679, was transported via Leith aboard the Crown of London bound for Barbados on 27 November 1679, was shipwrecked and drowned off Orkney on 10 December 1679. [RBM]

MIRRIE, JOHN, was warded in Edinburgh Tolbooth on 4 March 1684 and liberated on 8 March 1684. [ETR]

MITCHELL, JAMES, a minister who fought at Rullion Green, was sought by the Justice Court in August 1667 for his part in the late rebellion, and the assassination of Bishop Honeyman of Orkney in Edinburgh in July 1668, was imprisoned on the BassRock and executed in 1678. [GC.123] [RPCS.II.345][Z.197]

MITCHELL, JAMES, was captured at the Siege of Worcester in 1651, transported via London aboard the John and Sarah bound for Boston in December 1651, landed there in February 1652. [SD.1.5-6]

MITCHELL, JAMES, from Midlothian, a former student of theology at Edinburgh University and veteran of the Battle of Rullion Green, was accused of the attempted murder of Archbishop Sharp in Blackfriars Wynd, Edinburgh, was imprisoned on the Bass Rock for four years, trial papers, 1678, and executed. [NRS.JC39.30][Z.197/202]

MITCHELL, JOHN, in Braehead, Mauchline, Ayrshire, a prisoner in Canongait Tolbooth, having signed a bond was released on 23 August 1684. [RPCS.IX.314]

MITCHELL, JOHN, was transported via Leith to Jamaica in August 1685. [RPCS.XI.136]

MITCHELL, ROBERT, was killed at Ingliston in 1685. [Nithsdale Martyrs Monument, Dumfries-shire]

MOFFATT, JAMES, a prisoner in Edinburgh or Canongait Tolbooth, a rebel, was banished to the Plantations in Carolina on 8 August 1684. [RPCS.IX.95]

MOFFAT, JEAN, was transported via Leith aboard the Henry and Francis bound for East New Jersey on 5 September 1685, landed there on 7 December 1685. [RPCS.XI.154/290][NWI.I.423]

MOLLISON, ALEXANDER, was captured at the Siege of Worcester in 1651, transported via London aboard the John and Sarah bound for Boston in December 1651, landed there in February 1652. [SD.1.5-6]

MONCREIFF, ALEXANDER, was baptised on 16 December 1613 in Dunbarney, was educated at Edinburgh University, minister at Scoonie, Fife, from 1643 until 1661, was accused of holding conventicles and imprisoned in Edinburgh Castle in August 1660, [RPCS.VIII.465]; in 1671 he was accused of holding conventicles, he died on 6 October 1688 and was buried in Grayfriars, Edinburgh. [F.V.117]

MONCREIFF, JOHN, born 1605, was educated at St Andrews University, minister at Collessie, Fife, from 1628 to 1639, then minister of Kinghorn Easter, Fife, from 1639 until his death in

1650, he accompanied the army to England and was present at the Battle of Marston Moor in 1644. [F.V.94]

MONORGAN, GILBERT, was transported via Leith aboard the Henry and Francis bound for East New Jersey on 5 September 1685, died at sea. [RPCS.XI.162][NWI.I.423]

MONRO, ALEXANDER, of Beircrofts, a prisoner in Edinburgh Tolbooth, was transferred to either Stirling, Dunbarton or Blackness Castles on 19 September 1684. [ETR]

MONRO, DONALD, was captured at the Siege of Worcester in 1651, transported via London aboard the John and Sarah bound for Boston in December 1651, landed there in February 1652. [SD.1.5-6]

MONRO, GEORGE, a Captain of Lord Angus's Regiment, [the Cameronians], who fought at the Battle of Killiecrankie in 1689. [BK]

MONRO, HUGH, was captured at the Siege of Worcester in 1651, transported via London aboard the John and Sarah bound for Boston in December 1651, landed there in February 1652. [SD.1.5-6]

MONRO, JOHN, was captured at the Siege of Worcester in 1651, transported via London aboard the John and Sarah bound for Boston in December 1651, landed there in February 1652. [SD.1.5-6]

MONRO, ROBERT, was captured at the Siege of Worcester in 1651, transported via London aboard the John and Sarah bound for Boston in December 1651, landed there in February 1652. [SD.1.5-6]

MONROE, ROBERT, a Colonel of the Covenanters pre 1640, a Major General in the 1640s [NRS.GD188.19.1]; a Captain of Lord Angus's Regiment, [The Cameronians], who fought at the Battle of Dunkeld in August 1689. [BK]

MONTEITH, ALEXANDER, 'a sweet singer', [a cult], was transported via Leith to New York in May 1684. [RPCS.VIII.709]

MONTGOMERY, ADAM, son of Adam Montgomery of McViehill, a merchant and guildsbrother of Edinburgh, was killed at the Siege of Worcester in 1651. [EBR, a petition in 1659]

MONTGOMERY, ALEXANDER, a sievewright from Linlithgow, West Lothian, was transported via Leith to Carolina in June 1684. [RPCS.VIII.524/630]

MONTGOMERY, HUGH, Viscount Ards, supported fervently Calvinist ministers in Ulster, such as Josias Welsh. [SHR.99]

MONTGOMERY, HUGH, from Falkirk, Stirlingshire, fought at the Battle of Bothwell Bridge in 1679, was transported via Leith aboard the Crown of London bound for Barbados on 27 November 1679, was shipwrecked off Orkney on 10 December 1679, later transported to Jamaica. [RBM] [SW.201] [CEC.212/5]

MONTGOMERY, JOHN, of Ballevegley, County Antrim, fought at the Battle of Dunbar on 1 September 1650, and at the Siege of Worcester in September 1651 where he was captured and transported to Virginia, a petition in 1661. [SP.Ire.306/959]

MONTGOMERY. .........., of Langshaw, was tried for treason as an accessory to the Rebellion of 1679, in 1666. [NRS.JC39.66]

MONTROSE [?], LAUGHLIN, was captured at the Siege of Worcester in 1651, transported via London aboard the John and Sarah bound for Boston in December 1651, landed there in February 1652. [SD.1.5-6]

MOODIE, INGRAM, was captured at the Battle of Dunbar in 1650, transported via London aboard the Unity bound for Boston in November 1650. [SCF.1226]

MOORE, DONALD, was banished to the colonies on 7 August 1685, transported via Leith to East New Jersey in September 1685. [RPCS.XI.126/131/136]

MOORE, GEORGE, probably from Glasgow, was banished to the colonies on 18 August 1685, and transported via Leith aboard the

Henry and Francis bound for East New Jersey on 5 September 1685, landed there on 7 December 1685. [RPCS.XI.154/290/292] [NWI.I.423]

MOORE, JAMES, was captured at the Siege of Worcester in 1651, transported via London aboard the John and Sarah bound for Boston in December 1651, landed there in February 1652. [SD.1.5-6]

MOORE, JOHN, was captured at the Siege of Worcester in 1651, transported via London aboard the John and Sarah bound for Boston in December 1651, landed there in February 1652. [SD.1.5-6]

MOORE, ROBERT, from Carluke, Lanarkshire, was transported via Leith to Jamaica in 1685, landed at Port Royal in November 1685. [RPCS.XI.136] [LJ.169]

MOOR, WILLIAM, from Stirling, was transported to the colonies in March 1685. [RPCS.X.206]

MORCOT, [?], ALEXANDER, was captured at the Siege of Worcester in 1651, transported via London aboard the John and Sarah bound for Boston in December 1651, landed there in February 1652. [SD.1.5-6]

MORE,......, was captured at the Siege of Worcester in 1651, transported via London aboard the John and Sarah bound for Boston in December 1651, landed there in February 1652. [SD.1.5-6]

MORE, ......, from Bothwell, Lanarkshire, fought at the Battle of Bothwell Bridge in 1679, was transported via Leith aboard the Crown of London bound for Barbados on 27 November 1679, was shipwrecked off Orkney on 10 December 1679, later transported to Jamaica. [RBM] [SW.198] [CEC.212/5]

MORRIS, ROBERT, was killed in Sanquhar, Dumfries-shire, 16... [Nithsdale Martyrs Monument, Dumfries-shire]

MORRISON, DONALD, from Argyll, in Argyll's Rebellion, was transported via Leith to Jamaica in August 1685. [RPCS.XI.136]

MORISON, JAMES, in Halls, the younger, a rebel, subscribed to a bond of the peace in October 1668. [RPCS.II.548]

MORISON, JOHN, in Huikheid, a rebel, subscribed to a bond of the peace in October 1668. [RPCS.II.548]

MORRISON, JOHN, from Airth, Stirlingshire, fought at the Battle of Bothwell Bridge in 1679, was transported via Leith aboard the Crown of London bound for Barbados on 27 November 1679, was shipwrecked and drowned off Orkney on 10 December 1679. [RBM]

MORRISON, JOHN, from Erickstane, Dumfries-shire, was transported to the colonies in October 1684. [RPCS.X.275]

MORISON. ........, daughters of Steven Morison a ropespinner in Greenock, who attended a conventicle near Greenock, was to be captured and imprisoned in Edinburgh Tolbooth in August 1684. [RPCS.IX.131]

MORRIS, WALTER, in Arlary, for attending conventicles, was outlawed on 29 August 1672. [RPCS.III.583]

MORRIS, WILLIAM, in Midtoun, for attending conventicles, was outlawed on 29 August 1672. [RPCS.III.583]

MORTON, DAVID, guilty of conducting an irregular marriage, was transported via Leith to America on 22 June 1671. [RPCS.III.13/688]

MORTON, JAMES, a maltman in Greenock, who attended a conventicle near Greenock, was to be captured and imprisoned in Edinburgh Tolbooth in August 1684. [RPCS.IX.131]

MORTON, JOHN, a tenant in Evandale, a prisoner in Canongait Tolbooth, having signed a bond was released on 23 August 1684. [RPCS.IX.315]

MORTON, PATRICK, was captured at the Siege of Worcester in 1651, transported via London aboard the John and Sarah bound for Boston in December 1651, landed there in February 1652. [SD.1.5-6]

MOSMAN, GEORGE, a merchant in Edinburgh, was fined for attending a conventicle in widow Paton's house in February 1669. [RPCS.II.626]

MOSSMAN, JAMES, of Mount, was transported via Leith aboard the St Michael of Scarborough bound for East New Jersey on 12 December 1678. [RPCS.VI.76]

MOWAT, MATTHEW, born 1603, was educated at Glasgow University, a minister in Kilmarnock, Ayrshire, from 1641, was at the Battle of Mauchline Moor in June 1648, for refusing to take the Oath of Allegiance, was deposed and ordered to move out of the parish, on 16 September 1662, he died in December 1669. [RPCS.I263] [F.III.105]

MOWATT, ROBERT, a minister who was warded in Edinburgh Tolbooth on 27 November 1684. [ETR]

MOWBRAY, DAVID, a shoemaker, was accused of rioting in Edinburgh in 1686. [NRS.JC39.90]

MOWBRAY, JOHN, a shoemaker in Strathmiglo, Fife, for attending conventicles, was outlawed on 29 August 1672. [RPCS.III.583]

MOUBRAY, THOMAS, from Kirkliston, West Lothian, was transported via Leith aboard the St Michael of Scarborough bound for East New Jersey on 12 December 1678. [RPCS.VI.76]

MUDIE, SARA, in Dalricket Mill, Ayrshire, a rebel in 1684. [RPCS.IX.544]

MUIR, ADAM, was taken from Edinburgh Tolbooth on 29 July 1685, then transported via Leith to the conies in July 1685. [ETR] [RPCS.XI.114]

MUIR, ALEXANDER, in Drumclog, a rebel, subscribed to a bond of the peace in October 1668. [RPCS.II.548]

MUIR, GEORGE, in Rutherglen, who attended a conventicle near Greenock, was to be captured and imprisoned in Edinburgh

Tolbooth in August 1684. [RPCS.IX.131], was transported via Leith to America in August 1685. [RCS.XI.154]

MUIR, GILBERT, in Arminnie, was accused in Kirkcudbright of conversing with a rebel and fugitive, William Russell, in 1684. [RPCS.IX.374]

MUIR, HELEN, spouse to Patrick Carsan, was accused of rioting in Kirkcudbright in the parish of Irongray, in 1663. [RPCS.I.373]

MUIR, JAMES, from Lesmahagow, was transported via Leith to New York in May 1684. [RPCS.VIII.516]

MUIR, JAMES, of Cessford boat, was executed in the Grassmarket of Edinburgh, 'for denying authority', on 22 February 1684. [ETR]

MUIR, JANET, daughter of James Muir in Balgredane, Buittle, Kirkcudbrightshire, a fugitive and fanatic in 1684. [RPCS.IX.571]

MUIR, MARION, spouse of James Scott a seaman in Greenock, who attended a conventicle near Greenock, was to be captured and imprisoned in Edinburgh Tolbooth in August 1684. [RPCS.IX.131]

MUIR, PATRICK, brother of the laird of Rowallan, was brought from Tweedmouth, England, and was warded in Edinburgh Tolbooth on 20 October 1684, was liberated on 13 December 1684. [ETR]

MUIR, ROBERT, took part in Argyll's Rebellion, was banished to the Plantations on 31 July 1685, then transported via Leith aboard the Henry and Francis bound for East New Jersey on 5 September 1685, landed there. [RPCS.XI.129/130/136/137/330] [NJSA.EJD.Liber A, fo.226]

MUIR, THOMAS, a prisoner in Canongait Tolbooth, subscribed to a bond that he would behave regularly and attend his parish church, subject to a fine of 500 merks, dated 22 September 1684. [RPCS.IX.391]

MUIR, WILLIAM, of Caldwell, was sought by the Justice Court in August 1667 for his part in the late rebellion. [GC.123]

MUIR, WILLIAM, from Stirling, was transported via Leith aboard the Henry and Francis bound for East New Jersey on 5 September 1685, landed there. [RPCS.X.206]

MUIRHEAD, GAVIN, from Cambusnethan, Lanarkshire, was transported via Leith t New York in May 1684. [RPCS.VIII.516]

MUIRHEAD, JAMES, in Strachan, Holywood, for conversing with rebel John Smith in April 1684, was declared to be a rebel and fugitive, a prisoner in Edinburgh or Canongait Tolbooth, a rebel, was banished to the Plantations in Carolina on 8 August 1684. [RPCS.IX.95/370]

MUIRHEAD, JAMES, of Bredisome, was warded in Edinburgh Tolbooth on 24 December 1684, was transported via Leith aboard the Henry and Francis bound for East New Jersey on 5 September 1685, landed there on 7 December 1685.
[ETR][RPCS.XI.126/129/159/330][NWI.I.423]

MUIRHEAD, JOHN, a baillie of Dumfries, was captured near Carbelly Hill in 1684, died in Leith Tolbooth in 1685. [Nithsdale Martyrs Monument, Dumfries-shire] [GC.374]

MUIRHEAD, JOHN, a prisoner in Edinburgh Tolbooth, was transported via Leith aboard the Henry and Francis bound for East New Jersey in August 1685. [ETR]

MUIRHEAD, MARGARET, a prisoner in Edinburgh or Canongait Tolbooth, a rebel, was banished to the Plantations in Carolina on 8 August 1684. [RPCS.IX.95]

MUNCIE, JAMES, was warded in Edinburgh Tolbooth on 28 May 1685. [ETR]; died in Edinburgh Tolbooth, 16... [Nithsdale Martyrs Monument, Dumfries-shire]

MUNDELL, JOHN, a prisoner in Edinburgh Tolbooth, to be transported to the Plantations on 11 August 1685, but died in Edinburgh Tolbooth in 1685. [Nithsdale Martyrs Monument, Dumfries-shire] [ETR]

MUNGALL, WILLIAM, was captured at the Siege of Worcester in 1651, transported via London aboard the John and Sarah bound for Boston in December 1651, landed there in February 1652. [SD.1.5-6]

MUNRO, HUGH, a prisoner in Edinburgh Tolbooth, willing to go to America was released to go there on 17 December 1685, was transported via Leith aboard the John and Nicholas bound for Barbados in December 1685. [ETR]

MUNRO, WILLIAM, born 1625, was captured at the Siege of Worcester in 1651, transported via London aboard the John and Sarah bound for Boston in December 1651, landed there in February 1652. [SG.14.2.46]

MUNSIE, JAMES, for seeing young Thomas Harkness a rebel who had escaped from Dumfries Tolbooth, and not reporting it was declared a rebel and fugitive in 1684. [RPCS.IX.359]

MURDOCH, ANDREW, from Kinneil, Bo'ness, West Lothian, fought at the Battle of Bothwell Bridge in 1679, was transported via Leith aboard the Crown of London bound for Barbados on 27 November 1679, was shipwrecked and drowned off Orkney on 10 December 1679. [RBM]

MURDOCH, HUGH, servant to Andrew Brown in Boghead, a prisoner in Canongait Tolbooth, having signed a bond, was released in 1684. [RPCS.IX.315]

MURIE, ANDREW, from Glen Devon, Perthshire, fought at the Battle of Bothwell Bridge in 1679, was transported via Leith aboard the Crown of London bound for Barbados on 27 November 1679, was shipwrecked and drowned off Orkney on 10 December 1679. [RBM]

MURIE, JOHN, from Glen Devon, Perthshire, fought at the Battle of Bothwell Bridge in 1679, was transported via Leith aboard the Crown of London bound for Barbados on 27 November 1679, was shipwrecked and drowned off Orkney on 10 December 1679. [RBM]

MURRAY, ALEXANDER, fought at the Battle of Bothwell Bridge in 1679, was transported via Leith aboard the Crown of London bound for Barbados on 27 November 1679, was shipwrecked off Orkney on 10 December 1679, later was transported to Jamaica. [RBM] [CEC.212/5][SW.202]

MURRAY, ANNA, a prisoner in Edinburgh Tolbooth, to be transported to the Plantations on 11 August 1685. [ETR]

MURRAY, ANTHONY, minister at Kirkmichael, was warded in Edinburgh Tolbooth, on 15 October 1684, and released on 23 October 1684. [ETR]

MURRAY, HUGH, a cottar in Auchenleck, Ayrshire, a prisoner in Canongait Tolbooth, having signed a bond was released on 23 August 1684. [RPCS.IX.315]

MURRAY, JAMES, was captured at the Siege of Worcester in 1651, transported via London aboard the John and Sarah bound for Boston in December 1651, landed there in February 1652. [SD.1.5-6]

MURRAY, JAMES, was banished to the Plantations on 30 July 1685, then transported via Leith aboard the Henry and Francis bound for East New Jersey on 5 August 1685, landed there on 7 December 1685. [RPCS.XI.330][NWI.I.423]

MURRAY, JOHN, a minister, was accused of holding conventicles and imprisoned in Edinburgh Castle in August 1660. [RPCS.VIII.465]

MURRAY, JOHN, was captured at the Siege of Worcester in 1651, transported via London aboard the John and Sarah bound for Boston in December 1651, landed there in February 1652. [SD.1.5-6]

MURRAY, JOHN, a prisoner in Edinburgh Tolbooth in May 1685. [ETR]

MURRAY, JONAS, was captured at the Siege of Worcester in 1651, transported via London aboard the John and Sarah bound for

Boston in December 1651, landed there in February 1652. [SD.1.5-6]

MURRAY, NEIL, was captured at the Siege of Worcester in 1651, transported via London aboard the <u>John and Sarah</u> bound for Boston in December 1651, landed there in February 1652. [SD.1.5-6]

MURRAY, ROBERT, of Guilfoot, Dumfries-shire, was indicted for 'hearing and recepting rebellious preachers', in 1684. [RPCS.IX.555]

MUTRAY, ALEXANDER, from Midcalder, Midlothian, fought at the Battle of Bothwell Bridge in 1679, was transported via Leith aboard the <u>Crown of London</u> bound for Barbados on 27 November 1679, was shipwrecked and drowned off Orkney on 10 December 1679. [RBM]

NAIRN, ALEXANDER, of St Ford in Fife, and his wife Elizabeth, were fined 3,300 pounds Scots, on 24 July 1683, for attending conventicles. [RPCS.IX.110]

NAIRN, GEORGE, a minister, was accused of holding conventicles and imprisoned in Edinburgh Castle in August 1660, [RPCS.VIII.465]

NAIRN, ROBERT, a shoemaker in Bonhill, Dunbartonshire, died on 15 April 1685. [Bonhill gravestone]

NAPIER, JAMES, was warded in Edinburgh Tolbooth on 20 May 1685, but having subscribed to the Test Act, was released on 28 May 1685. [ETR]

NASMITH, JAMES, of Heughhead, born 1614, was educated at Edinburgh University, a minister at Dalmellington from 1641 until 1645. then in Hamilton, Lanarkshire from 1645 until 16 September 1662, when for refusing to take the Oath of Allegiance, was deposed and order to move out of the parish, in 1647 he was chaplain to Major General Holburn's Regiment, he returned to Hamilton in 1672, and died on 3 September 1674. [F.III.254] [RPCS.I263]

NEAL, JOHN, was captured at the Siege of Worcester in 1651, transported via London aboard the John and Sarah bound for Boston in December 1651, landed there in February 1652. [SD.1.5-6]

NEAVE, JOHN, born 1606, was educated at King's College, Aberdeen, was at the Battle of Mauchline Moor in June 1648, on 23 December 1662 he was banished from HM Dominions and went to Holland where he died in 1672. [F.III.120]

NEILSON, JOHN, from St Ninian's, Stirlingshire, fought at the Battle of Bothwell Bridge in 1679, was transported via Leith aboard the Crown of London bound for Barbados on 27 November 1679, was shipwrecked and drowned off Orkney on 10 December 1679. [RBM]

NEILSON, JOHN, of Corsock Castle, fought in the Pentland Rising, captured at the Battle of Rullion Green, and hanged in Edinburgh on 14 December 1686. [Kirkpatrick-Durham gravestone, Kirkcudbrightshire]

NEILSON, ROBERT, of Corsock, fought at the Battle of Rullion Green in 1666, was imprisoned and tortured. [Z.195]

NEWBIGGING, ANDREW, from Bowden, Roxburghshire, fought at the Battle of Bothwell Bridge in 1679, was transported via Leith aboard the Crown of London bound for Barbados on 27 November 1679, was shipwrecked and drowned off Orkney on 10 December 1679. [RBM] [ETR]

NICOL, JAMES, a vagabond in Peebles-shire, was tried in 1684 for his part in the 1679 Rebellion. [NRS.JC39.50]; he had judicially disowned the king, adhered to the Covenant also to the Sanquhar and Rutherglen Declarations, and would fight for the Covenant, August 1684. [RPCS.IX.109]; was executed for rebellion in the Grassmarket of Edinburgh on 27 September 1684. [ETR]

NICOLL, JOHN, was transported via Leith to Jamaica in August 1685. [RPCS.XI.236]

NICOLL, SIMON, was warded in Edinburgh Tolbooth on 28 May 1685, but having subscribed to the Test Act, was released on 28 May 1685. [ETR]

NIMMO, WILLIAM, a tailor in West Calder, a rebel and rioter, was banished and transported to Virginia, on 30 July 1668. [RPCS.II.503]

NIMMO, Mrs, wife of William Nimmo a rioter in Calder and now a fugitive, to be imprisoned in Edinburgh Tolbooth in June 1668. [RPCS.II.470]

NISBET, ALEXANDER, of Tarbolton, Ayrshire, was at the Battle of Rullion Green in 1666. [Z.193]

NISBET, JAMES, of Highside, Darvel, Ayrshire, was executed at Howgate Head on 5 June 1684. [Townhead Martyrs Memorial, Glasgow]

NISBET, JOHN, a woolfiner in Glasgow, a rebel in Glasgow Tolbooth, was banished to the Plantations in June 1684, and transported via Glasgow aboard the Pelican bound for Carolina, bond by Walter Gibson, a merchant in Glasgow, dated 20 June 1684. [RPCS.IX.208]

NISBET, JOHN, a minister in exile in Utrecht in the Netherlands from 1685 to 1686. [SEC]

NISBET, JOHN, of Hardhill, a Covenanter in 1679, fought at the Battles of Pentland, Drumclog, and Bothwell Bridge, was tried in 1685, and executed on 4 December 1685. [NRS.JC39.69]

NISBET, ROBERT, of Greenholme, a prisoner in Edinburgh Tolbooth, having subscribed to a bond was released on 27 August 1684. [RPCS.IX.318]

NISBET, SAMUEL, from Nenthorn, Berwickshire, fought at the Battle of Bothwell Bridge in 1679, was transported via Leith aboard the Crown of London bound for Barbados on 27 November 1679, was shipwrecked and drowned off Orkney on 10 December 1679. [RBM]

NIVEN, WILLIAM, from Cathcart, Glasgow, was transported via Leith aboard the <u>St Michael of Scarborough</u> bound for the West Indies on 12 December 1678. [RPCS.VI.76]

NIVEN, WILLIAM, a tenant farmer of Maxwell of Pollock, was transported via Leith aboard the <u>Henry and Francis</u> bound for East New Jersey on 5 September 1685, landed there on 7 December 1685. [RPCS.XI.155][NWI.I.423]

NIVISON, ALEXANDER, in Kirkboig, a rebel and fugitive in 1684. [RPCS.IX.360]

OCHILTREE, DAVID, was transported via Leith to Jamaica in August 1685. [RPCS.XI.329]

OLIPHANT, JOHN, minister at Stonehouse, Lanarkshire, was warded in Edinburgh Tolbooth, on 15 October 1684. [ETR]

OLIPHANT, WILLIAM, then in Edinburgh Tolbooth, was transferred to Dunnottar Castle, Kincardineshire, on 29 July 1685, was banished to the Plantations on 18 August 1685, then transported via Leith aboard the <u>Henry and Francis</u> bound for East New Jersey on 5 August 1685, landed there on 7 December 1685. [ETR][RPCS.XI.154/289/292][NWI.I.423]

OLIPHANT, WILLIAM, a Lieutenant of Lord Angus's Regiment, [The Cameronians], fought at the Battle of Dunkeld in August 1679. [BK]

OLIVER, JAMES, from Jedburgh Forest, Roxburghshire, then in Edinburgh Tolbooth, put in irons and imprisoned in Canongait Tolbooth on 29 July 1685, then transported via Leith bound for Jamaica in August 1685, landed at Port Royal in November 1685. [ETR][RPCS.XI.329][LJ.175]

OLIVER, JOHN, from Hobkirk, Roxburghshire, fought at the Battle of Bothwell Bridge in 1679, was transported via Leith aboard the <u>Crown of London</u> bound for Barbados on 27 November 1679, was shipwrecked and drowned off Orkney on 10 December 1679. [RBM]

O'NEIL, DANIEL, fought at the Siege of Worcester in 1651, then transported via London aboard the John and Sarah bound for Boston in December 1651, landed there in February 1652. [SD.1.5-6]

ORR, ROBERT, from Milnbank, was sought by the Justice Court in August 1667 for his part in the late rebellion, was transported to the colonies on 16 August 1670. [GC.123] [RPCS.XI.345; 111.320]

OSBURN, ALEXANDER, a minister in Dublin, latterly in Ayr, testament, 1690, Comm. Glasgow. [NRS]

OSBURNE, JOHN, minister at Dundonald, Ayrshire, in 1672, was accused of keeping conventicles at Tarbolton in 1674, in 1683 the Privy Council gave him the choice of immediately leaving the kingdom or abstaining conventicles, he chose the latter. [F.3.35]

OSBURNE, JOHN, in Penfilland, Keir parish, was accused of holding conventicles, in 1666. [GC.114]; a fugitive in May 1683. [RPCS.VIII.609]

OSBURN, JOHN, in Macalstoun, for aiding rebels John MacCall, Gilbert Gilchrist and William Milligan, and failing to report it was declared to be a rebel and fugitive in October 1684. [RPCS.IX.365]

PANTON, ROBERT, from Dalmany, West Lothian, was transported via Leith aboard the St Michael of Scarborough bound for the West Indies on 12 December 1678. [RPCS.VI.76]

PARK, JOHN, a rebel imprisoned in Edinburgh Tolbooth, was released on 25 September 1684. [RPCS.IX.180]

PARK, JOHN, tenant of Kennishead farm, Eastwood, Renfrewshire, refused to take the Test Act Oath, consequently he was hanged on Paisley Green on 3 July 1685. [Woodside gravestone, Paisley, Renfrewshire]

PARK, JOHN, a weaver from Lanark, a prisoner in Edinburgh Tolbooth, who refused to take an Oath of Allegiance, was banished to the American Plantations on 17 December 1685, was transported via Leith aboard the John and Nicholas in December 1685. [ETR][ RPCS.XI.254]

PATERSON, ALEXANDER, from Muirkirk, Ayrshire, fought at the Battle of Bothwell Bridge in 1679, was transported via Leith aboard the Crown of London bound for Barbados on 27 November 1679, was shipwrecked and drowned off Orkney on 10 December 1679. [RBM]

PATERSON, ANDREW, from Hamilton, Lanarkshire, was banished to the colonies on 18 August 1685, then transported via Leith aboard the Henry and Francis bound for East New Jersey on 5 September 1685, landed there on 7 December 1685. [RPCS.XI.154/291/292/295][NWI.I.423]

PATERSON, DAVID, from Eaglesham, Renfrewshire, fought at the Siege of Worcester in 1651, then transported via London aboard the John and Sarah bound for Boston in December 1651, landed there in February 1652. [SD.1.5-6]

PATERSON, DAVID, a prisoner in Edinburgh Tolbooth, who refused to take an Oath of Allegiance, was banished to the American Plantations on 17 December 1685, was transported via Leith aboard the John and Nicholas bound for Barbados in January 1686. [ETR] [RPCS.XI.254]

PATERSON, GAVIN, late of Bothwellshiells, a prisoner in Canongait Tolbooth for having been a rebel at the Battle of Bothwell Bridge on 22 June 1679, a bond on 12 January 1684. [RPCS.VIII.665]; trial papers, 1687. [NRS.JC39.99]

PATERSON, JAMES, fought at the Siege of Worcester in 1651, then transported via London aboard the John and Sarah bound for Boston in December 1651, landed there in February 1652. [SD.1.5-6]

PATERSON, JAMES, a prisoner in Edinburgh or Canongait Tolbooth, a rebel, was banished to the Plantations in Carolina on 8 August 1684. [RPCS.IX.95]

PATERSON, JOHN, in Keolston, Tynron, for seeing rebels James Corsan and Samuel MacKeoun in the house of Robert Smith in Upper Bellibught, and not reporting it, was declared to be a rebel and fugitive in October 1684. [RPCS.IX.368]

PATTERSON, ROBERT, was killed at the Battle of Aird's Moss on 22 July 1680. [Muirkirk Monument Ayrshire]

PATHESON, JOHN, in Craignee, for conversing with rebels Alexander Gibson and Walter Smith last summer, was declared to be a rebel and fugitive in October 1684. [RPCS.IX.368/373]

PATON, MATTHEW, , for his part in the Pentland Rising of 1666, was hanged in Glasgow on 19 December 1666. [Glasgow Cathedral]

PATON, Captain JOHN, of Meadowhead, Fenwick, Ayrshire, fought at the Battles of Mauchline Moor, Rullion Green, and Bothwell Bridge, was sentenced to death in Edinburgh on 9 May 1684.

PATON, JOHN, in Monkland, Lanarkshire, a rebel in Glasgow Tolbooth, was banished to the Plantations in June 1684, and transported via Glasgow aboard the Pelican bound for Carolina, bond by Walter Gibson, a merchant in Glasgow, dated 20 June 1684. [RPCS.IX.208]

PATON, MATTHEW, for his part in the Pentland Rising of 1666, was beheaded in Glasgow on 19 December 1666. [Glasgow Cathedral]

PATON, MATTHEW, fought at Bothwell Bridge, Lanarkshire, on 22 June 1679. [Glasgow Cathedral plaque]

PATON, ROBERT, born 1598, was educated at Glasgow University, was involved in the Pentland Rising, was sought by the Justice Court in August 1667 for his part in the late rebellion. [GC.123] [RPCS.II.345]; was banished to Virginia on 10 June 1669, [RPCS.III.22]; minister at Barnweil Ayrshire, from 1691 until his death in 1699. [F.III.77]

PATRICK, JAMES, a prisoner in Canongait Tolbooth, who refused to take an Oath of Allegiance, was banished to the American Plantations on 17 December 1685, transported via Leith aboard the John and Nicholas bound for Barbados in December 1685. [ETR][RPCS.XI.386]

PATTISON, JAMES, fought at the Siege of Worcester in 1651, then transported via London aboard the John and Sarah bound for Boston in December 1651, landed there in February 1652. [SD.1.5-6]

PEARSON, JOHN, was warded in Edinburgh Tolbooth on 28 May 1685. [ETR]

PEDEN, ALEXANDER, born in Auchenloich farm, Sorn, Ayrshire, in 1626, was educated at Glasgow University, former minister at New Luce, Galloway, from 1659 until 1662, was accused of holding conventicles, in 1666. [GC.114]; was sought by the Justice Court in August 1667 for his part in the late rebellion. [GC.123] [RPCS.II.345]; fled to Ireland in 1669, [Cal.SPIre.1669]; took refuge in Glenwherry, County Antrim, between 1682 and 1685, was imprisoned on Bass Rock, died on 26 January 1686. [NRS.E100.39.1] [Cumnock Old gravestone, Ayrshire]

PEDDIN, ALEXANDER, was transported via Leith aboard the St Michael of Scarborough bound for the West Indies on 12 December 1678. [RPCS.VI.76]

PEEBLES, HUGH, of Mainshill, bon 1614, was educated at Glasgow University, minister at Lochwinnoch, Renfrewshire, from 1647, he refused to conform to Episcopacy, was deprived in 1665, he was restored in 1676, and died in May 1691. [F.III.153][RPCS.II.383]

PEEBLES, THOMAS, a licentiate of the Church of Scotland, chaplain of Lord Eglinton's Regiment in Ireland in 1642, minister in Dundonald, Ireland, in 1645, died in 1670. [F.VII.532]

PENDAR, JOHN, from Torpichen, West Lothian, fought at the Battle of Bothwell Bridge in 1679, was transported via Leith aboard the Crown of London bound for Barbados on 27 November 1679, was shipwrecked off Orkney on 10 December 1679, later transported to Jamaica. [RBM] [CEC.212/5][SW.201]

PENMAN, JAMES, from Quathquan, Lanarkshire, fought at the Battle of Bothwell Bridge in 1679, was transported via Leith aboard the Crown of London bound for Barbados on 27

November 1679, was shipwrecked off Orkney on 10 December 1679, later transported to Jamaica. [RBM][CEC.212/5][SW.199]

PETER, WILLIAM, a chapman in Linlithgow, West Lothian, to be arrested and imprisoned in Edinburgh Tolbooth, a warrant dated 12 December 1684, he was warded there on 13 December 1684. [ETR]

PETTIGREW, THOMAS, from Shettleston Green, Lanarkshire, was warded in Edinburgh Tolbooth on 20 May 1685, but considering his old age and his paralysis, and his undertaking not to rebel again, was released on 28 May 1685. [ETR]

PETTY, JOHN, was transported via Leith to the colonies in July 1685. [RPCS.XI.114]

PHILP, THOMAS, from Muiravonside, Stirlingshire, fought at the Battle of Bothwell Bridge in 1679, was transported via Leith aboard the Crown of London bound for Barbados on 27 November 1679, was shipwrecked and drowned off Orkney on 10 December 1679. [RBM]

PIRIE, ALEXANDER, from Glasgow, fought at the Battle of Bothwell Bridge in 1679, was transported via Leith aboard the Crown of London bound for Barbados on 27 November 1679, was shipwrecked and drowned off Orkney on 10 December 1679. [RBM]

PIRIE, ANDREW, from Fife, fought at the Battle of Bothwell Bridge in 1679, was transported via Leith aboard the Crown of London bound for Barbados on 27 November 1679, was shipwrecked and drowned off Orkney on 10 December 1679. [RBM]

PIRIE, GEORGE, fought at the Siege of Worcester in 1651, then transported via London aboard the John and Sarah bound for Boston in December 1651, landed there in February 1652. [SD.1.5-6]

PLIVER, WILLIAM, servant to Alexander Williamson in Blackcraig, to be imprisoned in Edinburgh Tolbooth in August 1684. [RPCS.IX.126]

POE, DAVID, in Pokelly, was sought by the Justice Court in August 1667 for his part in the late rebellion. [GC.123] [RPCS.II.345]

POLLOCK, JOHN, of Bagra, was warded in Edinburgh Tolbooth on 1 November 1684, was transferred to Dunnottar Castle, Kincardineshire, on 29 July 1685, transported via Leith aboard the Henry and Francis bound for East New Jersey on 5 September 1685, landed there on 7 December 1685. [ETR][RPCS.XI.154/291/292][NWI.I.423]

POLLOCK, ROBERT, a shoemaker in East Kilbride, a Covenanter in 1679, imprisoned in Edinburgh Tolbooth, was tried in 1685 then hanged at the Gallowlee on 28 January 1685. [NRS.JC39.67] [ETR]

POLLOCK, WILLIAM, was warded in Edinburgh Tolbooth, on 3 December 1684. [ETR]

PORTEOUS, EDWARD, a merchant from Newbattle, Midlothian, was transported to Virginia in 1685, settled in Petsworth, Gloucester County, died in1700, probate Gloucester County in 1700, probate 1700 PCC. [NRS.GD297.114]

PORTEOUS, GEORGE, a servant of John Telfer a painter in Edinburgh, a rioter, was banished to the Plantations on 13 September 1666, probably was transported on the Ewe and Lamb bound for Virginia. [RPCS.II.195/201]

PORTEOUS, STEVEN, a tailor from Canongait, Edinburgh, was transported via Leith aboard the St Michael of Scarborough bound for the West Indies on 12 December 1678. [RPCS.VI.76]

PORTEOUS, STEPHEN, a rebel imprisoned in Edinburgh Tolbooth, was released on 25 September 1684. [RPCS.IX.180]

PORTER, JAMES, born in Nithsdale, educated at Glasgow University, minister of Kirkpatrick-Juxta and Dungree from 1654 until deprived in 1662, in 1670 and in 1677 he was accused of holding conventicles. [F.II.211]

PORTER, JAMES, in Gilroy, Dunscore, for aiding rebels, John Weir and Robert Lauchlison, was declared a rebel and fugitive in October 1684. [RPCS.IX.370]

PORTERFIELD, ALEXANDER, was sought by the Justice Court in August 1667 for his part in the late rebellion. [GC.123]; was warded in Edinburgh Tolbooth on 20 November 1684. [ETR]

PORTERFIELD, ALEXANDER, of Fullwood, was imprisoned in Edinburgh Tolbooth on 20 November 1684, was released on parole on 27 March 1685, and returned on 12 April 1685. [ETR]

PORTERFIELD, JOHN, of Duchall, was tried for treason having assisted his brother Alexander Porterfield and others, in 1684. [NRS.JC39.52]

PORTERFIELD, WILLIAM, of Quarreltoun, was sought by the Justice Court in August 1667 for his part in the late rebellion. [GC.123] [RPCS.II.345]

POTTER, MICHAEL, born around 1642, from St Ninian's parish, Stirlingshire, a minister in exile in Rotterdam, Holland, from 1677 until 1680. [SEC]

PRINGLE, JOHN, from Castleton, Roxburghshire, fought at the Battle of Bothwell Bridge in 1679, was transported via Leith aboard the Crown of London bound for Barbados on 27 November 1679, was shipwrecked and drowned off Orkney on 10 December 1679. [RBM]

PRINGLE, JOHN, an Ensign of Lord Angus's Regiment, [The Cameronians], fought at the Battle of Dunkeld in August 1679. [BK]

PRINGLE, THOMAS, from Stow, Midlothian, fought at the Battle of Bothwell Bridge in 1679, was transported via Leith aboard the Crown of London bound for Barbados on 27 November 1679, was shipwrecked and drowned off Orkney on 10 December 1679. [RBM] [ETR]

PRYDE, JAMES, a weaver from Strathmiglo, Fife, was transported via Leith aboard the St Michael of Scarborough bound for the West Indies on 12 December 1678. [RPCS.VI.76]

RAE, ELSPETH, spouse of John Thomson, for seeing rebel Peter Coudan at his own house, and not reporting it, was declared to be a rebel and fugitive in October 1684. [RPCS.IX.370]

RAE, HECTOR, was educated at Edinburgh University, minister at Hownam, Roxburghshire, from 1609 until 1639, his signature appears on the copy of the National Covenant preserved in Cavers. [F.III.132]

RAE, JAMES, from Uddingston, Lanarkshire, a prisoner in Edinburgh Tolbooth, who refused to take an Oath of Allegiance, was banished to the American Plantations on 17 December 1685, was transported via Leith aboard the John and Nicholas on 12 December 1685. [RPCS.XI.254][ETR]

RAE, JOHN, minister of Symington, Lanarkshire, was warded in Edinburgh Tolbooth on 4 March 1644. [ETR]

RAE, JOHN, an agent in Edinburgh, was fined for attending a conventicle in widow Paton's house in February 1669. [RPCS.II.626]

RALSTOUN, DAVID, from Bathgate, West Lothian, fought at the Battle of Bothwell Bridge in 1679, was transported via Leith aboard the Crown of London bound for Barbados on 27 November 1679, was shipwrecked and drowned off Orkney on 10 December 1679. [RBM]

RALSTON, JAMES, in Westhairburnhead, undertook not to rise in arms against the king, under a penalty of 500 merks, a bond dated 8 July 1684. [RPCS.IX.211]

RAMSAY, DAVID, son of Matthew Ramsay, was imprisoned for keeping conventicles in 1679. [F.III.165]

RAMSAY, GEORGE, born 1628, was educated at the University of St Andrews, minister at Kilmaurs, Ayrshire, from 1655 until deprived in 1662, was bound to join the Pentland Rising in November 1666, died in September 1677. [F.III.113]

RAMSAY, GILBERT, a licentiate of the Church of Scotland, was ordained in Bangor, Ireland, in 1646, was deprived in 1661, and died in August 1670. [F.VII.532]

RAMSAY, MATHEW, was educated at Glasgow University, a minister in Old Kirkpatrick, from 1648 was deposed for keeping conventicles, on 18 August 1663, minister in Paisley from 1669, died in May 1671. [RPCS.I.409; III.165]

RAMSAY, ROBERT, from Kirkmichael, Ayrshire, fought at the Battle of Bothwell Bridge in 1679, was transported via Leith aboard the Crown of London bound for Barbados on 27 November 1679, was shipwrecked and drowned off Orkney on 10 December 1679. [RBM]

RAMSAY, THOMAS, a minister, was accused of holding conventicles and imprisoned in Edinburgh Castle in August 1660, [RPCS.VIII.465]

RAMSAY, THOMAS, was educated at the University of St Andrews, minister at Mordington and Lamberton, Berwickshire, from 1648 until he was deprived in 1682, he was imprisoned in Edinburgh Castle in 1660 and again in 1680, he died in June 1695. [F.II.57]

RAMSAY, ....., in the Mains of Arniston, was sought by the Justice Court in August 1667 for his part in the late rebellion. [GC.123] [RPCS.II.345]

RANKEN, JAMES, was warded in Edinburgh Tolbooth on 2 July 1684. [ETR]

RANKIN, JOHN, from Bonhardpans, was transported to the colonies in August 1670. [RPCS.III.206]

RANKIN, JOHN, from Biggar, Lanarkshire, fought at the Battle of Bothwell Bridge in 1679, was transported via Leith aboard the

Crown of London bound for Barbados on 27 November 1679, was shipwrecked and drowned off Orkney on 10 December 1679. [RBM]

RAYNING, JOHN, in Hemisfieldtoun, for seeing rebel Peter Coudan on Hemisfieldtounmoor, and not reporting it, was declared to be a rebel and fugitive in October 1684. [RPCS.IX.370]

REANIE, JEAN, a widow, was accused of rioting in Kirkcudbright in the parish of Irongray, in 1663, she subscribed to a bond on 17 August 1663, undertaking to stand at the market cross of Kirkcudbright bearing a notice accepting fault for causing a tumult. [RPCS.I.373/408]

REDDY, JAMES, a mason in Kinswaid, for attending conventicles, was outlawed on 29 August 1672. [RPCS.III.583]

REID, ANDREW, from Argyll, in Argyll's Rebellion, a prisoner in Edinburgh Tolbooth, to be transported to the Plantations on 11 August 1685, via Leith bound for Jamaica in August 1685. [ETR][RPCS.XI.328]

REID, JAMES, in Blairhead, and his son Charles, for attending conventicles, were outlawed on 29 August 1672. [RPCS.III.583]

REID, JOHN, in Dalgoner, and his wife, for aiding rebels Robert Stewart in Manquehill, William Hunter in Clachan, and eight others after the ambush at Enterkin, also Daniel Carmichael and two other rebels, were declared to be a rebel and fugitive in October 1684. [RPCS.IX.365]

REID, ROBERT, a weaver from Glasgow, was transported via Leith aboard the St Michael of Scarborough bound for the West Indies on 12 December 1678. [RPCS.VI.76]

REID, WILLIAM, from Mauchline, Ayrshire, fought at the Battle of Bothwell Bridge in 1679, was transported via Leith aboard the Crown of London bound for Barbados on 27 November 1679, was shipwrecked and drowned off Orkney on 10 December 1679. [RBM]

REID, WILLIAM, from Musselburgh, Midlothian, fought at the Battle of Bothwell Bridge in 1679, was transported via Leith aboard the Crown of London bound for Barbados on 27 November 1679, was shipwrecked and drowned off Orkney on 10 December 1679. [RBM]

REID, WILLIAM, born in Scotland, was educated at Glasgow University, late minister in Galloway, was accused of holding conventicles, in 1666. [GC.114]; a minister in Ballywalter and in Balllynahinch, died on 7 May 1708. [Killinchy gravestone, County Down], [RGS.10.217] [FI.47]

REID, WILLIAM, from Lanark, a prisoner in Edinburgh Tolbooth, willing to go to America [sic] was released to go there on 17 December 1685, transported via Leith aboard the John and Nicholas bound for Barbados in December 1685. [ETR]

RENNIE, JOHN, was transported via Leith aboard the Henry and Francis bound for East New Jersey on 5 September 1685, died on voyage. [RPCS.XI.154/290/292][NWI.I.423]

RENNIE, MARION, was transported via Leith aboard the Henry and Francis bound for East New Jersey on 5 September 1685, died on voyage. [RPCS.XI.154/290/292][NWI.I.423]

RENWICK, Reverend JAMES, born in Moniaive, a field preacher, or conventlicer, was declared a fugitive on 16 September 1684, [RPCS.IX.175]; was tried in 1684, and hanged in the Greenmarket in Edinburgh on 17 February 1688. [NRS.JC39.47]; a prisoner in Edinburgh Tolbooth, having taken the Oath of Allegiance, was released on 5 March 1685. [ETR] [Greyfriars Monument, Edinburgh] [Nithsdale Martyrs Cross, Dumfries-shire]

RENWICK, JOHN, from Barnsalloch, was transported to the colonies in 1684. [RPCS.X.258]

RENWICK, JOHN, was hanged in the Greenmarket, Edinburgh, in 1685. [Nithsdale Martyrs Monument, Dumfries-shire]

RESTON, JAMES, from Grangeburn Mill, was warded in Edinburgh Tolbooth on 29 October 1684, but having taken the Test Act in Edinburgh Tolbooth on 19 December 1684, was released. [ETR]

RESTON, JAMES, was transported via Leith aboard the Henry and Francis bound for East New Jersey on 5 September 1685, landed there on 7 December 1685.
[RPCS.XI.154/166/291/292/374][NWI.I.423]

RICHARD, THOMAS, from Muirkirk, Ayrshire, was warded in Edinburgh Tolbooth on 10 July 1685; to be transported to the Plantations on 11 August 1685, was shipped via Leith bound for Jamaica in August 1685. [ETR] [RPCS.XI.329]

RICHARDSON, BARBARA, and Sophia Richardson, sometime in Logan, Buittle, Kirkcudbrightshire, fanatics and fugitives in 1684. [RPCS.IX.573]

RICHARDSON, JOHN, from Borgue, Kirkcudbrightshire, fought at the Battle of Bothwell Bridge in 1679, was transported via Leith aboard the Crown of London bound for Barbados on 27 November 1679, was shipwrecked off Orkney on 10 December 1679, later shipped to Jamaica. [RBM][CEC.212/5][SW.203]

RICHARDSON, JOHN, in Barholm, was accused, in Kirkcudbright in October 1684, of conversing with rebel Hendry McCulloch, sometime in Barholme, in June 1683. [RPCS.IX.376]

RICHARDSON, WILLIAM, was transported to the colonies on 17 November 1679. [RPCS.VI.343]

RICHMOND, ANDREW, from Auchenleck, Ayrshire, fought at the Battle of Bothwell Bridge in 1679, was transported via Leith aboard the Crown of London bound for Barbados on 27 November 1679, was shipwrecked and drowned off Orkney on 10 December 1679. [RBM]

RICHMOND, JOHN, for his part in the Pentland Rising of 1666, was hanged in Glasgow on 19 December 1666. [Glasgow Cathedral]

RICHMOND, JOHN, the younger of Knowe, fought at Bothwell Bridge on 22 June 1679. [Glasgow Cathedral plaque]

RIDDELL, ARCHIBALD, from Kippen Stirlingshire, was transported via Leith aboard the Henry and Francis bound for East New Jersey on 5 September 1685, landed there on 7 December 1685. [RPCS.X.79][NWI.I.423]

RIDDELL, HUGH, was transported via Leith to New York in 1683. [RPCS.VIII.253]

ROBB, RONALD, in Dalnaskin, to be tried accused of rebellion, 3 June 1684. [RPCS.IX.205]

ROBERTSON, ALEXANDER, a minister in Galloway, was accused of holding conventicles within the Presbytery in 1666. [GC.107]

ROBERTSON, ALEXANDER, a minister from Edinburgh, at the Battle of Rullion Green in 1666. [Z.193]

ROBERTSON, GEORGE, a weaver in Nethertoun, for attending conventicles, was outlawed on 29 August 1672. [RPCS.III.583]

ROBERTSON, JAMES, a merchant in Hazeldean, was executed in the Greenmarket, Edinburgh, on 5 December 1682. [ETR]

ROBERTSON, PATRICK, fought at the Siege of Worcester in 1651, then transported via London aboard the John and Sarah bound for Boston in December 1651, landed there in February 1652. [SD.1.5-6]

ROBERTSON, THOMAS, portioner of Hiselldean, a prisoner in Canongait Tolbooth, a witness against some rebels, to be released, in July 1684. [RPCS.IX.72]; a bond, dated 31 July 1684. [RPCS.IX.215]

ROBERTSON, THOMAS, tenant in Stains, a fugitive, was warded in Edinburgh Tolbooth on 2 July 1684. [ETR]

ROBINSON, ALESTER, fought at the Siege of Worcester in 1651, then transported via London aboard the John and Sarah bound for Boston in December 1651, landed there in February 1652. [SD.1.5-6]

ROBINSON, CHARLES, fought at the Siege of Worcester in 1651, then transported via London aboard the John and Sarah bound for Boston in December 1651, landed there in February 1652. [SD.1.5-6]

ROBINSON, DANIEL, fought at the Siege of Worcester in 1651, then transported via London aboard the John and Sarah bound for Boston in December 1651, landed there in February 1652. [SD.1.5-6]

ROBINSON, JAMES, fought at the Siege of Worcester in 1651, then transported via London aboard the John and Sarah bound for Boston in December 1651, landed there in February 1652. [SD.1.5-6]

ROBINSON, JOHN, fought at the Siege of Worcester in 1651, then transported via London aboard the John and Sarah bound for Boston in December 1651, landed there in February 1652. [SD.1.5-6]

ROBSON, JAMES, was killed at Bothwell Bridge, Lanarkshire, on 22 June 1679. [Nithsdale Martyrs Monument, Dumfries-shire]

ROBSON, JOHN, a rebel imprisoned in Dumfries Tolbooth, having subscribed to the bond of peace, was released on 23 February 1669. [RPCS.II.608]

ROGER, GEORGE, a boatman in Greenock, Renfrewshire, a prisoner in Canongait Tolbooth, having signed a bond was released on 23 August 1684. [RPCS.IX.315]

ROGER, RALPH, minister in Kilwinning, was warded in Edinburgh Tolbooth on 11 December 1684, there on 17 June 1685. [ETR]

ROGER, ROBERT, a maltman in Greenock, who attended a conventicle near Greenock, was to be captured and imprisoned in Edinburgh Tolbooth in August 1684. [RPCS.IX.131]

RODGER, WILLIAM, from Maybole, Ayrshire, fought at the Battle of Bothwell Bridge in 1679, was transported via Leith aboard the

Crown of London bound for Barbados on 27 November 1679, was shipwrecked and drowned off Orkney on 10 December 1679. [RBM]

RODGER, WILLIAM, from Kilbride, Lanarkshire, fought at the Battle of Bothwell Bridge in 1679, was transported via Leith aboard the Crown of London bound for Barbados on 27 November 1679, was shipwrecked and drowned off Orkney on 10 December 1679. [RBM]

ROGERSON, JOHN, a shoemaker in Halbank, for aiding a rebel, was declared a rebel and fugitive, 1684. [RPCS.IX.361]

ROME, CHARLES, was banished to the colonies on 6 August 1684, then transported via Leith to Carolina in 1684. [RPCS.IX.95]

ROME, GEORGE, of Beach, was tried for participating in the tumult in the parish of Irongray, Kirkcudbrightshire, in 1663. [RPCS.I.376]; a prisoner in Canongait Tolbooth, having taken the Oath of Allegiance was released on 1 August 1667, [RPCS.II.319]; imprisoned in Edinburgh or Canongait Tolbooth, a rebel, was banished to the Plantations in Carolina on 8 August 1684, then transported via Leith to Carolina in 1684. [RPCS.IX.95]

ROME, GEORGE, a prisoner in Edinburgh Tolbooth, having 'sworn never to rise in arms against His Majestry', was released on 27 March 1685. [ETR]

ROME, JEAN, a rioter, was imprisoned in Kirkcudbright Tolbooth, then to stand at the market cross there on two days in September 1683. [GC.105]

ROME, THOMAS, of Cloudan, Dumfries-shire, for aiding rebels, John Wallet son of John Wallet in Glenhead, and John Hepburn a vagrant preacher, also conventlicker John Hepburn, was declared a rebel and fugitive in October 1684. [RPCS.IX.372/555]

ROSE, DERMOT, was captured at the Battle of Dunbar in 1650, was transported via London to Carolina in 1684. [NWI.I.159]

ROSPER, THOMAS, was killed at Scarvating, in 1679. [Nithsdale Martyrs Monument, Dumfries-shire]

ROSPER, THOMAS, from Glencairn, Dumfriesshire, fought at the Battle of Bothwell Bridge in 1679, was transported via Leith aboard the Crown of London bound for Barbados on 27 November 1679, was shipwrecked and drowned off Orkney on 10 December 1679. [RBM]

ROSS, ALESTAR, fought at the Siege of Worcester in 1651, then transported via London aboard the John and Sarah bound for Boston in December 1651, landed there in February 1652. [SD.1.5-6]

ROSS, ALEXANDER, with a company of foot soldiers, fought at the Battle of Bothwell Bridge, Lanarkshire, on 2 June 1679.

ROSS, ALEXANDER, imprisoned in Canongait Tolbooth, accused of attending conventicles, in August 1684. [RPCS.IX.100]

ROSS, GEORGE, of Galstrich, Barony parish, Glasgow, absent as in Ireland in 1683. [RPCS.VIII.644]

ROSS, DANIEL, fought at the Siege of Worcester in 1651, then transported via London aboard the John and Sarah bound for Boston in December 1651, landed there in February 1652. [SD.1.5-6]

ROSS, DAVID, fought at the Siege of Worcester in 1651, then transported via London aboard the John and Sarah bound for Boston in December 1651, landed there in February 1652. [SD.1.5-6]

ROSS, JAMES, fought at the Siege of Worcester in 1651, then transported via London aboard the John and Sarah bound for Boston in December 1651, landed there in February 1652. [SD.1.5-6]

ROSS, JOHN, was captured at the Battle of Dunbar in 1650, transported via London aboard the Unity bound for Boston in November 1650. [CEB]

ROSS, JOHN, fought at the Siege of Worcester in 1651, then transported via London aboard the John and Sarah bound for

Boston in December 1651, landed there in February 1652. [SD.1.5-6]

ROSS, JONAS, fought at the Siege of Worcester in 1651, then transported via London aboard the John and Sarah bound for Boston in December 1651, landed there in February 1652. [SD.1.5-6]

ROSS, WILLIAM, a vagrant chapman, deceased, was in the rebellion, his widow Margaret Barclay in Largs, Ayrshire, in 1684. [RPCS.IX.550]

ROW, JAMES, fought at the Siege of Worcester in 1651, then transported via London aboard the John and Sarah bound for Boston in December 1651, landed there in February 1652. [SD.1.5-6]

ROW, JAMES, a merchant in Edinburgh, was accused of attending a conventicle in the widow Paterson in Edinburgh in February 1669. [RPCS.II.621]

ROW, WILLIAM, born 1614, was educated at Edinburgh University, minister at Ceres, Fife, from 1644 until deposed in 1665, he was accused of keeping conventicles in 1671; chaplain to the laird of Scotstarvet, was sought by the Justice Court in August 1667 for his part in the late rebellion. [GC.123] [RPCS.II.345], minister at Ceres from 1689, he died in 1698. [F.V.131]

ROWAT, JAMES, was educated at the University of Glasgow, a minister in Kilmarnock, Ayrshire, from 1649, for refusing to take the Oath of Allegiance, was deposed and order to move out of the parish, on 16 September 1662. [RPCS.II.263] [F.III.107]

ROXBURGH, ALEXANDER, in Minnigaff, was accused, in Kirkcudbright in October 1694, of conversing with rebel, Archibald Stewart. [RPCS.IX.375]

ROXBURGH, JOHN, in Minnigaff, was accused, in Kirkcudbright in October 1694, of conversing with rebel, William Kennedy in January 1684. [RPCS.IX.375]

ROY, DONALD, fought at the Siege of Worcester in 1651, then transported via London aboard the John and Sarah bound for Boston in December 1651, landed there in February 1652. [SD.1.5-6]

RULE, GILBERT, born 1629, from Fife, a minister in exile in Leiden and Rotterdam in the Netherlands, from 1662 to 1679, also in 1687. [SEC]

RUSSELL, DAVID, a tenant in Stains, a fugitive, was warded in Edinburgh Tolbooth on 2 July 1684, and liberated on 14 August 1684. [ETR]

RUSSELL, GAVIN, was accused of participating in the Earl of Argyll's Rebellion, in 1685. [NRS.JC39.72]; was warded in Edinburgh Tolbooth on 10 July 1685, later, executed in the Grassmarket of Edinburgh on 12 August 1685. [ETR] [RPCS.XI.114/119/125]

RUSSELL, JAMES, was transported to the colonies in October 1684 [RPCS.X.251]

RUSSELL, JAMES, in Easter Lenzie, and his brother John Russell, fugitives, were tried in Glasgow in October 1684, denied they were in the rebellion, were imprisoned. [RPCS.IX.709]

RUSSELL, JOHN, from Calder, Midlothian, fought at the Battle of Bothwell Bridge in 1679, was transported via Leith aboard the Crown of London bound for Barbados on 27 November 1679, was shipwrecked and drowned off Orkney on 10 December 1679. [RBM]

RUSSELL, ......, an assassin of Archbishop Sharp, who fled to Ireland, was captured there on 7 October 1680. [RPCS.VI.559]

RUSSELL, JOHN, was transported to the colonies in October 1684 [RPCS.X.251]

RUSSELL, PATRICK or PETER, then in Edinburgh Tolbooth, was transferred to Dunnottar Castle, Kincardineshire, on 29 July 1685, was banished to the Plantations on 18 August 1685, then transported via Leith aboard the Henry and Francis bound for

East New Jersey on 5 September 1685, landed there on 7 December 1685. [ETR][RPCS.XI.154/289/292][NWI.I..423]

RUSSELL, ROBERT, was transported via Leith to the colonies in November 1679. [ETR]

RUSSELL, ROBERT, in Mulrin, was warded in Edinburgh Tolbooth on 22 July 1685, was released on 1 October 1685. [RPCS.IX.163]

RUSSELL, SIMON, fought at the Siege of Worcester in 1651, then transported via London aboard the John and Sarah bound for Boston in December 1651, landed there in February 1652. [SD.1.5-6]

RUSSELL, THOMAS, was suspected in complicity in the assassination of Archbishop Sharp, who fled to Ireland, was captured there on 7 October 1680. [RPCS.VI.559], imprisoned in Edinburgh Tolbooth, was transferred to Dunnottar Castle, Kincardineshire, on 29 July 1685, [ETR], was transported via Leith aboard the Henry and Francis bound for East New Jersey on 5 September 1685, died on voyage. [RPCS.XI.154/166/291][NWI.I.423]

RUTHERFORD, GEORGE, fought at the Battle of Bothwell Bridge in 1679, was transported via Leith aboard the Crown of London bound for Barbados on 27 November 1679, was shipwrecked and drowned off Orkney on 10 December 1679. [RBM]

RUTHERFORD, Reverend SAMUEL, born 1600, educated at Edinburgh University, minister at Anwoth from 1627 until 1639, signed the National Covenant in 1638, was ejected in 1660, died there in March 1661, testament 2 November 1661, Comm. St Andrews. [Anwoth, Boreland Hill Monument, Kirkcudbrightshire]

RUXTON, JOHN, fought at the Battle of Dunbar in 1650, transported via London aboard the Unity bound for Boston in November 1650. [SCF.1226]

RYMER, HENRY, was educated at St Andrews University, minister at Carnbee, Fife, from 1644 until deposed in 1664 for not conforming to Episcopacy, died in Edinburgh on 17 October 1694. [F.V.188]

SAMUEL, DAVID, from East Calder, Midlothian, fought at the Battle of Bothwell Bridge in 1679, was transported via Leith aboard the Crown of London bound for Barbados on 27 November 1679, was shipwrecked off Orkney on 10 December 1679, later was shipped to Jamaica. [RBM][SW.202][CEC.212/5]

SANDERS, JOHN, in Annocreiche, for attending conventicles, was outlawed on 29 August 1672. [RPCS.III.583]

SANDS, JAMES, from Gargunnock, Stirlingshire, fought at the Battle of Bothwell Bridge in 1679, was transported via Leith aboard the Crown of London bound for Barbados on 27 November 1679, was shipwrecked off Orkney on 10 December 1679, later shipped to Jamaica. [RBM] [CEC.212/5][SW.201]

SANDS, ROBERT, from Orewell, Kinross, fought at the Battle of Bothwell Bridge in 1679, was transported via Leith aboard the Crown of London bound for Barbados on 27 November 1679, was shipwrecked off Orkney on 10 December 1679, later shipped to Jamaica. [RBM]

SCHAW, Mrs, spouse of James Schaw a miller in Greenock, who attended a conventicle near Greenock, was to be captured and imprisoned in Edinburgh Tolbooth in August 1684. [RPCS.IX.131]

SCOTT, ADAM, tenant of Blaikwood in Lesmahagow, a rebel in 1666, imprisoned in Edinburgh Tolbooth or Canongait Tolbooth, having taken the Oath of Allegiance, was released on 11 July 1667. [RPCS.II.308]

SCOTT, ANDREW, from Teviotdale, Roxburghshire, in Edinburgh Tolbooth, was put in irons and imprisoned in Canongait Tolbooth on 29 July 1685, then transported via Leith to Jamaica in July 1685, landed at Port Royal in November 1685. [ETR][RPCS.XI.329][LJ.195]

SCOTT, CHRISTIAN, was taken from Leith Tolbooth, put in irons and imprisoned in Edinburgh Tolbooth, in 1685. [ETR]; then transported via Leith aboard the Henry and Francis bound for East New Jersey on 5 September 1685. [RPCS.XI.166]

SCOTT, DAVID, in Irongray, was sought by the Justice Court in August 1667 for his part in the late rebellion. [GC.123]

SCOTT, DAVID, of Bargansholme, Old Monkland, failed to take the Test Oath, absent in Ireland, in 1683. [RPCS.VIII.642]

SCOTT, DAVID, a baillie of Rutherglen, Lanarkshire, was warded in Edinburgh Tolbooth on 10 July 1685, and released on 19 July 1685. [ETR]

SCOTT, DAVID, was taken from Leith Tolbooth, put in irons and imprisoned in Edinburgh Tolbooth, in 1685. [ETR]

SCOTT, JANET, was taken from Leith Tolbooth, put in irons and imprisoned in Edinburgh Tolbooth, in 1685. [ETR]

SCOTT, JOHN, chaplain to Major General Munro's Regiment in Ireland in 1642. [FI.48]

SCOTT, JOHN, fought at the Siege of Worcester in 1651, then transported via London aboard the John and Sarah bound for Boston in December 1651, landed there in February 1652. [SD.1.5-6]

SCOTT, JOHN, born 1615, was educated at Edinburgh University, minister at Oxnam, Roxburghshire, from 1645, was accused of holding conventicles and imprisoned in Edinburgh Castle in August 1660, [RPCS.VIII.465]; was imprisoned in Edinburgh Castle refusing to convert to Episcopacy was deprived in 1662, he died on 22 November 1681. [F.II.135]

SCOTT, JOHN, from Ancrum, Roxburghshire, fought at the Battle of Bothwell Bridge in 1679, was transported via Leith aboard the Crown of London bound for Barbados on 27 November 1679, was shipwrecked and drowned off Orkney on 10 December 1679. [RBM] [ETR]

SCOTT, JOHN, was educated at Edinburgh University, fought at the Battle of Rullion Green in 1666, minister at Hawick,

Roxburghshire, from 1657 until he was deprived in 1662, he took part in conventicles. [F.III.113][Z.193]

SCOTT, JOHN, in Fordell, Fife, for attending conventicles, was outlawed on 29 August 1672. [RPCS.III.583]

SCOTT, JOHN, was warded in Edinburgh Tolbooth on 20 May 1685, but having subscribed to the Test Act was released on 28 May 1685. [ETR]

SCOTT, ROBERT, for his part in the Pentland Rising of 1666, was beheaded in Glasgow on 19 December 1666. [Glasgow Cathedral]

SCOTT, ROBERT, fought at Bothwell Bridge on 22 June 1679. [Glasgow Cathedral plaque]

SCOTT, WILLIAM, from Castletoun, Roxburghshire, fought at the Battle of Bothwell Bridge in 1679, was transported via Leith aboard the Crown of London bound for Barbados on 27 November 1679, was shipwrecked and drowned off Orkney on 10 December 1679. [RBM]

SCOTT, Sir WILLIAM, the younger of Harden, was tried for treason as an accessory to the Rebellion of 1666, in 1679. [NRS.JC39.66]; to be brought from Jedburgh Tolbooth to Edinburgh Tolbooth, in July 1684. [RPCS.IX.69/100]; was imprisoned in Edinburgh Tolbooth on 5 March 1685. [ETR]

SCOTT, WILLIAM, a cottar in Cormstoun, was imprisoned in the Canongait Tolbooth as a rebel, having taken the oath of allegiance, was released in 1684. [RPCS.IX.16]

SCOTT, WILLIAM, a tailor in Greenock, who attended a conventicle near Greenock, was to be captured and imprisoned in Edinburgh Tolbooth in August 1684. [RPCS.IX.131]

SCOTT, WILLIAM, of Langhop, was warded in Edinburgh Tolbooth on 31 December 1684. [ETR]

SCROTCHETT, MARION, in Felland, was accused, in Kirkcudbright in October 1684, of conversing with rebel John Corsan in June 1684. [RPCS.IX.376]

SCOULLAR, JOHN, for his part in the recent rebellion was imprisoned in Edinburgh Tolbooth, having subscribed to a bond was released on 18 February 1669. [RPCS.II.602]

SCOULLAR, WILLIAM, from Cambusnethan, Lanarkshire, fought at the Battle of Bothwell Bridge in 1679, was transported via Leith aboard the Crown of London bound for Barbados on 27 November 1679, was shipwrecked off Orkney on 10 December 1679, later shipped to Jamaica. [RBM] [CEC.212/5][SW.198]

SELKRIG, JAMES, a tobacco-cutter in Edinburgh, a rebel imprisoned in Edinburgh Tolbooth, was released on 25 September 1684. [RPCS.IX.180]

SEMPLE, GABRIEL, of Towhead, at the Battle of Rullion Green in 1666, [Z.193]; was sought by the Justice Court in August 1667 for his part in the late rebellion. [GC.123] [RPCS.II.345]; fled to Ireland in 1669. [Cal.SP.Ire.1669]; was hanged at the Gallowlee on 24 November 1684. [ETR]

SEMPLE, GILBERT, former minister in Kilpatrick of the Muir, was accused of holding conventicles, in 1666. [GC.114]

SEMPLE, JEAN, then in Edinburgh Tolbooth, was transferred to Dunnottar Castle, Kincardineshire, on 29 July 1685, was taken from Leith Tolbooth, put in irons and imprisoned in Edinburgh Tolbooth, [ETR]

SEMPLE, JOHN, a minister, was accused of holding conventicles and imprisoned in Edinburgh Castle in August 1660, [RPCS.VIII.465]; was sought by the Justice Court in August 1667 for his part in the late rebellion. [GC.123]

SEMPLE, JOHN, in Craighthorm, Glassford, Lanarkshire, was accused of treason for refusing to abjure the Apologetical Declaration in 1684. [NRS.JC39.49]; was tortured, tried and hanged at the Gallowlee on 24 November 1684. [ETR]

SEMPLE, WILLIAM, born 1624, was educated at the University of Glasgow, minister of a Presbyterian congregation in Letterkenny, County Donegal, from 1647, returned to Scotland in 1649, minister at Neilston, Renfrewshire, from 1649 until 1653, returned to Letterkenny, died there on 19 October 1674, [F.III.157]; a non-conformist minister, who was imprisoned in Lifford, Ireland, in 1669. [Cal.SP.Ire.1669]

SESSOR, DANIEL, fought at the Siege of Worcester in 1651, then transported via London aboard the John and Sarah bound for Boston in December 1651, landed there in February 1652. [SD.1.5-6]

SHANKILAW, JOHN, in Whytfall Dumfries-shire, for seeing rebel William Milligan since he broke prison on Dumfries, and not reported it, was declared to be a rebel and fugitive in October 1684. [RPCS.IX.373]

SHARPE, PATRICK, was educated at Glasgow University, minister at Foulden, Berwickshire, from 1665 until deprived in 1681. [F.II.48]

SHARP, ROBERT, was transported via Leith to Jamaica in August 1685. [RPCS.XI.329]

SHARPRAW, JOHN, a servant of Thomas Watson in Potthouse, having conversed with John Fraser a fugitive in August 1684 and after the ambush at Enterkin, Lanarkshire, was declared a fugitive in October 1684. [RPCS.IX.360]

SHAW, ANTHONY, born 1619, was educated at Edinburgh University, a minister in Belfast from 1646 until 1650, then at Colmonell until deprived in 1662, minister in Loudoun, Ayrshire, from 1674 until 1684, was warded in Edinburgh Tolbooth on 10 January 1684, and released on 22 January 1684 on condition that he did not keep conventicles, marry or baptise, died by 1687. [F.III.120; VII.532][ETR]

SHAW, JOHN, born around 1634, portioner of Thrieve, admitted attending three conventicles, in 1684. [RPCS.IX.517]

SHAW, JOHN, of Balloch, admitted conversing with vagrant preachers Samuel Arnot and ...... Vernour, in 1683. [RPCS.IX.517]

SHAW, ROBERT, in Pluntoun, was accused, in Kirkcudbright on 4 October 1684, of aiding fugitive William Campbell. [RPCS.IX.375]

SHEILLS, ARCHIBALD, a prisoner in Canongait Tolbooth, took an oath to live orderly, attend ordinances, and compear when required, subject to a penalty of 500 merks, a bond of caution by Mungo Spotswood dated 4 July 1684. [RPCS.IX.210]

SHEMAN, JOHN, in Nether Barnrosh, was accused in Kirkcudbright on 7 October 1684, of conversing with rebel John Charters. [RPCS.IX.374]

SHERON, ANSELL, [?], fought at the Siege of Worcester in 1651, then transported via London aboard the John and Sarah bound for Boston in December 1651, landed there in February 1652. [SD.1.5-6]

SHERRON, DANIEL, SCOTT, JOHN, fought at the Siege of Worcester in 1651, then transported via London aboard the John and Sarah bound for Boston in December 1651, landed there in February 1652. [SD.1.5-6]

SHIELDS, ALEXANDER, born 1661, from Berwickshire, was educated in Edinburgh and in Utrecht, imprisoned in London and in Edinburgh, a minister in exile in Utrecht, in the Netherlands, from 1680 to 1681, and from 1687 to 1690, a preacher who was accused of treason in 1685, died in Port Royal, Jamaica, on 14 June 1700. [NRS.JC39.73] [SEC][F.VII.655][F.V.239]

SHILESTON, THOMAS, from Dunspurn, was transported via Leith aboard the Henry and Francis bound for East New Jersey on 5 September 1685. [RPCS.XI.155]

SHIRRINGLAW, JAMES, fought at the Battle of Bothwell Bridge in 1679, was captured and imprisoned in Canongait Tolbooth, having signed the Test Act, was released in July 1684. [RPCS.IX.59/75]; a bond dated 31 July 1684. [RPCS.IX.215]

SHISH, JAMES, from Bo'ness, West Lothian, was transported to the colonies in August 1670. [RPCS.III/206]

SHIVAS, SAMUEL, fought at the Siege of Worcester in 1651, then transported via London aboard the John and Sarah bound for Boston in December 1651, landed there in February 1652. [SD.1.5-6]

SHONE, JAMES, fought at the Siege of Worcester in 1651, then transported via London aboard the John and Sarah bound for Boston in December 1651, landed there in February 1652. [SD.1.5-6]

SHORT, GEORGE, was killed in Tongland parish in 1685. [Balmaghie gravestone, Kirkcudbrightshire]

SIMPSON, ALESTAR, fought at the Siege of Worcester in 1651, then transported via London aboard the John and Sarah bound for Boston in December 1651, landed there in February 1652. [SD.1.5-6]

SIMPSON, ALEXANDER, fought at the Siege of Worcester in 1651, then transported via London aboard the John and Sarah bound for Boston in December 1651, landed there in February 1652. [SD.1.5-6]

SIMPSON, DANIEL, fought at the Siege of Worcester in 1651, then transported via London aboard the John and Sarah bound for Boston in December 1651, landed there in February 1652. [SD.1.5-6]

SIMPSON, DAVID, fought at the Siege of Worcester in 1651, then transported via London aboard the John and Sarah bound for Boston in December 1651, landed there in February 1652. [SD.1.5-6]

SIMPSON, HUGH, from Dalmellington, Ayrshire, fought at the Battle of Bothwell Bridge in 1679, was transported via Leith aboard the Crown of London bound for Barbados on 27

November 1679, was shipwrecked and drowned off Orkney on 10 December 1679. [RBM]

SIMSON, JAMES, born 1621, from Airth, Stirlingshire, a minister there from 1650, in exile in the Netherlands from 1661 to 1666. [SEC][F.VII.533]

SIMPSON, JAMES, son of Richard Simpson of Sprostoun, Roxburghshire, was educated at Edinburgh University, an army chaplain in Ireland from 1642 to 1645, then a minister in Scotland from 1645 until 1660, was arrested in Portpatrick, Wigtownshire, when bound for Ireland, imprisoned then released on condition of exile, he died in Utrecht, the Netherlands, before August 1694. [FI.50]

SIMPSON, JOHN, from Garieside, Roxburghshire, was transported via Leith to Jamaica in August 1685, landed at Port Royal in November 1685. [ETR][LJ.15][RPCS.XI.330]

SIMPSON, JOHN, was warded in Edinburgh Tolbooth on 22 July 1685; a prisoner in Edinburgh Tolbooth, to be transported to the Plantations on 11 August 1685. [ETR]. [RPCS.IX.163]

SIMSON, MICHAEL, in Little Tilliry, for attending conventicles, was outlawed on 29 August 1672. [RPCS.III.583]

SIMPSON, PATRICK, fought at the Siege of Worcester in 1651, then transported via London aboard the <u>John and Sarah</u> bound for Boston in December 1651, landed there in February 1652. [SD.1.5-6]

SIMSON, PATRICK, born 2 October 1628, tutor to the family of the Marquis of Argyll, minister in Renfrew from 1658 until deprived in 1662, in 1678 he was accused of holding conventicles and was denounced as a rebel, he died on 24 October 1715. [F.III.186]

SIMPSON, ROBERT, in Parkhead of Burley, for attending conventicles, was outlawed on 29 August 1672. [RPCS.III.583]

SIMPSON, ROBERT, and his wife Helen Harper, in Lyne parish, fugitives in 1684. [RPCS.IX.501]

SIMSON, WILLIAM, a prisoner in Canongait Tolbooth, having taken the Oath of Allegiance, was released on 1 August 1667. [RPCS.II.318]

SINCLAIR, DUNCAN, was transported via Leith to Jamaica in August 1685. [RPCS.XI.136]

SINCLAIR, JOHN, in Delft in the Netherlands in 1684, formerly a minister in Ormiston, East Lothian. [NRS.JC39.48]

SINCLAIR, SOLOMAN, fought at the Siege of Worcester in 1651, then transported via London aboard the John and Sarah bound for Boston in December 1651, landed there in February 1652. [SD.1.5-6]

SITLINGTON, ROBERT, was killed at Bothwell Bridge, Lanarkshire, on 22 June 1679. [Nithsdale Martyrs Monument, Dumfries-shire]

SITLINGTON, THOMAS, was banished to the Plantations, died aboard the Henry and Francis bound for East New Jersey in 1685. [Nithsdale Martyrs Monument, Dumfries-shire]

SLOSS, ROBERT, of Arrothill, Ayr, was warded in Edinburgh Tolbooth on 28 October 1684, was transferred to Dunnottar Castle, Kincardineshire, on 29 July 1685, was transported to the colonies in 1686. [ETR] [RPCS.X.129]

SMELLIE, JOHN, in Watstounhead, a rebel, subscribed to a bond of the peace in October 1668. [RPCS.II.548]

SMISON, PATRICK, fought at the Siege of Worcester in 1651, then transported via London aboard the John and Sarah bound for Boston in December 1651, landed there in February 1652. [SD.1.5-6]

SMITH, ALEXANDER, then in Edinburgh Tolbooth, was transferred to Dunnottar Castle, Kincardineshire, on 29 July 1685. [ETR]

SMITH, GEORGE, in Evandale, a rebel in Glasgow Tolbooth, was banished to the Plantations in June 1684, and transported via Glasgow aboard the Pelican bound for Carolina, bond by Walter

Gibson, a merchant in Glasgow, dated 20 June 1684. [RPCS.IX.208]

SMITH, HELEN, was taken from Leith Tolbooth, put in irons and imprisoned in Edinburgh Tolbooth, in 1685. [ETR]

SMITH, HENRY, fought at the Siege of Worcester in 1651, then transported via London aboard the <u>John and Sarah</u> bound for Boston in December 1651, landed there in February 1652. [SD.1.5-6]

SMITH, HUGH, minister at Eastwood, Renfrewshire, from 1652, was deposed for keeping conventicles, on 18 August 1663. [RPCS.I.409]; he was denounced as a rebel in 1676, was dead by January 1679. [F.III.134]

SMITH, HUGH, having attended conventicles he was tried for treason in 1687. [NRS.JC39.100]

SMITH, ISOBEL, was warded in Edinburgh Tolbooth, on 3 December 1684, was transferred to Dunnottar Castle, Kincardineshire, on 29 July 1685. [ETR]

SMITH, JAMES, was sought by the Justice Court in August 1667 for his part in the late rebellion. [GC.123]

SMITH, JAMES, was executed in Glasgow on 13 June 1683. [Milton of Campsie gravestone, Stirlingshire]

SMITH, JAMES, was killed at Bothwell Bridge, Lanarkshire, on 22 June 1679. [Nithsdale Martyrs Monument, Dumfries-shire]

SMITH, JOHN, a minister in Edinburgh, was deposed and ordered to leave the town before 1 October 1662. [RPCS.I.264]

SMITH, JOHN, from Glencairn, Nithsdale, fought at the Battle of Bothwell Bridge in 1679, was transported via Leith aboard the <u>Crown of London</u> bound for Barbados on 27 November 1679, was shipwrecked off Orkney on 10 December 1679, later shipped to Jamaica. [RBM][CEC.212/5][SW.202]

SMITH, JOHN, from Dalry, Galloway, fought at the Battle of Bothwell Bridge in 1679, was transported via Leith aboard the

Crown of London bound for Barbados on 27 November 1679, was shipwrecked off Orkney on 10 December 1679, later shipped to Jamaica. [RBM][CEC.212/5][SW.203]

SMITH, JOHN, a tenant in Stains, a fugitive, was warded in Edinburgh Tolbooth on 2 July 1684, and liberated on 14 August 1684. [ETR]

SMITH, JOHN, from Hamilton, Lanarkshire, was transported via Leith to Carolina on 21 March 1684. [RPCS.VIII.710]

SMITH, JOHN, from Kirkintilloch, Dunbartonshire, was transported via Leith aboard the Henry and Francis bound for East New Jersey on 5 September 1685. [RPCS.XI.167]

SMITH, MICHAEL, was warded in Edinburgh Tolbooth on 28 May 1685, was liberated on 29 July 1685. [ETR]

SMITH, PETER, in Mid Claughrie, having seen the rebel Robert Morrein, at Wardlawshaw on Palgavin Muir, also John Frisell a rebel, also Robert Cowan a rebel, and nor reporting it, was declared a rebel and fugitive in October 1684. [RPCS.IX.361]

SMITH, ROBERT, in Smithstoun, was warded in Edinburgh Tolbooth, on 28 October 1684, and having taken the Oath of Allegiance was released on 13 December 1684. [ETR]

SMITH, ROBERT, in Upper Belibught, for aiding rebels William Herries from Kirkcudbright, Robert Greirson a chapman, James Corsan, and Samuel MacKeoan, was declared to be a rebel and fugitive in October 1684. [RPCS.IX.368]

SMITH, ROBERT, a cutler from Kilmaurs, Ayrshire, was at the Battle of Bothwell Bridge, Lanarkshire, in 1679. [RPCS.IX.548]

SMITH, ROBERT, was killed in Kirkcudbright in 1684. [Nithsdale Martyrs Monument, Dumfries-shire]

SMYTH, WALTER, and Elizabeth Milligan his wife in Craighill [?], fugitives in May 1683. [RPCS.VIII.609]

SMITH, WILLIAM, son of John Smith in Kingatyhill, Cambusnethan, Lanarkshire, was transported via Leith to Jamaica in August 1685, died at sea. [RPCS.XI.329][LJ.203]

SMITH, WILLIAM, in Carmunnock, Lanarkshire, a rebel in Glasgow Tolbooth, was banished to the Plantations in June 1684, and transported via Glasgow aboard the Pelican bound for Carolina, bond by Walter Gibson, a merchant in Glasgow, dated 20 June 1684. [RPCS.IX.208]

SNODGRASS, ANDREW, from Govan, Glasgow, fought at the Battle of Bothwell Bridge in 1679, was transported via Leith aboard the Crown of London bound for Barbados on 27 November 1679, was shipwrecked and drowned off Orkney on 10 December 1679. [RBM]

SOMERVILLE, JAMES, a fermorer from Cambusnethan, Lanarkshire, a prisoner in Edinburgh Tolbooth, who refused to take an Oath of Allegiance, was banished to the American Plantations on 17 December 1685, transported via Leith aboard the John and Nicholas bound for Barbados in December 1685. [ETR][RPCS.XI.254]

SOMERVELL, LUDOVIC, born 1630, was educated at Edinburgh University, minister at New Monkland, Lanarkshire, from 1656 until deprived in 1662, he died in July 1669. [F.III.271]

SOMERVILLE, PATRICK, a tailor in Canongait, Edinburgh, was transported via Leith aboard the St Michael of Scarborough bound for the West Indies on 12 December 1678. [RPCS.VI.76]

SOMERVILLE, WILLIAM, from Cambusnethan, Lanarkshire, a prisoner in Edinburgh Tolbooth, who refused to take an Oath of Allegiance, was banished to the American Plantations on 17 December 1685, transported via Leith on the John and Nicholas to Barbados in December 1685. [ETR][RPCS.XI.254]

SOUTHRUM, WILLIAM, factor to the laird of Largo, Fife, was accused of attending conventicles in 1668. [RPCS.II.491]

SPALDING, JOHN, was educated at St Andrews University, minister at Dreghorn, Ayrshire, from 1656 until deprived in 1662, was accused of keeping conventicles in 1669, returned to Dreghorn in 1670. [F.III.88]

SPENCE, ANDREW, in Hemisfieldtoun, for seeing rebel Peter Coudan and not reporting it, was declared to be a rebel and fugitive in October 1684. [RPCS.IX.370]

SPENCE, WILLIAM, a servant of the late Earl of Argyll, having participated in the Earl of Argyll's Rebellion was tried for treason in 1685. [NRS.JC39.71]; he was tortured until he revealed what he knew of the Earl's Rebellion, 24 July 1684, he was transferred to Dunbarton Castle in September 1684, he was sentenced to be handed at the Mercat Cross of Edinburgh on 22 July 1685, reprieved until 3 September 1685. [ETR] [RPCS.IX.68/73/179]

SPENCE, WILLIAM, born 1636, from Fossoway, Fife, a minister in exile in Utrecht, in the Netherlands, from 1684 until 1687. [SEC]

SPENCE, WILLIAM, was warded in Edinburgh Tolbooth on 6 June 1685. [ETR]

SPROT, ANDREW, from Borgue, Kirkcudbrightshire, fought at the Battle of Bothwell Bridge in 1679, was transported via Leith aboard the Crown of London bound for Barbados on 27 November 1679, was shipwrecked and drowned off Orkney on 10 December 1679. [RBM]

SPROTT, WILLIAM, in Crowburgh, was accused of fraudulently entering the signatures of the minister and elders onto a pass to enable him to go to Ireland, which was discovered at Port Patrick, Wigtownshire, in 1684. [RPCS.IX.381]

SPROTT, WILLIAM, from Clontarch, was banished to the Plantations on18 August 1685, then transported via Leith aboard the Henry and Francis bound for East New Jersey on 5 August 1685, landed there on 7 December 1685. [RPCS.X.154/612][NWI.I.423]

SPROUL, WILLIAM, was warded in Edinburgh Tolbooth on 28 November 1684, was transferred to Dunnottar Castle, Kincardineshire, on 29 July 1685. [ETR]

STEEL, JAMES, from Calder, Midlothian, , fought at the Battle of Bothwell Bridge in 1679, was transported via Leith aboard the Crown of London bound for Barbados on 27 November 1679, was shipwrecked and drowned off Orkney on 10 December 1679. [RBM]

STEELE, NINIAN, a Captain of Lord Angus's Regiment, [the Cameronians], who fought at the Battle of Killiecrankie in 1689. [BK]

STEELE, THOMAS, a rebel, was imprisoned in Edinburgh Tolbooth on 21 November 1683, was liberated on 10 February 1686. [RPCS.VIII.633][ ETR]

STEIDMAN, JOHN, a tailor in Kinross, for attending conventicles, was outlawed on 29 August 1672. [RPCS.III.583]

STEIDMAN, ROBERT, son of Robert Steidman of Bonnagall, for attending conventicles, was outlawed on 29 August 1672. [RPCS.III.583]

STEILL, WILLIAM, a notorious rebel in Glasgow Tolbooth, was to be tried for his life in October 1684, a prisoner in Edinburgh Tolbooth, was liberated on 10 February 1686. [RPCS.IX.710] [ETR]

STEPHENSON, JOHN, a Captain of Lord Angus's Regiment, [the Cameronians], who fought at the Battle of Killiecrankie in 1689. [BK]

STEVEN, JAMES, from Newport, Glasgow, was warded in Edinburgh Tolbooth on 20 May 1685, but, having sworn an Oath of Allegiance was released on 28 May 1685. [ETR]

STEVEN, JOHN, from Livingstone, West Lothian, fought at the Battle of Bothwell Bridge in 1679, was transported via Leith aboard the Crown of London bound for Barbados on 27

November 1679 was shipwrecked and drowned off Orkney on 10 December 1679. [RBM]

STEVEN, WILLIAM, from Glasgow, was transported via Leith aboard the St Michael of Scarborough bound for the West Indies on 12 December 1685. [RPCS.VI.76]

STEVENSON, ALEXANDER, minister at Dalmellington, Ayrshire, from 1648 until deposed for not conforming to Episcopacy. [F.3.31]

STEVENSON, JOHN, in Wester Camregan, Ayrshire, 1680. [NRS.GD117.117]

STEVENSON, JOHN, was killed at Caldons, Loch Trool, on 23 January 1685. [Newton Stewart gravestone, Kirkcudbrightshire]

STEVENSON, THOMAS, was killed at Caldons, Loch Trool, on 23 January 1685. [Newton Stewart gravestone, Kirkcudbrightshire]

STEWART, ALEXANDER, from Kirkliston, West Lothian, was transported via Leith aboard the St Michael of Scarborough bound for the West Indies on 12 December 1678. [RPCS.VI.76]

STEWART, ARCHIBALD, for his part in the Pentland Rising of 1666, was beheaded in Glasgow on 19 December 1666. [Glasgow Cathedral]

STEWART, ARCHIBALD, fought at Bothwell Bridge on 22 June 1679. [Glasgow Cathedral plaque]

STEWART, AUSTIN, fought at the Siege of Worcester in 1651, then transported via London aboard the John and Sarah bound for Boston in December 1651, landed there in February 1652. [SD.1.5-6]

STEWART, CHARLES, fought at the Siege of Worcester in 1651, then transported via London aboard the John and Sarah bound for Boston in December 1651, landed there in February 1652. [SD.1.5-6]

STEWART, DAVID, son of Thomas Stewart of Cultness, having participated in the Earl of Argyll's Rebellion of 1685, was tried for treason in 1685. [NRS.JC39.71] ; was warded in Edinburgh Tolbooth on 10 July 1685, then sentenced to be hanged at the Mercat Cross of Edinburgh on 22 July 1685, reprieved.[ETR]

STEWART, GILBERT, in Castle Mill, as he had attended a conventicle, was bound with rope and imprisoned, in 1684. [RPCS.IX.523/525]

STEWART, JAMES, of Fasnacloich, subscribed in Inveraray, Argyll, to a bond undertaking that he will not assist the Earl of Argyll or any other rebel under a penalty of 10,000 merks, dated 27 August 1684. [RPCS.IX.318]

STEWART, JAMES, of Hartwood, was warded in Edinburgh Tolbooth on 13 November 1684, was put in irons and imprisoned in Canongait Tolbooth on 29 July 1685. [ETR]; was transported via Leith bound for East New Jersey on 30 July 1685. [RPCS.XI.329]

STEWART, JAMES, son of Sir James Stewart the Provost of Edinburgh, having participated in the Earl of Argyll's Rebellion of 1685, was tried for treason in 1685. [NRS.JC39.71]

STEWART, JOHN, fought at the Battle of Dunbar in 1650, was transported via London aboard the Unity bound for Boston in 1650. [SCF.1226]

STEWART, JOHN, of Bellachylis, undertook not to assist the Earl of Argyll or any rebel, in a bond dated at Inveraray, Argyll, on 9 September 1684, subject to a penalty of 1000 pounds Scots. [RPCS.IX.349]

STEWART, JOHN, of Kilmoir, miller at Castle Mill, as he had attended a conventicle, was bound with rope and imprisoned, in 1684. [RPCS.IX.523]

STEUART, JOHN, in Edinburgh Tolbooth in May 1685. [ETR]

STEWART, NEIL, fought at the Siege of Worcester in 1651, then transported via London aboard the John and Sarah bound for Boston in December 1651, landed there in February 1652. [SD.1.5-6]

STEWART, PATRICK, from Argyll, fought in Argyll's Rebellion, was transported via Leith to Jamaica in August 1685. [RPCS.XI.329]

STEWART, ROBERT, fought at the Siege of Worcester in 1651, then transported via London aboard the John and Sarah bound for Boston in December 1651, landed there in February 1652. [SD.1.5-6]

STEWART, ROBERT, of Ardoch, in the parish of Dalry, a suspected Covenanter in 1665. [GC.111]

STEWART, ROBERT, son of Major Robert Stewart of Ardoch, was killed on 18 December 1684. [St John of Dalry gravestone, Kirkcudbrightshire]

STEWART, ROBERT, was killed on Auchencloy Moor in 1685. [Auchencloy Martyrs Monument, Kirkcudbrightshire]

STEWART, WILLIAM, fought at the Siege of Worcester in 1651, then transported via London aboard the John and Sarah bound for Boston in December 1651, landed there in February 1652. [SD.1.5-6]

STEWART, WILLIAM, of Allingtoun, was warded in Edinburgh Tolbooth on 13 November 1684. [ETR]

STEWART, WILLIAM, was killed near Lochenkit, in the parish of Kirkpatrick-Durham, on 2 March 1685. [Lochenkit gravestone]

STIRLING, DAVID, fought at the Siege of Worcester in 1651, then transported via London aboard the John and Sarah bound for Boston in December 1651, landed there in February 1652. [SD.1.5-6]

STIRLING, JAMES, born 1631, from Paisley, Renfrewshire, a minister in exile in Rotterdam, Holland, from 1679 to 1680. [SEC]

STIRLING, JOHN, fought at the Siege of Worcester in 1651, then transported via London aboard the John and Sarah bound for Boston in December 1651, landed there in February 1652. [SD.1.5-6]

STIRLING, JOHN, born 1620, son of Alexander Stirling a farmer in Stewarton, Ayrshire, was educated at the University of Glasgow, minister at Kilbarchan, Renfrewshire, from 1649 until deprived in 1662, then from 1672 until his death on 18 July 1683, [Wf.iii.149]; as accused of holding conventicles and imprisoned in Edinburgh Castle in August 1660, [RPCS.VIII.465]; possibly the preacher .... Stirling who returned from Holland, who was to be arrested for distributing a seditious pamphlet in 1667. [RPCS.II.376]

STITT, EDWARD, in Durisdear, Dumfriesshire, having aided the wounded rebel Robert Grier, a chapman, after the Enterkin ambush, was declared a rebel and fugitive in 1684. [RPCS.IX.358]; a prisoner in Edinburgh Tolbooth, to be put aboard a ship in Leith bound for Jamaica, on 11 August 1685. [ETR][RPCS.XI.145]

STOBIE, ADAM, from Lascar, Stirlingshire, was transported via Leith aboard the St Michael of Scarborough bound for the West Indies on 1 December 1678. [RPCS.VI.76]

STODDART, JOHN, born 1625, a tenant farmer of Williamhope, died on 15 July 1692. [Yarrow, Selkirkshire, gravestone]

STODDART, THOMAS, in Lesmahagow, Lanarkshire, was accused of participating in the Earl of Argyll's Rebellion, in 1685. [NRS.JC39.72]; then in Edinburgh Tolbooth, put in irons and imprisoned in Canongait Tolbooth on 29 July 1685, was executed in the Grassmarket of Edinburgh on 12 August 1685. [ETR]

STOT, DAVID, a rebel, to be imprisoned in Edinburgh Tolbooth in February 1669. [RPCS.II.608]

STOT, JOHN, died in Dunnottar Castle, Kincardineshire, in 1685. [Nithsdale Martyrs Monument, Dumfries-shire]

STRANG, CHRISTOPHER, from Kilbride, was transported via Leith aboard the Henry and Francis bound for East New Jersey on 5 September 1685. [RPCS.XI.154]

STRANG, JAMES, in Westdrum, Kilbride, a fugitive in 1683. [RPCS.VIII.648]

STRUTHERS, JOHN, from Kilbride, Lanarkshire, , fought at the Battle of Bothwell Bridge in 1679, was transported via Leith aboard the Crown of London bound for Barbados on 27

November 1679, was shipwrecked and drowned off Orkney on 10 December 1679. [RBM]

STUART, HENRY, a Lieutenant of Lord Angus's Regiment, [The Cameronians], fought at the Battle of Dunkeld in August 1679. [BK]

STUART, WILLIAM, from Galloway, was executed at Kirkpatrick, Irongray, Kirkcudbrightshire, in 1688. [Largshill Monument, Kirkcudbrightshire]

STURGEON, WILLIAM, in Nether Barncrosh, was accused, in Kirkcudbright on 4 October 1684, of conversing with rebels William Halliday and John Charters. [RPCS.IX.374]

SUMMERTON, JANET, was warded in Edinburgh Tolbooth, on 3 December 1684. [ETR]

SUTHERLAND, ANSELL, fought at the Siege of Worcester in 1651, then transported via London aboard the John and Sarah bound for Boston in December 1651, landed there in February 1652. [SD.1.5-6]

SUTHERLAND, PATRICK, fought at the Siege of Worcester in 1651, then transported via London aboard the John and Sarah bound for Boston in December 1651, landed there in February 1652. [SD.1.5-6]

SWAN, JOHN, was transported via Leith to East New Jersey on 39 July 1685. [RPCS.XI.329]

SWAN, THOMAS, from Carstairs, Lanarkshire, fought at the Battle of Bothwell Bridge in 1679, was transported via Leith aboard the Crown of London bound for Barbados on 27 November 1679, was shipwrecked off Orkney on 10 December 1679, later shipped to Jamaica. [RBM]

SWANSTON, WILLIAM, from Loudoun, Ayrshire, , fought at the Battle of Bothwell Bridge in 1679, was transported via Leith aboard the Crown of London bound for Barbados on 27 November 1679, was shipwrecked off Orkney on 10 December 1679, later shipped to Jamaica. [RBM] [NRS.JC41.2; JC27.10.3]

SWORD, ANDREW, in the parish of Borgue, later a weaver in the Stewartry of Kirkcudbright, confessed that he had taken up arms at Bothwell Bridge and had refused the Bond, one of the assassins of Archbishop Sharp on Magus Moor, Fife, on 3 May 1679, was hanged on 25 November 1679. [Magus Moor memorial] [GC.167][Z.203]

SYME, HUGH, from Eaglesham, Renfrewshire, a rebel in Glasgow Tolbooth, was banished to the Plantations in June 1684, and transported via Glasgow aboard the Pelican bound for Carolina, bond by Walter Gibson, a merchant in Glasgow, dated 20 June 1684. [RPCS.IX.208]

SYME, JOHN, in Eaglesham, Renfrewshire, a rebel in Glasgow Tolbooth, was banished to the Plantations in June 1684, and transported via Glasgow aboard the Pelican bound for Carolina, bond by Walter Gibson, a merchant in Glasgow, dated 20 June 1684. [RPCS.IX.208]

SYME, WILLIAM, in Eaglesham, Renfrewshire, a rebel in Glasgow Tolbooth, was banished to the Plantations in June 1684, and transported via Glasgow aboard the Pelican bound for Carolina, bond by Walter Gibson, a merchant in Glasgow, dated 20 June 1684. [RPCS.IX.208]

TACKET, ARTHUR, a rebel in Lanarkshire, to be tortured to reveal the names of accomplices in July 1684, to be executed. [RPCS.IX.22/70/71/73]

TAGGART, JOHN, from Annandale, Dumfriesshire, transported via Leith, aboard the Henry and Francis bound for East New Jersey on 5 September 1685. [RPCS.XI.155]

TAIT, ANDREW, in Mid Clauchrie, Closeburn, for aiding Archibald Hunter, Adam and James Harkness, Robert Grear, John Frisell, and other rebels, was declared a rebel and fugitive in October 1684. [RPCS.IX.360]; was interrogated about Archibald Hunter in Tarraran, refused to take the Test Oath, and was imprisoned in October 1684. [RPCS.IX.691]

TAIT, JOHN, from Camphill, Dumfries, was transported to the colonies in October 1684. [RPCS.X.591]

TANNIELL, [?], JOHN, fought at the Siege of Worcester in 1651, then transported via London aboard the John and Sarah bound for Boston in December 1651, landed there in February 1652. [SD.1.5-6]

TANNIS, AGNES, was transported via Leith aboard the Henry and Francis bound for East New Jersey on 5 September 1685. [RPCS.XI.154]

TAYLOR, DAVID, fought at the Siege of Worcester in 1651, then transported via London aboard the John and Sarah bound for Boston in December 1651, landed there in February 1652. [SD.1.5-6]

TAYLOR, EWAN, fought at the Siege of Worcester in 1651, then transported via London aboard the John and Sarah bound for Boston in December 1651, landed there in February 1652. [SD.1.5-6]

TAYLOR, JAMES, fought at the Battle of Dunbar in 1650, was transported via London aboard the Unity bound for Boston in 1650. [SCF.1226]

TAYLOR, JOHN, fought at the Battle of Dunbar in 1650, was transported via London aboard the Unity bound for Boston in 1650. [SCF.1226]

TAYLOR, WILLIAM, fought at the Battle of Dunbar in 1650, was transported via London aboard the Unity bound for Boston in 1650, landed there in February 1652. [SD.1.5-6]

TEMPLE, WILLIAM, from Linton, Roxburghshire, was transported via Leith aboard the St Michael of Scarborough bound for the West Indies on 12 December 1678. [RPCS.VI.76]

TENLOR, [?], JOHN, fought at the Battle of Dunbar in 1650, was transported via London aboard the Unity bound for Boston in 1650. [SCF.1226]

TENNANT, JAMES, a prisoner in Edinburgh or Canongait Tolbooth, a rebel, was banished to the Plantations in Carolina on 8 August 1684, then shipped via Leith to Carolina in August 1684. [RPCS.IX.95]

TENNANT, MARGARET, a widow in Barony parish, Glasgow, in 1683. [RPCS.VIII.644]

THOM, ROBERT, in Carmanock, was tried in 1684 for his part in the 1679 Rebellion. [NRS.JC39.50]

THOM, ROBERT, was killed at the Loan of Balmadie on 11 May 1685. [Cathcart gravestone, Glasgow]

THOM, ....., in Polmadie, Little Giveand, or Glasgow, who attended a conventicle near Greenock, was to be captured and imprisoned in Edinburgh Tolbooth in August 1684. [RPCS.IX.131]

THOMSON, ALEXANDER, fought at the Siege of Worcester in 1651, then transported via London aboard the John and Sarah bound for Boston in December 1651, landed there in February 1652. [SD.1.5-6]

THOMSON, ALEXANDER, feuar of Seggie, for attending conventicles, was outlawed on 29 August 1672. [RPCS.III.583]

THOMSON, ANDREW, fought at the Siege of Worcester in 1651, then transported via London aboard the John and Sarah bound for Boston in December 1651, landed there in February 1652. [SD.1.5-6]

THOMSON, ANDREW, from Dundonald, Ayrshire, , fought at the Battle of Bothwell Bridge in 1679, was transported via Leith aboard the Crown of London bound for Barbados on 27 November 1679, was shipwrecked off Orkney on 10 December 1679, later shipped to Jamaica. [RBM]CEC.212/5][SW.199]

THOMSON, ANDREW, from St Ninian's, Stirlingshire fought at the Battle of Bothwell Bridge in 1679, was transported via Leith aboard the Crown of London bound for Barbados on 27 November 1679, was shipwrecked off Orkney on 10 December 1679, later shipped to Jamaica. [RBM]CEC.212/5][SW.199]

THOMSON, ARCHIBALD, was transported via Leith to Jamaica in August 1685. [RPCS.XI.329]

THOMSON, DONALD, from Argyll, in Argyll's Rebellion was transported via Leith to Jamaica in July 1685. [RPCS.XI.94]

THOMSON, DUNCAN, from Argyll, in Argyll's Rebellion, was transported via Leith to Jamaica in August 1685. [RPCS.XI.130/329]

THOMSON, GABRIEL, a merchant in Glasgow, was transported via Leith aboard the St Michael of Glasgow bound for the West Indies on 12 December 1678. [RPCS.VI.76]

THOMSON, GABRIEL, in Gallowhill, was tried in 1684 for his part in the 1679 Rebellion. [NRS.JC39.50]; was killed on 1 May 1685. [Eaglesham gravestone, Renfrewshire]

THOMSON, GEORGE, fought at the Battle of Dunbar in 1650, was transported via London aboard the Unity bound for Boston in November 1650. [SCF.1226]

THOMSON, JAMES, fought at the Battle of Dunbar in 1650, was transported via London aboard the Unity bound for Boston in November 1650. [SCF.1226]

THOMSON, JAMES, a farmer from Tanhill, Lesmahagow, fought at the Battle of Drumclog on 1 June 1679, and was buried in St Ninian's graveyard, Stonehouse, Lanarkshire. [Stonehouse gravestone]

THOMSON, JAMES, from Quathquan, Lanarkshire, fought at the Battle of Bothwell Bridge in 1679, was transported via Leith aboard the Crown of London bound for Barbados on 27 November 1679, was shipwrecked and drowned off Orkney on 10 December 1679. [RBM]

THOMSON, JOHN, from Argyll, in Argyll's Rebellion, was transported via Leith to New England in July 1685. [RPCS.XI.94]

THOMSON, JOHN, son of Alexander Thomson in the Mains of Cleish, for attending conventicles, was outlawed on 29 August 1672. [RPCS.III.583]

THOMSON, JOHN, from Shotts, Lanarkshire, fought at the Battle of Bothwell Bridge in 1679, was transported via Leith aboard the Crown of London bound for Barbados on 27 November 1679, was shipwrecked off Orkney on 10 December 1679, later shipped to Jamaica. [RBM][CEC.212/5][SW.199]

THOMSON, JOHN, from Dalmeny, West Lothian, fought at the Battle of Bothwell Bridge in 1679, was transported via Leith aboard the Crown of London bound for Barbados on 27 November 1679, was shipwrecked and drowned off Orkney on 10 December 1679. [RBM]

THOMSON, JOHN, from Torpichen, West Lothian, fought at the Battle of Bothwell Bridge in 1679, was transported via Leith aboard the Crown of London bound for Barbados on 27 November 1679, was shipwrecked off Orkney on 10 December 1679. [RBM]

THOMSON, JOHN, at Tibers Mill, for aiding rebels John MacCall and William Milligan, was declared to be a rebel and fugitive in October 1684. [RPCS.IX.366]

THOMSON, JOHN, in Glengaber, for seeing rebels, .....Harper senior and junior in Kiroywood, Tinwald, and failed to report it, was declared to be a rebel and fugitive in October 1684. [RPCS.IX.370]

THOMSON, JOHN, in Hemesfield, for conversing with rebel Peter Coudan, was declared to be a rebel and fugitive in October 1684. [RPCS.IX.370]

THOMSON, JOSEPH, then in Edinburgh Tolbooth, was transferred to Dunnottar Castle, Kincardineshire, on 29 July 1685. [ETR]

THOMSON, NEIL, from Argyll, in Argyll's Rebellion, was transported via Leith to Jamaica in August 1685. [RPCS.XI.136]

THOMSON, ROBERT, a tailor in Seggie, for attending conventicles, was outlawed on 29 August 1672. [RPCS.III.583]

THOMSON, THOMAS, from St Ninian's, Stirlingshire, fought at the Battle of Bothwell Bridge in 1679, was transported via Leith aboard the Crown of London bound for Barbados on 27 November 1679, was shipwrecked off Orkney on 10 December 1679, later shipped to Jamaica. [RBM][CEC.212/5][SW.199]

THOMSON, THOMAS, of Cocklaw, a minister, and his wife Isabel Mercer, for holding conventicles, was fined, a bond dated 6 October 1684. [RPCS.IX.706]

THOMSON, WALTER, a smith in Midtoun, for attending conventicles, was outlawed on 29 August 1672. [RPCS.III.583]

THOMSON, WILLIAM, fought at the Battle of Dunbar in 1650, was transported via London aboard the Unity bound for Boston in November 1650. [SCF.1226]

THOMSON, WILLIAM, fought at the Battle of Bothwell Bridge in 1679, was transported via Leith aboard the Crown of London bound for Barbados on 27 November 1679, was shipwrecked and drowned off Orkney on 10 December 1679. [RBM]

THOMSON, WILLIAM, was educated at Edinburgh University, minister at Mearns, Renfrewshire, from 1653 until deprived in 1662, [F.III.155]; from Renfrew, a minister in exile in Rotterdam, Holland, from 1679 to 1680. [SEC]

THOMSON, WILLIAM, was transported via Leith bound for East New Jersey on 31 July 1685. [RPCS.XI.131]

THRESHIE, JAMES, a servant of Robert Greir at the Bridgend of Moniaive, a rebel in 1666, imprisoned in Edinburgh Tolbooth or Canongait Tolbooth, having taken the Oath of Allegiance, was released on 11 July 1667. [RPCS.II.308]

TINTO, JAMES, from Temple, Midlothian, fought at the Battle of Bothwell Bridge in 1679, was transported via Leith aboard the

Crown of London bound for Barbados on 27 November 1679, was shipwrecked and drowned off Orkney on 10 December 1679. [RBM]

TOD, JAMES, from Dunbar, East Lothian, fought at the Battle of Bothwell Bridge in 1679, was transported via Leith aboard the Crown of London bound for Barbados on 27 November 1679, was shipwrecked and drowned off Orkney on 10 December 1679. [RBM]

TOD, JOHN, in Kilmarnock, a rebel in 1666, imprisoned in Edinburgh Tolbooth or Canongait Tolbooth, having taken the Oath of Allegiance, was released on 11 July 1667. [RPCS.II.308]

TOD, ROBERT, from Fenwick, Ayrshire, fought at the Battle of Bothwell Bridge in 1679, was transported via Leith aboard the Crown of London bound for Barbados on 27 November 1679, was shipwrecked off Orkney on 10 December 1679, later shipped to Jamaica. [RBM]

TORRANCE, ANDREW, from Avondale, Lanarkshire, fought at the Battle of Bothwell Bridge in 1679, was transported via Leith aboard the Crown of London bound for Barbados on 27 November 1679, was shipwrecked and drowned off Orkney on 10 December 1679. [RBM]

TOSH, JAMES, born 1629, was transported to New England about 1650. [SCF.1226]

TOSH, JOHN, fought at the Battle of Dunbar in 1650, was transported via London aboard the Unity bound for Boston in November 1650. [SCF.1226]

TOSH, WILLIAM, fought at the Battle of Dunbar in 1650, was transported via London aboard the Unity bound for Boston in November 1650. [SCF.1226]

TOUGH, ALESTER, fought at the Siege of Worcester in 1651, then transported via London aboard the John and Sarah bound for Boston in December 1651, landed there in February 1652. [SD.1.5-6]

TOWER, PATRICK, fought at the Siege of Worcester in 1651, then transported via London aboard the John and Sarah bound for Boston in December 1651, landed there in February 1652. [SD.1.5-6]

TOWER, THOMAS, fought at the Battle of Dunbar in 1650, transported via London aboard the Unity bound for Boston in November 1650. [SCF.1226]

TRAILL, ROBERT, [I], born in Elie, Fife, around 1603, from Edinburgh, fought at Rullion Green in1666, was accused of holding conventicles and imprisoned in Edinburgh Castle in August 1660, later on the Bass Rock, [RPCS.VIII.465]; a minister in exile in Rotterdam and Utrecht in the Netherland from 1663 until 1670. [SEC][Z.201]

TRAILL, ROBERT, [2], born 1642, from Edinburgh, a minister in exile in Utrecht in the Netherland from 1667 until 1669. [SEC]

TRAIL, WILLIAM, born September 1640 in Elie, Fife, was educated at Edinburgh University, ordained at Lifford, Ireland, in 1671, minister there from 1673 until 1690, he was imprisoned there from 1681 to 1682, emigrated to America, minister on the Potomac River, Maryland, from 1684, returned to Scotland in 1690, minister at Borthwick, Mid Lothian, from 1690 until his death on 3 May 1714. [F.I.302; F.VII.666] [FI.81]

TRAILL, ......., son of Robert Traill, a suspected rebel, was sought in 1667. [RPCS.II.345]

TRUMBLE, Mrs, a rebel, was banished and transported to Virginia, on 30 July 1668. [RPCS.II.503]

TULLIDEPH, WILLIAM, a minister in Kilbirnie, was warded in Edinburgh Tolbooth on 11 December 1684, there on 17 June 1685. [ETR]

TURNBULL, ANDREW, with a troop of horse, fought at the Battle of Bothwell Bridge, Lanarkshire, on 2 June 1679.

TURNBULL, GEORGE, was warded in Edinburgh Tolbooth, on 15 October 1684. [ETR]

TURNBULL, JAMES, was warded in Edinburgh Tolbooth on 20 May 1685, but having subscribed to the Test Act was released on 28 May 1685. [ETR]

TURNBULL, THOMAS, of Knowe, Hassendean, Roxburghshire, born 1652, thought to have fought at the Battles of Drumclog on 1 June 1679, of Bothwell Bridge on 22 June 1679, of Beauly Hill, and in the attack on Drumlanrig's Tower in Hawick, Roxburghshire, died in 1730. [Minto gravestone, Roxburghshire]

TURNBULL, THOMAS, from Argyll, in Argyll's Rebellion, a prisoner in Edinburgh Tolbooth, was transported via Leith to Jamaica in August 1685. [ETR][RPCS.XI.330]

TURNBULL, WILLIAM, of Hornshole, born 1606, son of Thomas Turnbull of Minto, was educated at Edinburgh University, minister at Makerstoun from 1635 until 1667, was chaplain to a regiment of horse in 1645. [F.III.78]

TURNBULL, WILLIAM, was transported via Leith aboard the St Michael of Scarborough bound for the West Indies on 12 December 1678. [RPCS.VI.76]

TURNBULL, WILLIAM, was transported via Leith aboard the Henry and Francis bound for East New Jersey on 5 September 1685. [RPCS.XI.154]

TURNBULL, ......, of Ashieburn, two brothers, were transported to Virginia, for opposing a non Covenanter minister being imposed on Ancrum parish in 1665. [F.II.100] [F.III.100]

TURNER, JAMES, in Kirkland, was accused, in Kirkcudbright on 4 October 1684, of aiding James Garmorey in Ironanity a declared traitor. [RPCS.IX.378]

TURPNEY, JOHN, was transported via Leith aboard the Henry and Francis bound for East New Jersey on 5 September 1685. [RPCS.XI.154]

UNNESS, JOHN, from Castletoun, Roxburghshire, fought at the Battle of Bothwell Bridge in 1679, was transported via Leith aboard the Crown of London bound for Barbados on 27 November 1679, was shipwrecked and drowned off Orkney on 10 December 1679. [RBM]

URE, JAMES, from Shirgarton, Stirlingshire, a dissenter from 1670, sometime in Ireland, returned to fight at the Battle of Bothwell Bridge on 22 June 1679, tried in 1682, died in 1746. [Kippen gravestone, Stirlingshire]

URIE, JOHN, from Blairgorts, Newburgh, Fife, was transported via Leith aboard the St Michael of Scarborough bound for the West Indies on 12 December 1678. [RPCS.VI.76]

URIE, WILLIAM, from Cathcart, Glasgow, was transported via Leith aboard the St Michael of Scarborough bound for the West Indies on 12 December 1678. [RPCS.VI.76]

URIE, JOHN, a maltman in Glasgow, a rebel imprisoned in Canongait Tolbooth, was released in September 1684. [RPCS.IX.170]

URIE, JOHN, was banished to the Plantations on 5 September 1685, transported via Leith aboard the Henry and Francis bound for East New Jersey. [RPCS.XI.166]

URIE, JOHN, was killed at the Loan of Balmadie on 11 May 1685. [Cathcart gravestone, Glasgow]

URIE, PATRICK, a notorious rebel in Glasgow Tolbooth, was to be tried for his life in October 1684. [RPCS.IX.710]; was banished to the Plantations on 5 September 1685, transported via Leith aboard the Henry and Francis bound for East New Jersey. [RPCS.XI.155]

URIE, ROBERT, a weaver in Little Govan, a rebel in Glasgow Tolbooth, was banished to the Plantations in June 1684, and transported via Glasgow aboard the Pelican bound for Carolina, bond by Walter Gibson, a merchant in Glasgow, dated 20 June 1684. [RPCS.IX.208]

URIE, WILLIAM, from Cathcart, Glasgow, was transported via Leith aboard the St Michael of Scarborough bound for the West Indies on 12 December 1678. [RPCS.VI.76]

URQUHART, JAMES, a minister, in Edinburgh Tolbooth on 17 June 1685. [ETR]

URQUHART, THOMAS, was accused of holding conventicles in Moray in 1668, to be arrested. [RPCS.II.504]

URQUHART, JAMES, was transported to the colonies in 1685. [RPCS.X.165]

URRY, WILLIAM, a Lieutenant Colonel in the Army of the Solemn League and Covenant, Colonel of Urry's Regiment of Horse in 1651, was captured at the Siege of Worcester. [RHCA.398]

VALLANCE, ALEXANDER, from Ayr, then in Edinburgh Tolbooth, was transferred to Dunnottar Castle, Kincardineshire, on 29 July 1685, then transported to the colonies in 1685. [ETR][RPCS.X.129]

VALLANCE, HUGH, having attended conventicles he was tried for treason in 1687. [NRS.JC39.100]

VALLANCE, JAMES, of Possill, escaped to Ireland in 1680. [NRS.GD61.71]

VEITCH, JAMES, minister at Mauchline, Ayrshire, from 1656 until 1662 when he was deprived for refusing to take the Oath of Allegiance, was re-admitted in 1669 until 1684, he went to Holland but returned to Mauchline in 1687 and died in 1694. [F.I.49] [RPCS.I.264]

VEITCH, JOHN, born 2 March 1620, son of Reverend John Veitch in Roberton, Lanarkshire, was educated at Glasgow University, minister at Westruther from 1648 until 1662 when he refused to conform to Episcopacy, he was declared an outlaw on 5 October 1680 and imprisoned in Edinburgh Tolbooth on 5 September 1685, released on 14 January 1686, he died in Dalkeith, Midlothian, on 16 December 1702. [F.II.165] [ETR]

VEITCH, WILLIAM, later a minister in Dumfries, in the 1666 Rising, trial papers, 1667. [NRS.JC39.29]; was sought by the Justice Court in August 1667 for his part in the late rebellion. [GC.123]

VERNOUR, THOMAS, a minister in Galloway, was accused of holding conventicles within the Presbytery in 1666. [GC.107]; a rebel who fled to Ireland, 7 October 1680. [RPCS.VI.560]

VIOLENT, WILLIAM, minister at Ferry-Port-on-Craig, Fife, from 1656 until derived in 1662, indulged minister of Cambusnethan, Lanarkshire, was accused of preaching at conventicles, was warded in Edinburgh Tolbooth on 31 July 1684, he was released in December 1684 on condition that he left the kingdom. [RPCS.IX.78/126]; he returned to Ferry-Port-on-Craig in 1690. [F.III.240][ETR]

WADDELL, ALEXANDER, from Castletoun, Roxburghshire, fought at the Battle of Bothwell Bridge in 1679, was transported via Leith aboard the Crown of London bound for Barbados on 27 November 1679, was shipwrecked and drowned off Orkney on 10 December 1679. [RBM]

WADDELL, JAMES, from Monklandsshire, fought at the Battle of Bothwell Bridge in 1679, was transported via Leith aboard the Crown of London bound for Barbados on 27 November 1679, was shipwrecked and drowned off Orkney on 10 December 1679. [RBM][ETR]

WADDELL, WALTER, from Sproustoun, Roxburghshire, fought at the Battle of Bothwell Bridge in 1679, was transported via Leith aboard the Crown of London bound for Barbados on 27 November 1679, was shipwrecked and drowned off Orkney on 10 December 1679. [RBM]

WADDELL, WADDELL, from Monklands, Lanarkshire, fought at the Battle of Bothwell Bridge in 1679, was transported via Leith aboard the Crown of London bound for Barbados on 27 November 1679, was shipwrecked off Orkney on 10 December 1679, later shipped to Jamaica. [RBM][CEC.212/5][SW.198]

WALKER, ALEXANDER, from Shotts, Lanarkshire, WADDELL, ALEXANDER, from Castletoun, Roxburghshire, fought at the Battle of Bothwell Bridge in 1679, was transported via Leith aboard the Crown of London bound for Barbados on 27 November 1679, was shipwrecked and drowned off Orkney on 10 December 1679. [RBM]

WALKER, DONALD, a farmer from Otter, Argyll, a prisoner to be returned to the ship at Leith bound for Jamaica on 12 August 1685, transported via Leith to Jamaica in August 1685. [ETR]

WALKER, DUNCAN, from Argyll, in Argyll's Rebellion, was transported via Leith bound for Jamaica in August 1685. [RPCS.XI.136]

WALKER, ELSPETH, was taken from Leith Tolbooth, put in irons and imprisoned in Edinburgh Tolbooth, in 1685. [ETR]

WALKER, GEORGE, a servant on Kirkcalle Farm, Wigtownshire, was executed in 1685. [Wigtown gravestone]

WALKER, JOHN, in Loudoun, imprisoned in Canongait Tolbooth suspected of being a rebel, having taken the Oath of Allegiance, was released on 18 July 1667. [RPCS.II.399]

WALKER, PATRICK, born around 1666, was warded in Edinburgh Tolbooth on 16 July 1684, to be transported by Robert Malloch a merchant in Edinburgh, aboard his ship bound for the Plantation in Carolina, in July 1684. [RPCS.IX.69] to be brought ashore to be tried for killing a soldier, 4 August 1684. [RPCS.IX.100]; then in Edinburgh Tolbooth, was transferred to Dunnottar Castle, Kincardineshire, on 29 July 1685, transported via Leith aboard the Henry and Francis bound for East New Jersey on 5 September 1685. [ETR][RPCS.XI.155]

WALKER, ROBERT, a violer in Minniegaff, was accused, in Kirkcudbright in October 1684, of conversing with rebels Anthony Stewart and William Kennedy. [RPCS.IX.375]

WALKER, WILLIAM, was transported via Leith to Jamaica in August 1685. [RPCS.XI.136]

WALLACE, ANDREW, a prisoner in Edinburgh Tolbooth, was transported via Leith to the colonies on 27 November 1679. [ETR]

WALLACE, Colonel JAMES, of Auchans, former Governor of Belfast, led the Pentland Rising of 1666, fought at Rullion Green on 28 November 1666, consequently, was forfeited by the Justice Court in August 1667. [GC.123]; he took refuge in Holland where he died. [RPCS.II.345][Z.193]

WALLACE, JAMES, born 1623, was educated at Edinburgh University, minister at Inchinnan, Renfrewshire, from 1649 until 1663 when he was deprived for not conforming to Episcopacy, in 1674 he was accused of holding conventicles in Killellan, he returned as minister at Inchellan in 1690, and died in 1692. [F.III.144]

WALLACE, JOHN, of Monkcastle, minister at Largs from 1652 until deprived in 1662, as having held conventicles a warrant for his apprehension was issued in 1679. [F.III.215]

WALLACE, JOHN, late minister at Kirkmahoe, Dumfries-shire, for aiding rebels, Robert Lauchlieson and five others in Auchincairn, was declared a rebel and fugitive in October 1684. [RPCS.IX.372]

WALLACE, JOHN, from Galloway, was executed at Kirkpatrick, Irongray, Kirkcudbrightshire, on 2 March 1685. [Largshill Monument, Kirkcudbrightshire]

WALLACE, NICHOLAS, fought at the Siege of Worcester in 1651, then transported via London aboard the John and Sarah bound for Boston in December 1651, landed there in February 1652. [SD.1.5-6]

WALLACE, ROBERT, from Fenwick, Ayrshire, fought at the Battle of Bothwell Bridge in 1679, was transported via Leith aboard the Crown of London bound for Barbados on 27 November 1679, was shipwrecked off Orkney on 10 December 1679, later shipped to Jamaica. [RBM]

WALLACE WILLIAM, a prisoner in Canongait Tolbooth, to be liberated if he agrees to live orderly and attend his parish church, in August 1684. [RPCS.IX.80]

WALLET, ANDREW, was killed at Scarvating in 1667. [Nithsdale Martyrs Monument, Dumfries-shire]

WALLET, ANDREW, from Irongray, Dumfriesshire, fought at the Battle of Bothwell Bridge in 1679, was transported via Leith aboard the Crown of London bound for Barbados on 27 November 1679, was shipwrecked and drowned off Orkney on 10 December 1679. [RBM]

WALLET, JOHN, was warded in Edinburgh Tolbooth on 28 November 1684, was transferred to Dunnottar Castle, Kincardineshire, on 29 July 1685, then transported via Leith to the colonies in May 1685. [ETR][RPCSXI.289]

WALLS, HERBERT, in Lanridding, Tynwald, for seeing rebel Peter Coudan with a gun before the ambush at Enterkin, Lanarkshire, also seeing rebel in Tynwald, and rebel John Mundell visiting his mother on her deathbed, also rebel James Glover in Auchnean, was declared to be a rebel and fugitive in October 1684, was transported to the colonies in October 1684. [RPCS.IX.370; X.206]

WALLS, JAMES, in Hemisfieldtoun, for seeing rebel Peter Cowdan in July 1684 and not reporting it, was declared to be a rebel and fugitive in October 1684. [RPCS.IX.370]

WARDEN, JAMES, a shopkeeper in Greenock, who attended a conventicle near Greenock, was to be captured and imprisoned in Edinburgh Tolbooth in August 1684. [RPCS.IX.131]

WARREN, JAMES, fought at the Battle of Dunbar in 1650, was transported via London aboard the Unity bound for Boston in November 1650. [SCF.1226]

WATSON, ALEXANDER, in Minnigaff, was accused, in Kirkcudbright, on 4 October 1684, of conversing with rebel Archibald Stewart in 1682. [RPCS.IX.375]

WATSON, GEORGE, portioner of Nethertoun, for attending conventicles, was outlawed on 29 August 1672. [RPCS.III.583]

WATSON, HELEN, spouse of William Miller at the Mill of Greenock, Renfrewshire, a prisoner in Canongait Tolbooth, having signed a bond was released on 23 August 1684. [RPCS.IX.315]

WATSON, JOHN, from Avondale, Lanarkshire, fought at the Battle of Bothwell Bridge in 1679, was transported via Leith aboard the Crown of London bound for Barbados on 27 November 1679, was shipwrecked and drowned off Orkney on 10 December 1679. [RBM]

WATSON, JOHN, in Hells, for aiding rebels, John Harper, the elder and the younger, was declared to be a rebel and fugitive in October 1684. [RPCS.IX.370]

WATSON, THOMAS, was killed at the Battle of Aird's Moss on 22 July 1680. [Muirkirk Monument, Ayrshire]

WATSON, WILLIAM, from Islay, Argyll, in Argyll's Rebellion in 1685, was transported via Leith to Jamaica in August 1685. [RPCS.XI.136]

WATT, JOHN, in Easter Kilbride, who attended a conventicle near Greenock, was to be captured and imprisoned in Edinburgh Tolbooth in August 1684. [RPCS.IX.131]; was warded in Edinburgh Tolbooth on 1 November 1684, and was transferred to Dunnottar Castle, Kincardineshire, on 29 July 1685, transported via Leith aboard the Henry and Francis bound for East New Jersey on 5 September 1685. [ETR][RPCS.XI.167]

WATT, PATRICK, from Kilmarnock, Ayrshire, fought at the Battle of Bothwell Bridge in 1679, was transported via Leith aboard the Crown of London bound for Barbados on 27 November 1679, was shipwrecked off Orkney on 10 December 1679, later shipped to Jamaica. [RBM][CEC.212/5][SW.199]

WATTERSON, GEORGE, of Colliston, for attending conventicles, was outlawed on 29 August 1672. [RPCS.III.583]

WAUCH, JOHN, in Blackwood, for aiding the rebels John Harper the elder, and John Pagan, was declared to be a rebel and fugitive in October 1684. [RPCS.IX.361]

WAUGH, WILLIAM, in Cuill, for aiding Robert Lauchlison a rebel, was declared to be a rebel and fugitive in October 1684. [RPCS.IX.361]

WEDDELL, JOHN, from Monllands, Lanarkshire, one of the assassins of Archbishop Sharp on Magus Moor, Fife, on 3 May 1679, was executed on 25 November 1679. [Magus Moor memorial] [Z.203]

WEDDERBURN, ALEXANDER, born 1620, son of James Wedderburn minister of Moonzie, was educated at St Andrews University, minister at Forgan from 1647 until deprived in 1665, minister in Kilmarnock, Ayrshire, from 1670 until his death in November 1678. [F.III.105]

WEDDERBURN, ANDREW, born 1625, was educated at St Andrews University, minister at Liff, Angus, from 1650 until he was deprived in 1664, was accused of keeping conventicles and imprisoned, minister at Dysart, Fife, from 1688, later returned to Liff, he died in 1694. [F.V.89]

WEIR, ADAM, was executed in the Grassmarket of Edinburgh, 'for denying authority', on 22 February 1684. [ETR]

WEIR, HUGH, born 1628, was educated at St Andrews University, minister at Monkland, Lanarkshire, from 1653 until deprived in 1662, died before August 1664. [F.III.274]

WEIR, JOHN, born 1610, was educated at Glasgow University, minister at Dalserf from 1642, he was sent to administer the Solemn League and Covenant to the Protestants in Ulster in 1643, however on the voyage home he was taken prisoner by Alastair MacDonald son of Colla Ciotach, and imprisoned in Mingary Castle, Ardnamurchan, Argyll, where he died on 16 October 1644. [F.III.245]

WEIR, JOHN, of Newton, was accused of assisting the rebels in 1679, [NRS.JC39.54]; a Covenanter imprisoned in Edinburgh Tolbooth on 21 November 1683. [RPCS.VIII.633]; was transferred to Dunbarton Castle in September 1684. [RPCS.IX.179/351]

WEIR, ROBERT, from Lesmahagow, Lanarkshire, WADDELL, ALEXANDER, from Castletoun, Roxburghshire, fought at the Battle of Bothwell Bridge in 1679, was transported via Leith aboard the

Crown of London bound for Barbados on 27 November 1679, was shipwrecked and drowned off Orkney on 10 December 1679. [RBM]

WEIR, THOMAS, from Lesmahagow, Lanarkshire, in Edinburgh Tolbooth, was put in irons and imprisoned in Canongait Tolbooth on 29 July 1685, then transported via Leith to Jamaica in August 1685, landed at Port Royal in November 1685.
[ETR][RPCS.XI.329][LJ.225]

WELLS, HARBERT, in Laridden, Tynwald, 'was committed to the castle' in 1684. [RPCS.IX.703]

WELSH, ANDREW, from Ochiltree, Ayrshire, WADDELL, ALEXANDER, from Castletoun, Roxburghshire, fought at the Battle of Bothwell Bridge in 1679, was transported via Leith aboard the Crown of London bound for Barbados on 27 November 1679, was shipwrecked and drowned off Orkney on 10 December 1679. [RBM]

WELSH, JAMES, of Little Cludden, a prisoner in Dumfries for rebellion, to be transferred to Edinburgh Tolbooth, on 2 June 1684. [RPCS.IX.30]

WELSH, JOHN, former minister of Irongray, was accused of holding conventicles, in 1666. [GC.114]; was sought by the Justice Court in August 1667 for his part in the late rebellion. [GC.123]

WELSH, JOHN, of Scar, was sought by the Justice Court in August 1667 for his part in the late rebellion. [GC.123] [RPCS.II.345]

WELSH, JOHN, from Templepatrick, Ireland, fought at the Battle of Bothwell Bridge on 22 June 1679.

WELSH, WALTER, a prisoner in Dumfries Tolbooth for rebellion, to be banished to the Plantations, on 2 June 1684. [RPCS.IX.30]

WELSH, WILLIAM, was killed in Dumfries in 1667. [Nithsdale Martyrs Monument, Dumfries-shire]

WELSH, ........, of Cornley was sought by the Justice Court in August 1667 for his part in the late rebellion. [GC.123] [RPCS.II.345]

WEMYSS, JAMES, of Cask99iberran, General of the Artillery in 1648, fought at the Siege of Worcester in 1651. [RHCA.361]

WEMYSS, WILLIAM, born 1606, was educated at Edinburgh University, minister at Roxburgh from 1641 until his death on 17 March 1658, he was chaplain to the Earl of Roxburgh's Regiment in England. [F.III.86]9

WHARRY, JOHN, from Lesmahagow, was executed in Glasgow on 13 June 1683. [Milton of Campsie gravestone, Stirlingshire] [see a letter sent from Glasgow Tolbooth on 11 June 1683, [RPCS.VIII.609]

WHITE, ADAM, born in Scotland, was educated at Glasgow University, a minister at Clondevarrock from 1654 to 1672, he was a non-conformist minister imprisoned in Lifford, Ireland, in 1669, [Cal.SP.Ire]; at Ardstraw from 1672 until 1693, and at Billy from 1692, he died on 19 December 1708. [FI.51]

WHYT, HUGH, was educated at Edinburgh University, was denounced as a fugitive on 5 May 1684, was licensed as a Presbyterian minister in Newtown, Ireland, on 31 January 1688, and ordained in 1690, later a minister in Stirlingshire, died in 1716. [F.4.311]

WHITE, JAMES, was shot dead by Peter Ingles at Little Blackwood in 1685. [Fenwick gravestone]

WHITE, JOHN, in Cothill, for attending conventicles, was outlawed on 29 August 1672. [RPCS.III.583]

WHITE, JOHN, from Kirkoswald, Ayrshire, fought at the Battle of Bothwell Bridge in 1679, was transported via Leith aboard the Crown of London bound for Barbados on 27 November 1679, was shipwrecked and drowned off Orkney on 10 December 1679. [RBM]

WHYTE. JOHN, from Fenwick, Ayrshire, fought at the Battle of Bothwell Bridge in 1679, was transported via Leith aboard the Crown of London bound for Barbados on 27 November 1679, was shipwrecked and drowned off Orkney on 10 December 1679. [RBM]

WHYTE, MALCOLM, from Argyll, was transported via Leith to Jamaica in August 1685. [RPCS.XI.126]

WHYTFORD, JAMES, a prisoner in Edinburgh Tolbooth, was released having taken the bond, in August 1668. [RPCS.II.507]

WHYTHEAD, ANDREW, a rebel in Dunscore, Dumfries-shire, in 1684. [RPCS.IX.292]

WHYTHILL, JOHN, from Glasgow, was warded in Edinburgh Tolbooth on 20 May 1685, but, having sworn an Oath of Allegiance was released on 28 May 1685. [ETR]

WHITELAW, JOHN, fought at the Battle of Bothwell Bridge on 22 June 1679, a prisoner in Edinburgh Tolbooth, a confession and testimony before his execution on 28 November 1683. [RPCS.VIII.633]

WIGHT, WILLIAM, in Claffin, to be tried accused of rebellion, 3 June 1684. [RPCS.IX.205]

WILKIE, JAMES, in the Mains of Cliftounhall, was sought by the Justice Court in August 1667 for his part in the late rebellion. [GC.123] [RPCS.II.345]

WILKIE, JOHN, formerly minister in Twynholm, Galloway, was accused of holding conventicles within the Presbytery in 1666. [GC.107/114]; was imprisoned in Edinburgh Tolbooth, transferred to Moffat in September 1668. [RPCS.II.536]

WILKIE, THOMAS, born 1592, was educated at St Andrews University, minister at Crailing and Nisbet from 1621 until his death in 1651 or 1652, he was chaplain to The Earl of Lothian's Regiment in 1645. [F.III.108]

WILKIE, WILLIAM, was educated at St Andrews University, minister at Lilliesleaf from 1662, he refused to conform to Episcopacy in 1662. [F.II.182]

WILKIESON, JAMES, was accused of participating in the Earl of Argyll's Rebellion, in 1685. [NRS.JC39.72]; his execution was reprieved until December 1685. [ETR]

WILLIESON, JAMES, then in Edinburgh Tolbooth, put in irons and imprisoned in Canongait Tolbooth on 29 July 1685. [ETR]

WILLIAMSON, JOHN, was warded in Edinburgh Tolbooth on 28 May 1685, having taken the Oath of Abjuration was released on 21 July 1685. [ETR]

WILLIAMSON, THOMAS, from Cranston, Midlothian, fought at the Battle of Bothwell Bridge in 1679, was transported via Leith aboard the Crown of London bound for Barbados on 27 November 1679, was shipwrecked and drowned off Orkney on 10 December 1679. [RBM]

WILLIAMSON, THOMAS, a prisoner in Dumfries Tolbooth for rebellion, to be banished to the Plantations, on 2 June 1684. [RPCS.IX.30]

WILSON, ALEXANDER, minister at Cameron, Fife, from 1650 until he was deprived in 1662, in 1674 he was accused of holding conventicles, he fled to Holland in November 1678 but returned after 1683. [F.V.186]

WILSON, ANDREW, fought at the Siege of Worcester in 1651, then transported via London aboard the John and Sarah bound for Boston in December 1651, landed there in February 1652. [SD.1.5-6]

WILSON, ANDREW, in Bousie, was accused of attending conventicles in Fife during 1668. [RPCS.II.491]

WILSON, CHRISTOPHER, fought at the Siege of Worcester in 1651, then transported via London aboard the John and Sarah bound for Boston in December 1651, landed there in February 1652. [SD.1.5-6]

WILSON, HUGH, was educated at Glasgow University, minister at Inch and Saulseat, Wigtownshire, from 1660 until 1662 when he was deposed, he then went to Castlereagh in Ireland, 'where he was sure he would survive the troubles of the time.', returned to Scotland in 1690, minister at Inch in 1692. [F.II.336; VII.533]]

WILSON, JAMES, in Larghie, was accused, in Kirkcudbright on 4 October 1684, of aiding several rebels in 1684. [RPCS.IX.377]

WILSON, JAMES, a chapman, a rebel in 1684. [RPCS.IX.358]

WILSON, JANET, spouse to John Patheson in Craignee, for aiding rebels, Walter Smith, Alexander Gibson, and Thomas Hunter in Breckinside, was declared a rebel and a fugitive in October 1684. [RPCS.IX.369]

WILSON, JANET, in Crawfordtoun, for aiding rebels and fugitives, William Herries, James Corsan, James McMichael, and other rebels a little after the ambush at Enterkin, Lanarkshire, were declared to be rebels and fugitives, in September 1684. [RPCS.IX.373]

WILSON, JOHN, fought at the Siege of Worcester in 1651, then transported via London aboard the John and Sarah bound for Boston in December 1651, landed there in February 1652. [SD.1.5-6]

WILSON, JOHN, in Kilbryde, a fugitive in 1683. [RPCS.VIII.647]

WILSON, JOHN, a gardener in Kirkton of Kilmaurs, Ayrshire, was in the rebellion, a deposition of 21 October 1684. [RPCS.IX.548/549]

WILSON, MARGARET, born 1667, daughter of Gilbert Wilson, a farmer in Glen Vernock, was accused of attending a conventicle, and was drowned in the Solway at Wigtown on 11 May 1685. [Wigtown Monument] [GC.415]

WILSON, MARIE, spouse of Robert Herries, for aiding William Herries and other rebels and fugitives, was declared to be a rebel and fugitive, in September 1684. [RPCS.IX.373]

WILSON, MARION, spouse of William Pathieson in Clonrae, and his son John Pathieson, for aiding rebels, Walter Smith, John MacCall, and one of the Corsans from Jedburgh, was declared a rebel and a fugitive in October 1684. [RPCS.IX.369]

WILSON, PATRICK, from Livingston, West Lothian, fought at the Battle of Bothwell Bridge in 1679, was transported via Leith aboard the Crown of London bound for Barbados on 27 November 1679, was shipwrecked and drowned off Orkney on 10 December 1679. [RBM][ETR]

WILSON, THOMAS, from Quathquan, Lanarkshire,

WADDELL, ALEXANDER, from Castletoun, Roxburghshire, fought at the Battle of Bothwell Bridge in 1679, was transported via Leith aboard the Crown of London bound for Barbados on 27 November 1679, was shipwrecked and drowned off Orkney on 10 December 1679. [RBM]

WILSON, THOMAS, and his wife Jean Glencorse in Camling, for aiding Alexander Gibson, Walter Smith, and other rebels and fugitives, were declared to be rebels and fugitives, in September 1684. [RPCS.IX.373]

WILSON, WILLIAM, from Galloway, was transported via Leith aboard the Henry and Francis bound for East New Jersey on 5 September 1685. [RPCS.XI.154]

WILSON, ......, a prisoner in Blackness Castle, West Lothian, to be transferred to Edinburgh Tolbooth in June 1684. [RPCS.IX.17]

WINNING, JAMES, for his part in the Pentland Rising of 1666, was beheaded in Glasgow on 19 December 1666. [Glasgow Cathedral]

WINNING, JAMES, fought at Bothwell Bridge on 22 June 1679. [Glasgow Cathedral plaque]

WINTER, EDWARD, a prisoner in Edinburgh Tolbooth, willing to go to America, was released to go there on 17 December 1685. [ETR]

WISHART, WILLIAM, a student at the University of Utrecht was warded in Edinburgh Tolbooth on 27 April 1684, a rebel, was banished to the Plantations in Carolina on 8 August 1684. [ETR][RPCS.IX.95]

WITHERSPOON, GAVIN, portioner of Old Monkland, Lanarkshire, failed to take the Test Oath and became a fugitive in 1683. [RPCS.VIII.642]

WODROW, FRANCIS, from Glasgow, fought at the Battle of Bothwell Bridge in 1679, was transported via Leith aboard the Crown of London bound for Barbados on 27 November 1679, was shipwrecked and drowned off Orkney on 10 December 1679. [RBM]

WOOD, ALEXANDER, from Nunlaws, parish of Bothwell, was tried in 1684 for his part in the 1679 Rebellion, [NRS.JC39.51]; was executed in Glasgow on 24 October 1684. [Townhead Martyrs Memorial, Glasgow]

WOOD, GEORGE, one of the assassins of Archbishop Sharp on Magus Moor, Fife, on 3 May 1679, was executed on 25 November 1679. [Magus Moor memorial]

WOOD, GEORGE, was shot dead by trooper John Reid at Tinkhornhill in 1688. [Sorn gravestone]

WOOD, JAMES, from Newmilns, Ayrshire, one of the assassins of Archbishop Sharp on 3 May 1679, was executed on 25 November 1679. [Z.203]

WOOD, THOMAS, in Kirkmichael, was accused of being at Bothwell Bridge in 1679, later with the rebels at Blackloch, and killing a soldier of the king at a recent ambush, on 2 July 1684. [RPCS.IX.29]

WOODALL, JOHN, fought at the Siege of Worcester in 1651, then transported via London aboard the John and Sarah bound for Boston in December 1651, landed there in February 1652. [SD.1.5-6]

WOTHERSPOON, GRIZZELL, was transported via Leith aboard the Henry and Francis bound for East New Jersey on 5 September 1685. [RPCS.XI.155]

WRIGHT, JOHN, a rebel in 1666, imprisoned in Edinburgh Tolbooth, was banished to Virginia on 4 August 1668. [RPCS.II.507]; he was granted to Captain Lightfoot, master of the

Convertin at Leith bound for the Plantations in September 1668.
[RPCS.II.534]

WRIGHT, JOHN, in Auchinnaight, and his wife, for aiding rebels Thomas Hunter of Breckinside and John MacCall, were declared to be rebels and fugitives in October 1684. [RPCS.IX.365]

WYLLIE, ANDREW, from Stewarton, Ayrshire, fought at the Battle of Bothwell Bridge in 1679, was transported via Leith aboard the Crown of London bound for Barbados on 27 November 1679, was shipwrecked and drowned off Orkney on 10 December 1679. [RBM]

WYLLIE, JOHN, from Fenwick, Ayrshire, fought at the Battle of Bothwell Bridge in 1679, was transported via Leith aboard the Crown of London bound for Barbados on 27 November 1679, was shipwrecked and drowned off Orkney on 10 December 1679. [RBM]

WYLLIE, MATTHEW, in Dewgley, for attending conventicles, was outlawed on 29 August 1672. [RPCS.III.583]

WYLLIE, ROBERT, from Stewarton, Ayrshire, fought at the Battle of Bothwell Bridge in 1679, was transported via Leith aboard the Crown of London bound for Barbados on 27 November 1679, was shipwrecked and drowned off Orkney on 10 December 1679. [RBM]

WYLLIE, THOMAS, of Barclay, born 1618, was educated at Edinburgh University, minister at Borgue in 1642, then at Mauchline, Ayrshire, from 1646, was at the Battle of Mauchline Moor in June 1648, transferred to Kirkcudbright in 1655 until deprived in 1662, then minister in Coleraine, Ulster, in 1669, finally was minister in Fenwick, Ayrshire, from 1672 until his death on 3 September 1676. [F.III.94]

WYLLIE, THOMAS, from Loudoun, Ayrshire, fought at the Battle of Bothwell Bridge in 1679, was transported via Leith aboard the Crown of London bound for Barbados on 27 November 1679, was shipwrecked and drowned off Orkney on 10 December 1679. [RBM]

WYLLIE, THOMAS, from Stewarton, Ayrshire, fought at the Battle of Bothwell Bridge in 1679, was transported via Leith aboard the Crown of London bound for Barbados on 27 November 1679, was shipwrecked and drowned off Orkney on 10 December 1679. [RBM]

WYLLIE, THOMAS, a prisoner in Canongait Tolbooth, who refused to take an Oath of Allegiance, was banished to the American Plantations on 17 December 1685, was transported via Leith aboard the John and Nicholas bound for Barbados in December 1685. [ETR][RPCS.XI.254]

WYNET, JOHN, from Monklands, Lanarkshire, fought at the Battle of Bothwell Bridge in 1679, was transported via Leith aboard the Crown of London bound for Barbados on 27 November 1679, was shipwrecked and drowned off Orkney on 10 December 1679. [RBM]

YEAMAN, JOHN, from Edington, Berwickshire, was transported via Leith aboard the St Michael of Scarborough bound for the West Indies on 12 December 1678. [RPCS.VI.76]

YEAMAN, WILLIAM, from Edington, Berwickshire, was transported via Leith aboard the St Michael of Scarborough bound for the West Indies on 12 December 1678. [RPCS.VI.76]

YOUNG, ANDREW, from Airth, Stirlingshire, fought at the Battle of Bothwell Bridge in 1679, was transported via Leith aboard the Crown of London bound for Barbados on 27 November 1679, was shipwrecked and drowned off Orkney on 10 December 1679. [RBM]

YOUNG, GEORGE, from Teviotdale, Roxburghshire, in Edinburgh Tolbooth, put in irons and imprisoned in Canongait Tolbooth on 29 July 1685, then was transported via Leith to Jamaica in August 1685, landed at Port Royal in November 1685. [ETR][RPCS.XI.329][LJ.17]

YOUNG, JAMES, from Irvine, Ayrshire, was transported to the colonies in 1679. [Irvine gravestone]

YOUNG, JAMES, from Netherfield, Avondale, Lanarkshire, in Edinburgh Tolbooth, a prisoner to be returned to the ship at Leith bound for Jamaica on 12 August 1685. [ETR][RPCS.XI.129]

YOUNG, JASON, fought at the Battle of Bothwell Bridge in 1679, was transported via Leith aboard the Crown of London bound for Barbados on 27 November 1679, was shipwrecked and drowned off Orkney on 10 December 1679. [RBM]

YOUNG, JOHN, from Melrose, Roxburghshire, fought at the Battle of Bothwell Bridge in 1679, was transported via Leith aboard the Crown of London bound for Barbados on 27 November 1679, was shipwrecked and drowned off Orkney on 10 December 1679. [RBM]

YOUNG, JOHN, at Eaglesham Kirk, a rebel in Glasgow Tolbooth, was banished to the Plantations in June 1684, and transported via Glasgow aboard the Pelican bound for Carolina, bond by Walter Gibson, a merchant in Glasgow, dated 20 June 1684. [RPCS.IX.208]

YOUNG, MARK, from Barnhills, Roxburghshire, was transported to the colonies in October 1684. [RPCS.IX.449]

YOUNG, RICHARD, from Cavers, Roxburghshire, fought at the Battle of Bothwell Bridge in 1679, was transported via Leith aboard the Crown of London bound for Barbados on 27 November 1679, was shipwrecked and drowned off Orkney on 10 December 1679. [RBM]

YOUNG, ROBERT, from Galashiels, Selkirkshire, fought at the Battle of Bothwell Bridge in 1679, was transported via Leith aboard the Crown of London bound for Barbados on 27 November 1679, was shipwrecked and drowned off Orkney on 10 December 1679. [RBM]

YOUNG, ROBERT, in Midtoun, for attending conventicles, was outlawed on 29 August 1672. [RPCS.III.583]

YOUNG, ROBERT, from Muirhead, Dalserf, in Glasgow Tolbooth, gave up a bond that he would live properly or be fined 1000 merks, in October 1684. [RPCS.IX.710]

YOUNG, ROBERT, from Avondale, then in Edinburgh Tolbooth, was transferred to Dunnottar Castle, Kincardineshire, on 29 July 1685, was transported via Leith aboard the Henry and Francis bound for East New Jersey on 5 September 1685. [ETR][RPCS.XI.154]

YOUNG, WILLIAM, a tailor from Evandale, was executed in the Grassmarket of Edinburgh for rebellion on 9 October 1684. [ETR]

YOUNGER, JAMES, from Galston, Ayrshire, fought at the Battle of Bothwell Bridge in 1679, was transported via Leith aboard the Crown of London bound for Barbados on 27 November 1679, was shipwrecked and drowned off Orkney on 10 December 1679. [RBM]

YOUNGER, JOHN, in Falkland, Fife, a rebel in 1666, imprisoned in Edinburgh Tolbooth or Canongait Tolbooth, having taken the Oath of Allegiance, was released on 11 July 1667. [RPCS.II.308]

YOUNGER, WILLIAM, from Livingston, West Lothian, fought at the Battle of Bothwell Bridge in 1679, was transported via Leith aboard the Crown of London bound for Barbados on 27 November 1679, was shipwrecked and drowned off Orkney on 10 December 1679. [RBM][ETR]

www.ingramcontent.com/pod-product-compliance
Lightning Source LLC
Chambersburg PA
CBHW070022010526
44117CB00011B/1671